How to R
Academy School

HOW TO RUN AN ACADEMY SCHOOL

Katie Paxton-Doggett FCIS

Trust through governance

Published by
ICSA Publishing Ltd
Saffron House
6–10 Kirby Street
London EC1N 8TS

Typeset in 9½ on 12½ pt Kuenstler by Hands Fotoset, Woodthorpe, Nottingham
Printed in Great Britain by Hobbs the Printers Ltd, Totton, Hampshire

British Cataloguing in Publication Data
A catalogue record for this book is available from the British Library.

ISBN 978 1 86072 610 1

Contents

Foreword

On behalf of the National Governors' Association (NGA) I am very pleased to be able to write a foreword for this publication. ICSA is the chartered membership and qualifying body for people working in governance, risk and compliance, including company secretaries. Its work is therefore complementary to the National Governors' Association: the membership organisation for all state-funded school governing bodies and academy boards of trustees.

The past ten years have seen seismic changes in how schools are run, managed and governed. There has been a significant increase in the number of schools that are academies. Over half of secondary schools and 10% of primary and special schools are now academies, many of whom are 'Gold Members' of the NGA. Academies are independent state schools, answerable to the Secretary of State for Education both through statute and by the school's individual funding agreement.

The NGA has always championed the need for governing bodies, as the accountable body of the school, to be strategic. In terms of academies, they now need to understand the different responsibilities of trustees, directors, members and governors. This publication distinguishes these differences and provides a template of how an academy should be run corporately. As an academy is self-governing, it is vital that everybody involved in its management and leadership understands its different roles and responsibilities. It is apparent to the NGA from the numerous questions asked of our helpline that there is a level of confusion and misunderstanding about the different roles of trustees, directors, members and governors, particularly within multi-academy trusts. Confusion and misunderstandings will inevitably lead to problems within the corporate governance of an academy and detract from the effective running of any school.

This publication not only details this from the standpoint of a governor, but more especially from the point of view of the clerk or company secretary of the organisation. Again, professional clerking is something that the NGA has actively pushed for a number of years. We believe that this is a vital part of the good governance of any school – someone clerking all governing body meetings, who can provide advice, but who is independent of the school. The NGA has been running a 'Clerking Matters' campaign with SOLACE (the Society for Local Authority Chief Executives) and is very pleased that the National College for Teaching and Leadership will shortly be launching training programmes specifically for clerks of schools. This training will again be complementary to the comprehensive information in this publication.

Since September 2012, Ofsted has, quite rightly, focused on the role of the governing body/board of trustees of a school and its effectiveness in holding the senior leaders to account. Without professional clerking, with minutes of meetings that show an equal measure of support and challenge, the governing body will struggle to attain the necessary accolade of being a 'Good' or 'Outstanding' school.

The constant theme of this book is that the right people must be around the table to ensure effective governance of an academy. This, again, is something that the NGA will always support: the first of our 'eight elements of effective governance'. The second is that everybody around the table understands their roles and responsibilities, followed by good chairing, professional clerking and leading onto a commitment to asking challenging questions followed by courageous conversations. All of these elements of effective governance are dealt with in detail here. What will also be of interest are the chapters on risk assessment, risk management and skills audits – areas that many governors are not as familiar with as they should be.

This book contains many examples of good practice from existing academies and multi-academy trusts. These move the publication from being a theory-driven book to a practical day-to-day application of the legal and regulatory compliance necessary for good governance of any organisation.

Whilst the NGA cannot trace its history back to 1902 (the year that ICSA was granted its Royal Charter) the commonality of approach around the detail of corporate governance is gratifying. The NGA sees this publication as an essential guide to the legal and regulatory compliance to fulfil the company secretary role in an Academy.

Duncan Haworth
Chair, National Governors' Association
May 2014

Preface

Becoming an academy brings significant challenges. The greatest challenge is often the transformation from a maintained school under the auspices of a local authority to a charitable company, with all the legal and regulatory requirements that the new status brings. It is essential that new academies not only recognise these requirements, but that they also embrace them to establish robust governance capable of underpinning the organisation.

This book is a practical guide for those involved in the day-to-day administration of an academy. It provides real-life case studies along with useful precedents that can be used.

It is the book that I would have liked if I had found myself required to do the job without any experience.

The terminology around academies is confusing and it is important that anyone working in this area is clear about what the various expressions mean. Most confusion arises around the terms 'member', 'trustee', 'director' and 'governor'. Members are *not* trustees. In fact, the last three terms apply simultaneously to the same group of people: by virtue of their roles as charitable trustees, directors of a limited company and governors of a school, they have a number of different responsibilities. However, generally the roles are indistinguishable. This book clarifies the terms in current usage within academies and helps the officers fulfil their roles effectively.

The current terminology contains many unhelpful ambiguities. For example, strictly speaking, the individual schools within a multi-academy trust (MAT) are known as 'academies' themselves. However, I have referred to these as 'schools' to further differentiate between the different governance levels in the organisation.

The content of the book is based on the versions of the model documentation available at the time of writing and focuses on mainstream academies. I have taken a fairly generic approach. However, the specific terms will differ according to the type of academy or multi-academy, as well as when the documentation was drafted and agreed. It is, therefore, absolutely essential that reference is made to the original documentation: it should be the first task of anyone involved in the administrative function of an academy to read and be familiar with the contents of the funding agreement and Articles of Association for their own academy.

A well-run academy offers great opportunities both for those running it and for the students passing through it. The key to good outcomes for both groups is ensuring that the administrative function both supports and enables a fantastic learning experience for pupils.

I would like to thank all the talented and committed people working with academies who have contributed to the book as well as my four beautiful daughters who are my constant reminder of why it's so important to get the governance of academies right!

Katie Paxton-Doggett
May 2014

1 What are academies?

■ In this chapter

This chapter considers the importance of ensuring that an academy is run effectively by:

- outlining the background to 'academisation';
- explaining what an academy is and the implications of being a charitable company;
- summarising the greater freedoms available to academies;
- detailing the implications of charity status and the role of the trustee; and
- exploring the roles of company secretary and secretary to the board.

■ Background

The idea for publicly funded schools free from local authority (LA) control was initially introduced by the Conservative government in the Education Reform Act 1988. City Technology Colleges (CTCs) specialise in subjects such as science, mathematics and technology and were intended to be located in urban areas. One-fifth of capital costs were to be met by private business sponsors.

However, the programme was met with significant opposition from local authorities who failed to identify suitable sites so that the schools were built on the outskirts of cities rather than centrally as planned. The cost of building the new schools was also much more expensive than anticipated, requiring a much higher level of government funding. The programme was abandoned after only 15 CTCs had been created.

In 2000, the Labour government introduced city academies which were intended to replace failing schools in deprived areas. The legislation for CTCs was amended by the Learning and Skills Act 2000. Again, sponsors were appointed, although the financial commitment was halved from that under the CTC scheme. Although the schools were independent of LA control, city academies were bound by the schools admission code. CTCs were encouraged to convert to city academies and the majority did so. In 2002, the name was changed to 'academies' by an amendment enacted by the Education Act.

David Cameron's Coalition government expanded the programme and streamlined the process to enable more schools to become academies. The first academies had been failing schools which were sponsored; the new academies were excellent schools which wanted autonomy. The Academies Act 2010 opened the way for all maintained schools, both primary and secondary, to become academies. Unlike the earlier 'Mark I' academies, no external sponsor was required. Initially, only schools assessed as 'Outstanding' by Ofsted were able to convert; the first schools became 'converter academies' in September 2010. In an effort to help raise achievement more widely, these converter academies were required to support at least one weaker school.

The Academies Act 2010 was a watershed in the move to a fully independent, yet state-funded, education system. Prior to this, only poorly performing secondary schools were covered by the academies programme. However, as only 'outstanding' schools could convert, the Act meant that suddenly academy status was something to aspire to, an indicator of quality.

Following the comprehensive spending review announcement on 20 October 2010, the programme was further expanded so that schools assessed as 'Good' with one or more outstanding features were able to convert to academy status. Other schools were also eligible if they were working in partnership with an 'Outstanding' or 'Good' school which had committed to assisting them with improvement. In January 2011, the policy was expanded to allow 'Outstanding' special schools to convert.

Since then, the programme has continued to grow exponentially with all schools now being given the opportunity to convert to academy status. The Department for Education's ('DfE') website states that: 'Any school or PRU which is performing well can now submit an application to convert into a stand-alone academy.' In addition, schools can now choose to join with other schools as part of a multi-academy or umbrella arrangement as long as they can demonstrate that at least one school is performing well and the group has the capacity to improve and sustain performance. The DfE considers each application on its own merits taking into consideration the financial management of the school as well as certain criteria:

- Results in relation to national averages in absolute attainment and progression, and assessment of performance against the floor standard:
  - Three/four-year GCSE results trajectory (where results should be stable or improving taking account of the starting point) for the percentage of pupils with five or more GCSEs at A* to C including English and mathematics.
  - Pupil progress measures: percentage of pupils making expected progress in English and mathematics from KS2 to KS4.
- Latest Ofsted report with a specific focus on capacity to improve, outcomes and leadership and management.

- Any other matters that the school may rely on to demonstrate that it is performing well (e.g. social context).

What is clear is that the academies programme is here to stay. Introduced by the Conservative government and embraced by successive Labour and Coalition governments, there is no formal opposition from any of the main political parties. With the funding to LAs declining rapidly and cutbacks in the services they provide, schools are left with little choice about whether to convert to academy status.

What is an academy?

An academy is a state-funded independent school. It is not under LA control and has greater freedom than a maintained school, particularly in relation to delivery of the curriculum and the ability to set its own pay and conditions for staff.

Academies are charitable companies limited by guarantee. They must be registered as a company with Companies House and governance must be undertaken in the same way as any other company. They are exempt charities, so are not required to register with the Charity Commission. Compliance with charities law is regulated by the DfE as the Secretary of State for Education is the 'principal regulator' for academies.

Academies receive their funding directly from the Education Funding Agency (EFA), the DfE agency specifically tasked with funding and compliance. Funding is calculated on a per-pupil basis in the same way as maintained schools. With the move to a national funding formula, inconsistencies between schools should reduce. Academies also receive additional funding to account for services that were previously provided by the LA. At the outset of the academies programme, this additional funding was significant, but it is expected to reduce over time. Initially, this additional funding was identified separately but it is now subsumed within the grant funding. Perhaps the most important feature of funding for academies is their increased freedom as to how budgets are utilised to best benefit their pupils.

The DfE has a series of model documents which schools are expected to use when the academy is created. This documentation forms the constitution and sets the rules for the business operations of the academy. There are several versions available depending on whether the academy is to stand alone or will join with others in a multi-academy or umbrella structure; the status of the converting school will also affect this choice, particularly if faith schools are involved. There is also a cooperative version of the documentation for free schools, studio schools and university technical colleges (UTCs). New model documents have been, and continue to be, introduced reflecting changes in policy and legislation. Any deviation will only be approved in 'exceptional circumstances'.

In the Mark 1 academies, underperforming schools were sponsored by an external sponsor who provided funding as well as taking responsibility for improvement in performance. Schools are no longer sponsored in this way. However, there have been high-profile cases, where a failing school has been 'taken over' and 'academised'. One such school, Downhills Primary School in Haringey, north London, fought hard to avoid conversion but eventually joined the Harris Federation and changed its name to the Harris Primary Academy Philip Lane. The school becomes one of a number of schools within a multi-academy structure, with the management taken over by that MAT. A range of organisations, such as successful schools, businesses, universities, charities and faith bodies, can act as a 'sponsor' although the terminology is not terribly helpful; in these situations, the failing school becomes legally part of the MAT rather than just being supported by it. This is an onerous task and MATs are unlikely to take it on if they did not believe that they could genuinely offer the support required.

In addition to academies, there are other structures: free schools, studio schools and UTCs. Although they offer different educational provision and come into being in different ways, they operate along the same lines as academies. Furthermore, new schools must either be a new academy or a free school.

All the necessary documentation and relevant provisions are explored in detail in this book. There are common themes throughout as, once up and running, sponsored and converter academies, free schools, studio schools and UTCs operate, on a legal basis, in much the same way. However, the details will differ and it is absolutely essential that all involved in the management of an academy are fully aware of the provisions contained within their own funding agreement and Articles of Association. It will be no defence to any potential action to be unaware of the requirements!

Academies sign a funding agreement which is essentially a contract with the Secretary of State. The academy must meet the requirements in the funding agreement to qualify for ongoing public funding. Despite its name, this document contains no details of funding that will be granted to the academy.

Continuing obligations

The governing body of a school is part of its leadership and management whether the school is maintained or an academy. However, the responsibilities borne by this group, who now become the directors of an academy, are greatly increased. The role of 'governor' needs to be 'professionalised' and nowhere is this clearer than in an academy where strict legal obligations already exist.

Directors and staff are not only to be entirely focused on developing and oper-ating an outstanding school with excellent pupil progress and achievement, they are also responsible for running a charitable company! Whereas previously, the LA took overall responsibility for many aspects relating to property, staffing or general legal requirements, now the academy must do so alone.

Funding for an academy comes directly from the EFA. Although the require-ments of an academy are more onerous in terms of accounting functions, the financial year is brought into line with the academic year rather than the situation under the maintained system where budgets ran from April to March, straddling two academic years. Academies must comply with Companies Act, Financial Handbook, Accounts Direction, charity SORP and charity law in a complex interrelation of rules unique to academies coupled with a reporting deadline equal to that of listed companies.

Freedom of 'academisation'

According to the DfE, academies benefit from 'greater freedoms to innovate and raise standards' which include:

- freedom from local authority control;
- the ability to set their own pay and conditions for staff;
- freedoms around the delivery of the curriculum; and
- the ability to change the length of terms and school days.

'Academisation' offers schools an opportunity to recreate themselves and become the organisation that they wish to be. The single biggest difference is the control over funding. Academies can allocate budgets as they wish, shop around to get better value and, in the case of MATs and umbrellas, take advantage of economies of scale.

EXPERIENCE

Bob Wintringham, Chair of the Board of Directors, Faringdon Academy of Schools expresses what becoming a MAT meant for them:

'The structure of a community Multi Academy Trust provides a mix of local expertise and knowledge, but also adds in a real desire for success born out of a sense of ownership.

Directors experience tangible empowerment that drives and focuses improvement and staff are set free to work together across the Academy, unhindered by notional school boundaries that can stifle innovation.

Academies have a golden opportunity to take the best of the old system and combine it with radical thinking and bold initiatives. The new freedoms allow us to think differently – but there are no guarantees of sure-fire success.'

The academy becomes the employer of all staff and, in theory, has the freedom to set its own pay and conditions. However, all staff who had previously worked for a school which has converted to academy status will be protected by the Transfer of Undertakings (Protection of Employment) Regulations 2006 (TUPE). This means that those employees automatically transfer on the same terms and conditions. There are also specific TUPE obligations in relation to notification to, and consultation with, unions and employee representatives.

Irrespective of the TUPE arrangements for existing staff, the academy is free to set its own terms and conditions for new members of staff and has the opportunity to pay a premium to attract and retain high-quality staff.

Following conversion, any subsequent changes to terms and conditions for staff who transferred under TUPE may only be put into effect following formal consultation with staff and their union representatives.

Teachers working in an academy are still subject to the Teachers' Pension Regulations 2010 and belong to the Teachers' Pension Scheme (TPS). The TPS is a defined benefit scheme with index-linked pensions. Contributions are made by both the employer (i.e. the academy) and the scheme member (i.e. the member of teaching staff). The TPS is a national scheme, but the academy will be responsible for all administrative matters in connection with it and will need to pay for an audit which is likely to be required annually. Liability for the TPS is long term and funded through contributions; the deficit represents a gap calculated under certain assumptions made by the actuary which is likely to represent an inflationary pressure on future funding in order to reduce the deficit.

MATs should give careful consideration and, if necessary, take advice regarding the eligibility of any Executive Head to join the TPS. Whilst headteachers will fall within the scheme where they are the academic head and responsible for the teaching and learning function, an executive head who occupies a mainly financial or administrative role would not. Eligibility is determined by the MAT on an individual basis and will depend on the particular circumstances of the case.

Non-teaching staff will be eligible for membership of the Local Government Pension Scheme (LGPS) although not all support staff choose to become members. The LGPS is a 'defined contribution' scheme so only the amount paid in by the staff member and employer is set. Therefore, an independent actuarial assessment is made which will take into account the age profile of the staff involved. The assessment is used to determine the academy's contributions. The LGPS is locally administered; the academy will become an 'admitted body' of the scheme in its local area. Annual reports from the LGPS actuary may be required at an additional cost to the academy.

The presence of the LGPS valuation does cause an issue in accounting terms, albeit theoretical. Often the pension fund will be found to be managing a deficit which transfers from the LA to the academy at conversion. This liability will impact on the bottom line of the accounts so that it appears that the academy is insolvent as liabilities are greater than assets. The Charity Commission has advised that this will not be indicative of insolvency because the deficit is being reduced by the contribution made. Nevertheless, it is good practice to provide a full explanation in the notes to the accounts.

■ Charity status

Since 1 August 2011, all academies are automatically classified as exempt charities (s.12(4) Academies Act 2010) and do not need to apply for charitable status. This means that they are exempt from registration and direct regulation by the Charity Commission; any academies previously registered must stop using their charity number and should be removed from the register. Academies must, however, inform HMRC that the company is charitable. Otherwise, they will have to complete tax returns, which will increase their administrative burden. A written application to HMRC for recognition as a charity for tax purposes should be made using Form ChA1.

According to the Charities Act 2011, a charity must:

- be established for charitable purposes only; and
- have a purpose that is for the public benefit.

For academies, the charitable purpose is 'the advancement of education'.

Charities must be independent and must not be controlled by another organisation. At present, academies cannot be run by a profit-making organisation.

The basic responsibilities of trustees are the same as those of a registered charity, but some Charities Act requirements do not apply.

The Secretary of State for Education is the principal regulator for academies, which means that the DfE is responsible for overseeing compliance with charity law. This role is undertaken by the EFA with support from the Charity Commission. According to the Charity Commission, principal regulators can provide information about charity law requirements and use their existing monitoring arrangements to check whether charities are complying with charity law. They have no additional powers, but can involve the Charity Commission if they have concerns about the way a charity they supervise is operating. In particular, the DfE, as principal regulator, will ensure that academies:

- comply with requirements in the governing document;
- act responsibly and in the interests of the charity and its beneficiaries;
- manage any conflicts of interest; and
- exercise reasonable care and skill, taking professional advice where necessary.

Endowments and other funds set up by the founders of an academy to provide additional funding may also benefit from this exempt status. If that fund is a charity, controlled by the academy and for one or more of the purposes of that academy, it will also be exempt (e.g. an academy endowment where the academy company is trustee, prize funds or scholarships). In these cases, where the administrative links are very close, the funds should be included in the academy's accounts.

Parent Teacher Associations are independent of the academy and are not exempt. They must register with the Charity Commission if they wish to benefit from charitable status. Alternatively, PTAs may choose to operate as a club or committee.

COMMENT

Chloe Brunton, Senior Associate with Veale Wasbrough Vizards, explained:

'All academies are operated by charitable companies called "academy trusts". Academy trusts are exempt charities which means that whilst they are charities, they are not regulated by the Charity Commission nor are they required to be registered with them. Instead, they are regulated by their "Principal Regulator" the Secretary of State for Education (supported by the Education Funding Agency).

Despite their exempt charity status, academy trusts remain subject to the key principles of charity law. The trustees (directors) of an academy trust have the same general duties and responsibilities as trustees of other charities. These are summarised by the Charity Commission in their guidance entitled *The Essential Trustee: What you need to know* (CC3):

> Trustees have and must accept ultimate responsibility for directing the affairs of a charity, and ensuring that it is solvent, well-run, and delivering the charitable outcomes for the benefit of the public for which it has been set up.

Being a charity means that certain additional restrictions apply to the academy trust's operation, including restrictions around non-charitable trading and payments being made to trustees or to connected parties. Academy trusts are also required to prepare accounts under the Charities' Statement of Recommended Practice (SORP).

The Department for Education and the Charity Commission have entered into a memorandum of understanding which details how they will work alongside one another including, for example, the circumstances when the Secretary of State might invite the Charity Commission to use its powers of intervention and investigation under the Charities Act 2011.'

The trustee

A director of an academy is also regarded as a trustee for the purposes of charity law. In a single academy, this will be the governors of the academy trust. In a MAT, the charity trustees are the directors of the academy trust; any governors sitting on an individual school's local governing body are akin to committee members and do not have trustee responsibility. In an umbrella arrangement, each school is a charity in its own right and the governors/directors of each academy will be charity trustees.

Trustees are required by law to 'have regard' to the public benefit guidance produced by the Charity Commission 'when exercising any powers or duties to which the guidance is relevant'. This means that trustees should be able to show that they are aware of the guidance and have taken it into account when making any decision to which it is relevant and have good reasons if they depart from the guidance. The Charities (Accounts and Reports) Regulations 2008 (SI 2008/629) also require trustees to confirm that they have done so in their annual report.

Trustees have ultimate responsibility for the charity and its property and must:

- make sure the charity complies with the law and its governing document;
- act responsibly, in the interests of the charity and its beneficiaries;
- manage any conflicts of interest; and
- exercise reasonable care and skill – using relevant personal knowledge or taking professional advice where appropriate.

It is paramount that trustees remember that their duty is owed to the charity, which must be uppermost in any decision making; despite the method of appointment or election, trustees do not represent any specific body or group. Trustees must not forget that the academy controls public funds. This introduces a further layer of regulatory requirements.

The company secretary

Since the Companies Act 2006 there has been no legal requirement to appoint a designated company secretary provided that there is no specific requirement to do so within the Articles of Association.

The Department for Education has provided model Memorandum and Articles of Association which schools are not expected to change (see Chapters 3 and 4). There is no specific requirement to appoint a company secretary included in the model articles. It is, of course, still open to an academy to choose to appoint a company secretary.

Normally, a company secretary will act as the chief administrative officer of the academy. Their specific responsibilities will differ depending on the requirements of the academy but they are likely to advise on legal and regulatory matters, finance and accounting, governance and the development of strategic planning. In fact, they could be responsible for any of the matters covered by this book – and more!

A company secretary is a high-ranking professional whose role is often combined with that of the director of finance. They enable the directors to retain a strategic focus managing the business of the academy. The company secretary will carry legal responsibilities; however, ultimate responsibility for administration of the academy lies with the directors.

Unfortunately, smaller academies or individual schools in an umbrella may not have the financial resources to appoint a specialist company secretary directly. Various organisations such as solicitors, offer a company secretarial service which will fulfil the requirements relating to Companies House and company law. However, many more academies are opting to appoint a member of staff to take responsibility for the company secretarial function rather than using external providers. Often this will be the bursar/director of finance or business manager.

Whatever the approach, academies must fulfil their obligations. The company secretarial function is fundamental and whoever undertakes the role should not underestimate the level of responsibility involved. It is incumbent on the directors to make sure that any person appointed knows what they are doing. As well as possible liability implications for the directors and company secretary, failure to meet these requirements could see academies threatened with fines from Companies House followed by a visit from the DfE or Ofsted!

The role of the company secretary is not dictated by legislation or regulation, so the remit of any person appointed will be established by the terms of their contract of employment. There is no 'typical' company secretary, but it should be recognised as a key operational role.

An academy is not legally bound to appoint a company secretary. Where no company secretary has been formally appointed, the liability will fall on the directors as a whole.

Secretary/clerk

The model articles provide that the directors should appoint a clerk or secretary to the board 'at such remuneration and upon such conditions as they may think fit'. The person appointed cannot be a director or principal, although the board may appoint a director to act as clerk for any meeting where the clerk fails to attend. The 'clerk' in this sense is akin to the clerk to the full governing body in a maintained school.

The clerk has a central role in organising and directing the work of the board just as in a maintained school. The importance of the position has not gone unnoticed. In their 'Report on the Role of School Governing Bodies' published in July 2013, the House of Commons Education Committee commented:

'As professional bodies, school governors need professional support. The role of clerk to a school governing body should be classed as a professional post.'

COMMENT

Emma Knights, Chief Executive of the National Governors' Association stated:

'For academy governance to be effective, they need the support of a professional clerk to advise those involved in every layer of governance on their duties and how best to fulfil them. The National Governors' Association is carrying out a piece of work called *Clerking Matters* alongside others, including the Society of Local Authority Chief Executives (SOLACE), to improve the profile of clerking, and encourage all schools to invest in this vital post. The House of Commons Education Select Committee inquiry on the role of school governing bodies concluded that "An effective clerk is vital to the success of a governing body. The evidence clearly indicates that this should be a professional role – similar to a company secretary."'

The clerk should be able to provide support on a much wider basis than simply attending to take the minutes of meetings. They should be well versed in the law and procedures relevant to meetings and the particular requirements of the funding agreement and Articles of Association adopted by their own academy. The requirements are often very different to those of the maintained sector and they should be well trained and conversant in the legalities.

Historically, the role of clerk to the governing body was undertaken by the school secretary. This is no longer appropriate. Not only is the role important in its own right, requiring particular knowledge and training, but it presents a difficult dilemma for the individual who reports to the head teacher as part of their day job, but to the board, and specifically to the chair, when they operate as clerk to the board. An independent and appropriately qualified clerk is recommended.

There is a legal obligation on the academy to compile and retain minutes of board meetings; a record of board decisions should also be kept, whether passed in a board meeting or via a written resolution. The requirements are too onerous not to be given the attention they deserve.

There is obviously a distinct overlap in the roles of clerk and company secretary and consideration should be given to the most appropriate arrangements to meet the needs of an academy.

COMMENT

Simon Osborne FCIS, Chief Executive of ICSA:

'The number of schools converting to academies increases year on year. There are now over 3,500 but many governors do not appreciate that, on conversion from school to academy, they become directors and trustees, as well as remaining as governors; and they take on a range of legal duties of which they may not be fully aware. The DfE audit findings in 2012, following the investigation at The Priory Federation of Academies Trust, referred, perhaps kindly, to a misunderstanding of responsibilities and unclear or inadequate policies. That case, and several others, demonstrate the need for academy governors to understand what constitutes good corporate governance; and that a fully qualified company secretary/clerk is indispensable in ensuring that good governance is applied in practice. The basic error into which governors will be well advised not to fall is to assume that they just need someone, anyone who is able to take a few minutes of meetings. The role is much wider than that.

Actually the role of secretary or clerk to academy governors is one for which chartered secretaries are well qualified and suited. They have been grounded in business and company law, governance, strategy, financial management and decision making as well as sound principles of secretaryship and administration. They have the know-how to advise the chair of governors and the governors as a whole across a wide spectrum of issues and about the appropriate governance framework for the organisation. In short, to borrow a slogan for a quite different industry, they know how to help keep an organisation like an academy "legal, honest, decent and truthful".'

▓ Summary

Background

- The idea for publicly funded schools free from local authority control dates back to 1988 and has been extended and expanded by successive Conservative, Labour and Coalition governments. The academies programme is here to stay.
- Initially, academies were converter CTCs as well as failing schools sponsored by a third party. Today, all maintained schools have the opportunity to convert to academy status.

What is an academy?

- An academy is a state-funded independent school free from local authority control.
- Academies are charitable companies limited by guarantee and must be registered as a company with Companies House. They are also exempt charities regulated by the DfE.
- Funding is received direct from the EFA and calculated in a similar way to maintained schools.
- Academies use DfE model documentation when they are created which forms the constitution and sets the rules for the business operations of the academy.
- External sponsors no longer provide funding to underperforming schools when taking responsibility for improvements in performance. A failing school may be able to join a MAT where it legally becomes part of that academy structure rather than just supported by it.

Continuing obligations

- There are greatly increased responsibilities on the directors of an academy.
- The academy must develop and operate an outstanding school with excellent pupil progress and achievement, as well as taking overall responsibility for property, staffing or general legal requirements.
- The requirements on an academy are more onerous in terms of accounting functions and it must prepare and publish audited annual accounts.

Benefits of 'academisation'

- Academies benefit from greater freedoms including:
  freedom from local authority control;
  the ability to set their own pay and conditions for staff;
  freedoms around the delivery of the curriculum; and
  the ability to change the length of terms and the school day.
- Staff who have previously worked for a school which has converted to academy status will be protected by TUPE and will transfer their employment on the same terms and conditions.
- Teachers belong to the TPS, a national defined benefit pension scheme. No individual liability is transferred to an academy.
- Non-teaching staff are eligible for membership of the LGPS, a defined contribution pension scheme. An academy is theoretically liable for any deficit in the scheme as it relates to their own staff which could lead to an adverse impact on the bottom line of academy accounts.

Charity status

- Academies are automatically classified as exempt charities and do not need to register with the Charity Commission but they do need to confirm their charitable status with HMRC.
- The DfE acts as principal regulator for academies and oversees compliance with charity law.

The trustee

- A director of an academy is also regarded as trustee for the purposes of charity law.
- Trustees must 'have regard' to the public benefit guidance produced by the Charity Commission 'when exercising any powers or duties'.

The company secretary

- There is no legal requirement to appoint a designated company secretary.

- The company secretary is a high-ranking professional who acts as the chief administrative officer of the academy.
- Whether a dedicated company secretary is appointed or not, academies must fulfil their obligations and directors could find themselves personally liable for any failures.

Secretary/clerk to the board

- The model articles provide that the directors should appoint a clerk or secretary to the board who cannot be a director or principal.
- The clerk has a central role in organising and directing the work of the board.
- An independent and appropriately qualified clerk is recommended. The legal obligations on the board are too onerous not to be given the attention they deserve.

2 Governance structures

▨ In this chapter

This chapter considers the different governance structures available for new and converter academies, specifically looking at:

- single academies as a separate legal entity;
- chains including multi-academies, umbrellas and the options for collaborative working;
- free schools or 'parent-led' academies;
- studio schools and University Technical Colleges; and
- the role of sponsors.

Becoming an academy, either through conversion or as a new endeavour, involves decisions about the way that the school is going to operate and collaborate long before the first pupil has walked through the door. This is not a simple decision.

The first academies were standalone, single academies, where the school was one company. This meant that the first of the academy converters were large secondary schools with significant resources and manpower to support the additional workload. The very first converters also had the benefit of an external sponsor which contributed significant financial resources. Unfortunately, for many smaller schools (particularly with the removal of sponsorship funding) the reality of setting up alone was not an option. Consequently, as time has gone on, different structures have evolved to enable schools to work together.

The Department for Education (DfE) is clear that schools cannot use the conversion process to change or remove their faith character, expand, become mixed or single sex or introduce selection. There is a presumption that schools will convert 'as is' with the governance structure unchanged. Of course, for the multi-academy arrangements this has proved difficult, with some level of modification in the governance structure being necessary.

Figure 2.1: Single academy governance structure

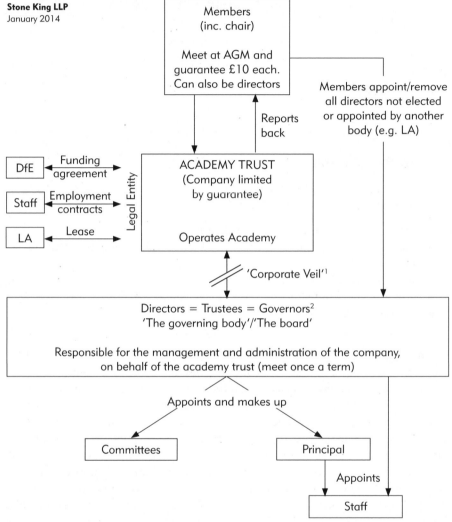

Stone King LLP
January 2014

Members (inc. chair)

Meet at AGM and guarantee £10 each. Can also be directors

Members appoint/remove all directors not elected or appointed by another body (e.g. LA)

Reports back

Funding agreement → DfE

ACADEMY TRUST (Company limited by guarantee)

Operates Academy

Legal Entity

Employment contracts → Staff

Lease → LA

'Corporate Veil'[1]

Directors = Trustees = Governors[2]
'The governing body'/'The board'

Responsible for the management and administration of the company, on behalf of the academy trust (meet once a term)

Appoints and makes up

Committees

Principal

Appoints

Staff

Notes:

[1]*Corporate veil*
The Directors/Trustees/Governors have no personal liability for their actions on behalf of the academy, unless they act outside their powers or continue to trade when they are aware the academy is insolvent. They may, however, be responsible for regulatory breaches.

[2]*Directors/Trustees/Governors*
The terms 'Directors', 'Trustees' and 'Governors' are interchangeable, as the role is essentially the same. The three terms are used as the responsibilities of the board are governed by three different branches of law – as the academy trust is set up as a company limited by guarantee and a charity, and the academy is an educational establishment. In education terminology, they are known as 'governors' of the school. In company law terms, they are 'directors' of the academy trust as a company. Under charity law, they are known as 'trustees' of the academy trust as a charity. Whatever terminology is chosen, they have the same duties and responsibilities.

Single academies

A single academy is a separate legal entity which is responsible for one school. It has its own funding agreement and Articles of Association with the Secretary of State.

Becoming a single academy is an onerous responsibility for a school. As well as the practical aspects of running a school outside of the local authority (LA), it is necessary to demonstrate that the school has the capacity to maintain high levels of achievement and attainment.

Any school considering conversion as a single academy should fulfil the following requirements:

- The most recent Ofsted grading is 'Good' or 'Outstanding'.
- Results are above floor targets and national averages.
- The school has the capacity to identify and support school improvement to raise standards further.
- The school has sufficient business support resources and finance skills.

However, the DfE has stated that each application will be considered on its own merits.

COMMENT

Graham Burns, Partner with Stone King:

The governance structure in single academies –
Flat governance v two-tier structure

In many academy trusts, every governor will consent to being a member. This is referred to as 'flat structure' because the members will consist of the same persons making up the governing body.

In other academy trusts, the members may be a small and distinct group from the governors (typically consisting of the chair of governors, vice chair and some other committee chairs). This is referred to as a 'two-tier structure' as the members have the authority to make a small number of decisions without consulting the governors.

Once the governors have grasped the differences between the role of the governors as the directors of the academy trust responsible for the running of the academy, and the role of the members who have reserved powers, such as amending the Articles of Association, it is easier to understand the distinction between a flat and a two-tier structure.

In cases where a flat structure has been adopted it is particularly relevant that the governors understand in which capacity they are making decisions concerning the academy (i.e. whether they are wearing their *governor's hat* or *member's hat*).

The DfE's current preferred approach is for the academy to adopt the two-tier structure. This is partly because the DfE has been resistant to the headteacher or other school employees being members (as recorded in a footnote to the DfE model articles). On this basis, it should be anticipated that as a matter of policy the DfE may request that the headteacher and any school employees are excluded from the membership.

Despite the flat structure not being the DfE's preferred approach, one of the key benefits of this structure is that as the powers reserved to the members (such as amending the Articles of Association) are not provided to a distinct group of persons from the directors, this results in a more democratic approach taken to the running of the academy.

There are, however, some practical considerations that will need to be factored in if a flat-structure is adopted; for instance, depending on the individual academy trust's needs, it may be advantageous to amend the DfE's model articles to provide that a governor who is also a member shall cease to be a governor where he ceases to be a member.

Academy chains

Many schools feel that they would be better working with others in an academy chain, particularly where they have enjoyed a close relationship as part of a partnership arrangement. Generally, it will be for the individual schools to decide if they wish to become an academy and to join a chain. However, if schools are in a hard federation, it will be necessary for a conversion to cover all member schools.

The governance structure put into place must be appropriate to the circumstances of the chain to facilitate effective school improvement support for all schools.

The DfE defines a chain in a very loose way so that it can apply to any collaboration between schools, whether that is done through a legal structure or a more informal approach. Working with other schools enables a pooling of resources which can be used to improve performance, expand the curriculum or get better value for money.

The DfE recognises the strength of schools working together and the Governors' Handbook (published in January 2014) encourages collaborative arrangements, stating: 'Working together delivers benefits to schools at many levels, including in relation to their governance.'

Not only is the importance of collaborative working recognised by the DfE, but it expects schools to support one or more other schools (which can be maintained or academies themselves). This measure is intended to raise standards as part of a 'self-improving school system'. Although this commitment is not regularly monitored by the DfE, it is clear that collaborative arrangements will be part of the educational landscape in the longer term. Government has encouraged more schools to embrace the approach, not least by offering a 'primary chain grant' where three or more schools, the majority of which are primary, convert to become a MAT.

COMMENT

Graham Burns, Partner with Stone King:

'Where a school is wishing to collaborate with other schools, it is recommended that the Governors carefully consider the trust's intended purpose from the outset. Form should follow function – i.e. the schools should consider how they wish to work together, and what they want to achieve before considering what form their collaboration should take.'

Multi-academy trusts

The most structured chain is a multi-academy trust (MAT) – where a number of schools combine to form a single academy. The MAT is set up as a company so there is only one legal entity, with one board of directors, which is accountable for all schools within the MAT. It is also the most common form of chain. Ofsted's Annual Report, published in December 2013, noted that 91% of academy chains are MATs.

There is a master funding agreement between the Secretary of State and the MAT with each individual school having a supplemental funding agreement.

Funding is calculated based on pupil numbers in relation to the individual schools. However, the MAT has the flexibility to set up central services such as HR, facilities management, finance and business support which are utilised by all schools in the MAT. Depending on the size of the MAT, many services which were previously provided by the LA can be secured on a cost-effective basis. The funding for these central services will be sourced from a contribution often based on a percentage of the individual schools' budgets. The MAT now has flexibility in the way that the general annual grant (GAG) is applied across schools.

The MAT is accountable for the performance of each of the individual schools. A MAT can choose to establish a local governing body in each school to which it delegates some governance functions. The local governing body is akin to a committee of the MAT and individuals appointed as governors of the local governing body are not directors by virtue of the position (though they could also be appointed as a director).

Alternatively, some MATs engage with schools through an advisory body which acts as a mechanism for gathering information from schools for board consideration and decision making. Such advisory bodies can also act as a way of disseminating information to the individual schools in the MAT. Advisory bodies in this context do not have any delegated authority.

It is particularly important to have a clear governance structure which is understood by everybody, together with a schedule of delegation setting out what functions and authorities have been delegated by the board to local governing bodies, head teachers in the schools or other individuals.

All staff in the schools are employed by the MAT, which can also facilitate the sharing of expertise and transfer of personnel across sites. Ultimately, the MAT must be able to provide effective support to any of the schools that require it.

Efforts have been made to enable schools with different governance structures to work together in MATs (i.e. community, foundation and faith schools in a single MAT).

As a single legal entity, the MAT will have a single vision and strategy which it will apply to all schools subject to agreed flexibilities and variation.

COMMENT

Graham Burns, Partner with Stone King:

'In the MAT model, the Academy trust is responsible for operating a number of academies. The MAT enters into a master funding agreement with the Secretary of State which sets out the overarching terms and conditions which apply to all of the academies the MAT operates.

The MAT also enters into a supplemental funding agreement with the Secretary of State for each of its academies. Each supplemental funding agreement sets out terms and conditions which are specific to that Academy. Each Academy must be run in accordance with the terms of the master funding agreement and the terms of the Academy's supplemental funding agreement.

The members of the MAT are not involved in the day-to-day management, but will usually have the power to appoint a certain number of directors to the MAT and have certain constitutional powers under company law (such as amending the company's articles or changing the company's name).' (See Figure 2.2 below.)

Figure 2.2: Multi-academy governance structure

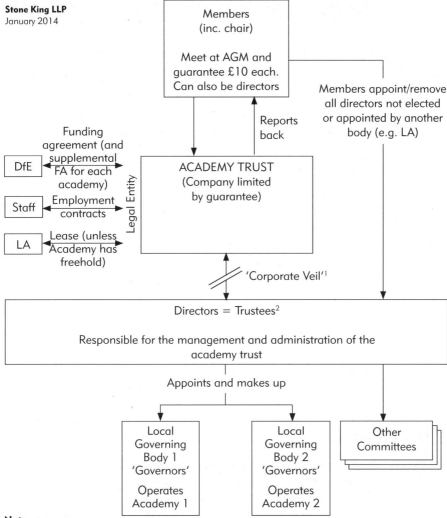

Stone King LLP
January 2014

Members (inc. chair)

Meet at AGM and guarantee £10 each. Can also be directors

Members appoint/remove all directors not elected or appointed by another body (e.g. LA)

Reports back

Funding agreement (and supplemental FA for each academy)

DfE

Employment contracts

Staff

Lease (unless Academy has freehold)

LA

Legal Entity

ACADEMY TRUST (Company limited by guarantee)

'Corporate Veil'[1]

Directors = Trustees[2]

Responsible for the management and administration of the academy trust

Appoints and makes up

Local Governing Body 1 'Governors' Operates Academy 1

Local Governing Body 2 'Governors' Operates Academy 2

Other Committees

Notes:

[1]*Corporate veil*
The Directors/Trustees/Governors have no personal liability for their actions on behalf of the academy, unless they act outside their powers or continue to trade when they are aware the academy is insolvent. They may, however, be responsible for regulatory breaches.

[2]*Directors/Trustees/Governors*
The terms 'Directors', 'Trustees' and 'Governors' are interchangeable, as the role is essentially the same. The three terms are used as the responsibilities of the board are governed by three different branches of law – as the academy trust is set up as a company limited by guarantee and a charity, and the academy is an educational establishment. In education terminology, they are known as 'governors' of the school. In company law terms, they are 'directors' of the academy trust as a company. Under charity law, they are known as 'trustees' of the academy trust as a charity. Whatever terminology is chosen, they have the same duties and responsibilities. They may, however, be responsible for regulatory breaches.

Table 2.1: Key advantages and disadvantages of MATs

Advantages	Disadvantages
■ Possibility of cohesive strategic leadership through MAT structure	■ Possibility of becoming a 'mini-LA' without LA equivalent economies of scale
■ Increased flexibility and operational efficiencies – less duplication of effort than two single academy trusts	■ No 'firewall' – risk of financial or educational failure for a single school affects all other schools
■ Increased value for money (VFM) and buying power through economies of scale	■ Academy budgets may be top sliced to support the central organisation
■ Top-down approach to driving school improvement allows academies to achieve strong collaboration and to use this collaboration and accountability to drive up school standards	■ No clear exit route for an academy which wishes to leave the MAT.
■ Sharing best practice and staff and leadership development opportunities	
■ Possibility of broader range of opportunities and benefits for students and staff	
■ One single employer – allowing greater flexibility for employer over staff teams	
■ Any future schools can easily be brought within the MAT family.	

▓ Umbrella trust

Schools can also join together in an umbrella arrangement. In this case, the over-arching body, or umbrella, is a charitable trust in its own right with its own board. Each of the individual schools is a single academy. An umbrella trust also allows schools of different status such as community, VC and VA to work together in a formal structure without having to alter their governance structure or change the representation by a faith or other foundation body.

There is a lot of flexibility in the model to decide on the level of collaboration and joint working. The umbrella often has the power to appoint members or directors to the individual academy schools providing a governance link. A close structure could be set up whereby the umbrella enables collaboration and shared governance which could include central services, employment of umbrella staff and a shared vision and strategy. A much looser arrangement may be preferred where the single academies wish to remain relatively independent.

COMMENT

Graham Burns, Partner with Stone King:

Umbrella trusts are usually established as a separate company limited by guarantee, and will have members and directors, in the same way as the individual academy trusts. Each academy trust will usually appoint members and directors 'up' to the umbrella trust.

The individual schools will need to decide who should be the members and directors of the umbrella trust. It is common for each academy trust to be a corporate member, although they will be represented at meetings by a nominated individual of their choice (see Figure 2.3).

The directors of the umbrella trust may be, for example, the principal, chair and vice-chair of directors of each academy trust. The directors will make decisions on behalf of the umbrella trust. Although they will be drawn from the member schools, the directors' duty will be to act in the best interest of the umbrella trust, and not the individual schools. Therefore, the directors will need to keep a close eye on any conflicts of interest they may have between their duty to act in the best interests of the umbrella trust and their interests in their respective academies.

One of the key benefits of using an umbrella trust is that member schools retain their autonomy, as each school has its own academy trust and its own funding agreement with the Secretary of State. Each governing body has responsibility for the running of their school, in the usual way. They are able to control what functions they devolve to the umbrella trust and, depending on the particular arrangements in place, they may extract themselves from these arrangements if they are no longer appropriate.

Another benefit is that the financial, performance or other issues in one member school should have less of an impact on the other member schools than if a closer collaborative structure, for example a multi-academy trust, was used. However, member schools still benefit from the support of working closely alongside other schools.

There are other notable benefits of collaborating as an umbrella trust, to include:

- encouraging a shared ethos and vision between member schools;
- procuring goods or services on behalf of member schools (with associated economies of scale);
- facilitating collaboration between member schools in areas of common interest, including leadership, professional development and best practice; and
- providing a governance link between the member schools.

Used properly, an umbrella trust can be a highly effective vehicle for collaboration. However, as it is a separate company limited by guarantee, it also represents an additional layer of administrative and regulatory burden (company law filing obligations, for example, and possible Charity Commission filing obligations). Therefore, schools should ensure that the benefits of the umbrella trust outweigh any additional time or cost that they will have to spend ensuring that it is properly run. It should also be noted that as a matter of DfE policy, the DfE may not approve a weaker school converting into an umbrella trust arrangement.

Figure 2.3: Umbrella trust governance structure

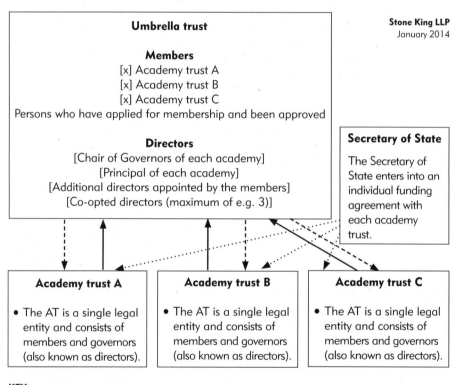

Umbrella trust

Stone King LLP
January 2014

Members
[x] Academy trust A
[x] Academy trust B
[x] Academy trust C
Persons who have applied for membership and been approved

Directors
[Chair of Governors of each academy]
[Principal of each academy]
[Additional directors appointed by the members]
[Co-opted directors (maximum of e.g. 3)]

Secretary of State

The Secretary of State enters into an individual funding agreement with each academy trust.

Academy trust A
- The AT is a single legal entity and consists of members and governors (also known as directors).

Academy trust B
- The AT is a single legal entity and consists of members and governors (also known as directors).

Academy trust C
- The AT is a single legal entity and consists of members and governors (also known as directors).

KEY

⟶ : Together the individual academy trusts will usually appoint all, or the majority of, the members and directors of the umbrella trust.

---▶ : The umbrella trust can be given the power to appoint members and/or directors of each individual academy trust, providing governance links between the academies.

·······▶ : Each Academy Trust enters into a funding agreement with the Secretary of State.

Table 2.2: Key advantages and disadvantages of umbrella structures

Advantages	Disadvantages
■ Academies retain level of autonomy as they have their own academy trust with separate governance arrangements ■ The umbrella trust may appoint members or governors in the individual academies, providing a clear governance link between the academies ■ The umbrella trust may set a joint vision for the academies or procure joint services and resources to reduce costs for the individual academies involved ■ Facilitates collaborative working amongst the academies and enables the academies to share good practice and to raise standards ■ May be beneficial where there is a group of schools of mixed categories (e.g. community, voluntary aided and voluntary controlled) which wish to collaborate ■ Easier for a school to leave the umbrella trust than a MAT.	■ The umbrella trust is a separate company limited by guarantee but is not an exempt charity and is likely to be required to register with the Charity Commission ■ Each academy trust is a separate legal entity with its own Company Law filing requirements – less cost saving opportunities than a MAT ■ Staff are employed by all different employers ■ Weaker schools who are ineligible to convert on their own need approval to join ■ Additional corporate structure adds extra layer of administration with associated costs.

■ Collaborative arrangements

Informal collaborative arrangements may be developed along the lines of partnerships to enable academies to work with each other and with maintained schools. It is possible to agree a memorandum of understanding between the various schools but there is no shared governance. Each academy involved in such an arrangement will have its own funding agreement and Articles of Association and will need to ensure their own corporate governance structures and company law compliance.

There are significant difficulties with a collaborative arrangement where there is the intention to set up central support to employ staff or to get the benefits of joint procurement. A collaborative arrangement such as this would be regarded as a partnership, which could have significant repercussions in terms of risk. The parties in a partnership are regarded as having 'joint and several' liability. This means that each individual party is liable to the full extent of the obligation in respect of a liability; one party could find themselves liable to pay the full extent of a claim to a claimant and then take action against the other partners for their respective elements of liability and payment. Consequently, it is more difficult to employ staff and run central services in a collaborative arrangement.

It is also possible for maintained schools and academies to collaborate through a 'school company' (ss. 11–13 Education Act 2002):

- to provide services or facilities for any schools;
- to exercise relevant LA functions; or
- to contract for goods or services from third parties on behalf of member schools.

CASE STUDY

Brian Walton, Headteacher at Headley Park Primary School, describes their collaborative arrangement:

'I am part of a collaboration called the Malago Learning Partnership (MLP and not to be confused with Malaga). We are a group of seven primaries and one secondary within South Bristol. Our schools have collaborated since 2011. All the primaries who joined the partnership have made significant improvements as illustrated through Ofsted inspections since 2012.

1 moved from good to outstanding.

1 from satisfactory to outstanding.

2 from satisfactory to good.

1 new academy (after a history of inadequate in its previous form) was graded good.

One school has an interim assessment deferring their inspection – good.

The last primary to join the partnership was at the time in special measures. It has since had, by far, its best ever results (High 80's and 90's L4+) and considering it has free school meals (FSM) at 80%+ and now has very stable leadership will be a strong school in its next full inspection.

Our secondary is currently graded "Requires Improvement" by Ofsted.

The schools sit in an area of social need with Pupil Premium figures on average at 49% compared to the Bristol average of 24%.

Our model of partnership involves:

- Two school improvement visits per year to each school
- Termly head's strategy meetings with three additional days of CPD

- MLP website to provide forums for CPD and share school led professional development
- Joint INSET training (Jan 2014 – Over 540 staff and 70 workshops (90% led by partnership staff))
- A joint Practice Development Group (JPDG) who identify and broker support within the MLP
- Joint analysis day leading to a risk matrix shared within the MLP and including production of a shared data pack and presentation to strategic partners
- Established clusters for specific areas including Early Years Foundation Stage (EYFS), Inclusion, Transition, ICT and NQTs.

I think what is most unique about the MLP is that it is a fully functioning system-led collaborative partnership (there's a mouthful!) which includes a sponsored academy (E-Act), CofE primary, maintained schools, independent academies and a secondary academy. It is a mixed bag and there is no law, we know of, that can bind us. Therefore, we are doing this because we see the impact it is having on our school communities. That is a VERY powerful incentive.'

CASE STUDY

Academies can also find themselves in a collaborative arrangement due to the nature of their governance structure. One company secretary acts for five of the grammar schools in Birmingham; these five schools are now academies:

- King Edward VI Aston School
- King Edward VI Camp Hill School for Boys
- King Edward VI Camp Hill School for Girls
- King Edward VI Five Ways School
- King Edward VI Handsworth School for Girls.

The company secretary's role ensures a robust and consistent approach to governance across each of these academies and items of common interest are shared across the five.

Although established as standalone academies, these schools enjoy a close relationship due to the underlying foundation and as a member of each academy trust may make appointments to the individual governing bodies.

The academies converted from former voluntary aided grammar schools and retain a selective admissions policy.

Free schools

Free schools were set up by the Coalition government following the general election in 2010. They were influenced by similar models in Sweden and New Zealand and the Charter movement in the US and Canada.

They are state-funded schools, independent of LA control. Academically non-selective free schools are nevertheless subject to the School Admissions Code of Practice (with the exception that they are allowed to give priority to founders' children). Free schools are charitable companies limited by guarantee in just the same way as academies. In other words, free schools are a type of academy. This has been recognised by the Labour shadow cabinet who plan to rebrand them 'Parent-led academies' if, and when, it gets into power.

Free schools can be set up by 'proposer groups' of parents, teachers, charities or other groups. Free schools can be mainstream, special, alternative provision or 16- to 19-year-old schools which have demonstrated evidence of demand in the area. The group applying to set up a free school will generally adopt complete respon-sibility for the management of the school on an ongoing basis. Alternatively, it may be possible for the group to either hand over day-to-day running of the school or transfer complete control to an external education provider. Many of the existing free schools have been set up by existing providers and academy chains. At present, free schools cannot be set up or be taken over by for-profit companies.

The proposer group must use the pre-opening period to identify appropriate directors. The DfE will provide guidance in designing governance structures and reporting arrangements to drive school improvement.

A number of independent schools have now converted to become free schools.

Studio schools and University Technical Colleges (UTCs)

Studio schools were also introduced by the Coalition government in 2010. Intended as innovative institutions offering project-based practical learning as well as mainstream academic qualifications, they are schools for 14- to 19-year-olds which are set up with the backing of local businesses and employers. Studio schools are small with around 300 students. They follow workplace opening hours with a 9 to 5 working day and year-round timetable.

Studio schools offer core academic qualifications together with more vocational qualifications, all of which are taught following a practical and project-based approach. Study is combined with paid work placements. Studio schools endeavour to provide students with the skills that are required by employers including punctuality, good communication, reliability and team-working, whilst ensuring a strong grounding in English, maths and science.

UTCs are technical academies for 14- to 19-year-olds and are sponsored by universities and employers. Typically, further education colleges and other educational institutions such as established academies, work in partnership with a UTC. The UTC programme is sponsored by the Baker Dearing Trust, an educational trust established by Lord Kenneth Baker, former Secretary of State for Education.

With around 500–800 students, UTCs offer technically orientated courses of study which are taught alongside core GCSEs. There is a focus on disciplines that require modern, highly specialised equipment such as engineering, manufacturing and construction, which are taught alongside general business and ICT skills. UTCs prepare students for a range of careers and continuing education at 19.

Studio schools and UTCs are both versions of the academy and model funding agreements and annexes for both are available.

Nominees of the employer and university sponsors must together form the majority on the board of directors.

Sponsors

Under-performing schools are usually sponsored, which means that the lead sponsor will have majority control of the academy and be able to appoint the majority of members. NCSL research published in 'The Growth of Academy Chains: Implications for Leaders and Leadership' identified eight different types of academy sponsor:

- successful school
- charitable non-faith-based organisation
- charitable faith-based organisation
- philanthropic individual
- further education college
- higher education institution
- corporate.

However, successful converter academies are now the most common sponsors and it may not be terribly useful to talk in terms of sponsors here. Where a failing school converts to join a MAT, the school is subsumed into the governance structure of the overall company; the MAT is responsible for its performance in the same way as any other school, whether struggling or 'Outstanding'.

Furthermore, academies can choose to involve a sponsor who can bring specialist expertise or knowledge. This is particularly apparent in the studio school and UTC format where employers and university sponsors may bring valuable input.

▣ Summary

Governance structures

- There is a presumption that schools will convert 'as is', though some modification of governance structure may be necessary in multi-academy arrangements.

Single academies

- A single academy is a separate legal entity with its own funding agreement and Articles of Association.

Academy chains

- Maintained schools in a hard federation must convert together.
- The DfE expects schools to support one or more other schools as part of a 'self-improving school system'.

Multi-academy trusts (MATs)

- The MAT is a single legal entity with one board of directors which is accountable for all schools within the MAT.
- There is a master funding agreement between the Secretary of State and the MAT with each individual school having a supplemental funding agreement.

Umbrella trust

- The over-arching body, or umbrella, is a charitable trust in its own right with its own board. Each school is set up as a single academy.
- An umbrella trust allows schools of different status to work together in a formal structure without having to alter their governance structure or change the representation by a faith or other foundation body.

Collaborative arrangements

- Informal collaborative arrangements may be developed along the lines of partnership to enable academies to work with each other and with maintained schools.
- Maintained schools and academies can collaborate through a 'school company'.

Free schools

- Free schools are a type of academy set up by 'proposer groups'.
- Free schools can be mainstream, special, alternative provision or 16–19 schools which have demonstrated evidence of demand in the area.

Studio schools and University Technical Colleges (UTCs)

- Studio schools offer project-based practical learning as well as main-stream academic qualifications for 14- to 19-year-olds and have the backing of local businesses and employers.
- UTCs are technical academies for 14- to 19-year-olds sponsored by a university and employers.
- Nominees of the employer and university sponsors together form the majority on the board of directors.

Sponsors

- Under-performing schools are usually sponsored with the lead sponsor having majority control of the academy.
- Successful converter academies are now the most common sponsors.
- Failing schools join, and are subsumed into, the governance structure of the MAT.

3 Funding agreement

In this chapter

This chapter explores the provisions of the funding agreement by looking at:

- the conditions of grant that need to be fulfilled by the academy;
- grants payable and the relevant financial and accounting requirements that apply;
- termination of the agreement including circumstances when it may take place and implications; and
- funding agreements for MATs.

The funding agreement

The funding agreement is effectively the contract by which the academy agrees to provide educational services in exchange for funding provided by the Department for Education (DfE). There are model versions of the funding agreement but these have been updated over time to reflect changes in policy and legislation.

The DfE does not expect schools to deviate from the model documents unless there are exceptional circumstances, although some variation may be agreed where the rationale can be satisfactorily justified. As a result, it is essential to refer directly to the academy's funding agreement to verify the particular requirements applicable.

Schools looking to convert must use the latest version of the funding agreement which incorporates the Memorandum and Articles of Association as appendices. Academies on older versions of the funding agreement can change to the latest version should they wish to do so.

COMMENT

Nick MacKenzie, Partner at Browne Jacobson:

'The funding agreement is the key contract between the Secretary of State and the academy trust. It governs the basis on which the academy trust will receive funding from central government. The academy trust is bound to conduct the academy in accordance with the terms of the funding agreement and it is therefore essential that the directors and senior management team have a comprehensive understanding of their obligations under the agreement.

The DfE updates its model funding agreement relatively regularly, for example to reflect changes in policy and to make clarificatory amendments. The DfE will sometimes contact existing academies asking them to agree to vary their existing funding agreement to adopt the latest model or a particular new clause. It is important that academies carefully consider the position before agreeing to vary their existing funding agreement. Ideally, legal advice should be sought on any proposed deed of variation issued by the DfE or EFA. There may be benefits to adopting a newer version of the funding agreement, but equally there may be less favourable implications.'

▦ Conditions of grant

Conditions and other requirements that the academy must fulfil are set out. These include that:

- the school will be at the heart of its community, promoting community cohesion and sharing facilities with other schools and the wider community;
- there will be assessments of pupils' performance as they apply to maintained schools and the opportunity to study for qualifications;
- the admissions policy and arrangements for the school will be in accordance with admissions law, and the DfE Codes of Practice;
- teachers' levels of pay and conditions of service will be the responsibility of the academy;
- there will be an emphasis on the needs of the individual pupils including those with special educational needs (SEN);
- there will be no charge in respect of admission to the school and the school will only charge pupils where the law allows maintained schools to charge; and
- the academy must be set up in a way that enables receipt and management of donations and it shall use reasonable endeavours to procure donations.

Governance
The academy will be governed by directors who must have regard to any guidance published by the Secretary of State for Education.

Conduct
The academy will be run in accordance with:

- the terms of the funding agreement;
- the Articles of Association; and
- any relevant legislative provisions.

Disclosure and Barring Service checks

Enhanced Disclosure and Barring Service (DBS) checks and any necessary further checks will be made for members of staff, supply staff and directors. A copy of an enhanced DBS certificate must be provided to the Secretary of State for Education on request.

COMMENT

Katie Michelon, Solicitor at Browne Jacobson:

'In terms of safe recruitment and vetting, academies are bound by the legislation that applies to independent schools, not maintained schools. This is made clear in the funding agreement which confirms that the academy trust must comply with the requirements of the Education (Independent School Standards) Regulations in relation to carrying out disclosure and barring service checks on all staff and governors. Importantly, these Regulations require an academy to carry out enhanced DBS checks on all its governors, which is different to the position for maintained schools.'

Pupils

The planned capacity of the academy is detailed, including the age range and whether there is a sixth form or nursery unit.

COMMENT

Katie Michelon, Solicitor at Browne Jacobson:

'The funding agreement sets out the academy's size, including the number of nursery and sixth-form places if applicable, and its age range. If any changes are made to these characteristics these will therefore need to be reflected in the funding agreement. The Secretary of State's agreement will be required as he will need to be party to the Deed of Variation that will legally amend the funding agreement. Remember though that it is the academy's capacity figure that should be included in the funding agreement, not its Published Admission Number (PAN), so a change to PAN will not necessarily trigger the need to amend the funding agreement.'

Designated teacher for looked-after children

The academy will act in accordance with, and be bound by, all relevant statutory and regulatory provisions, guidance and codes of practice in the same way as they apply to a maintained school.

Teachers and other staff

Under the terms of the latest model funding agreement documents, a mainstream academy can employ 'anyone it deems is suitably qualified or is otherwise eligible' as a teacher. Only a SEN coordinator and a designated teacher for looked-after children must hold qualified teacher status.

All staff must be given access to the relevant pension scheme: TPS for teachers and LGPS for all other employees.

If a teacher applies for a teaching post in another publicly funded organisation, the academy must advise in writing whether there have been any formal capability hearings over the past two years and details of any proceedings.

Curriculum, curriculum development and delivery and RE and collective worship

Academies do not have to follow the national curriculum, but they must provide a 'broad and balanced' curriculum for pupils up to the age of 16, including English, mathematics and science in mainstream academies. Information on the curriculum provision must be published by the academy including:

- content of the curriculum;
- approach to the curriculum;
- GCSE options, other Key Stage 4 qualifications or other future qualifications offered;
- names of any phonics or reading schemes in operation for Key Stage 1; and
- how parents (including prospective parents) can obtain further information.

The academy must make provision for the teaching of religious education and for a daily act of collective worship in both faith and non-faith academies.

Academies designated with a religious character must ensure that provision for religious education and collective worship are in accordance with the tenets and practice of the specific religion or religious denomination. The requirements will be slightly different depending on whether the academy is treated as a voluntary aided school with a religious character, a foundation school with a religious character or a voluntary controlled school.

The academy should have regard to guidance issued by the Secretary of State on sex and relationship education to ensure that pupils are 'protected from inappropriate teaching materials' and 'learn the nature of marriage and its importance for family life and for bringing up children'.

The promotion of partisan political views in teaching should be forbidden and political issues dealt with by offering a balanced presentation of opposing views.

This also applies to any extra-curricular activities offered at the academy. Pupils under 12 should be prevented from taking part in any political activities either in school or elsewhere if it is arranged by a member of staff or someone acting on behalf of the academy.

Assessment

The academy must ensure that pupils take part in assessments and in teacher assessments of pupils' performance and reporting will take place in the same way as in maintained schools. The academy will take part in monitoring and moderation of assessment arrangements in respect of all Key Stages.

Exclusions agreement

The academy can enter into an arrangement with a LA to the effect that payment will flow between the academy and the LA in the same way as it would do were the academy a maintained school.

School meals

Unless it would be unreasonable to do so, school lunches should be provided when they are requested by or on behalf of any pupil. A school lunch must be provided free of charge to any pupil entitled to free school lunches. From September 2014, free school lunches must be provided to all KS1 pupils.

Charging

An academy is treated in the same way as a maintained school in respect of charging, particularly in relation to the obligation to enter pupils for public examinations, charges, regulations about information about charges and school hours, voluntary contributions, recovery of sums as civil debt and interpretation regarding charges. The terms also place an obligation on an academy to have a charging and remissions policy.

International education surveys

The academy must provide such information as required by the Secretary of State for participation in international surveys such as Programme for International Student Assessment (PISA).

Pupil premium

The pupil premium is additional funding given to publicly funded schools in England to raise the attainment of disadvantaged pupils and close the gap between them and their peers.

Pupil premium funding is available to both mainstream and non-mainstream schools, such as special schools and pupil referral units. It is paid to schools according to the number of pupils who:

- have been registered as eligible for free school meals at any point in the last six years or
- have been looked after for one day or more
- were adopted from care on or after 30 December 2005 or left care under:
  - Special Guardianship Order on or after 30 December 2005
  - Residence Order on or after 14 October 1991.

In addition, there is a 'service child premium' payable at a lower rate for children who have parents in the armed forces.

Information must be published annually in relation to:

- the amount of pupil premium allocation that will be received in that financial year;
- what the pupil premium allocation will be spent on;
- how pupil premium was spent in the previous financial year; and
- the impact on educational attainment resulting from expenditure of pupil premium in the previous financial year.

Duration of school day and year

The academy can determine the duration of the school day, term dates and year. The provisions in respect of school sessions required for maintained schools do not apply and there are no other obligations in respect of the number of days or length of a school day.

Grants to be paid by the Secretary of State

The Secretary of State commits to pay grants towards 'recurrent expenditure' to cover the 'establishment, conduct, administration and maintenance of the academy'. Two separate and distinct grants are made: general annual grant (GAG) and earmarked annual grant (EAG).

Grants may also be made towards capital expenditure; however, there is no commitment on behalf of the Secretary of State to do so.

The academy cannot budget for expenditure in excess of expected income without the Secretary of State's prior agreement.

Capital grant

Specific prior written agreement by the Secretary of State must be obtained prior to incurring any capital expenditure on which capital grant payments are sought. Capital expenditure may include costs for building new premises or for substantially refurbishing existing premises.

The payment of the capital grant is subject to the following conditions:

- such grants are used solely to defray expenditure approved by the Secretary of State;

- the academy certifying and providing evidence that all planning and other consents necessary for the development and all related infrastructure to be completed have been obtained or put in place; and
- any other conditions that the Secretary of State may specify.

General annual grant

The general annual grant (GAG) will be paid to cover the normal running costs of the academy such as salary and administration costs. The funding is equivalent to that which would be received by a maintained school with similar characteristics, together with an additional element for functions which would be carried out by the LA if the academy were a maintained school.

A larger GAG may be available for the 'start-up period' of a newly opened academy to enable it to operate effectively.

The amount of GAG is determined annually and is notified to the academy in a funding letter preceding the academy's financial year. GAG is paid in monthly instalments on or before the twenty-fifth day of each month via BACS; the payment should be available in the academy's nominated bank account on the first working day of each month. A monthly remittance advice is also issued. Each instalment should be used to fund the salaries and other payroll costs for the relevant month of all monthly paid employees and all other costs payable during the following month.

Earmarked annual grant

The earmarked annual grant (EAG) may be paid for either recurrent expenditure or capital expenditure for such specific purposes as have been agreed between the Secretary of State and the academy. EAG may only be spent in accordance with the scope, terms and conditions of the grant set out in the relevant funding letter.

To apply for an EAG, the academy must submit a letter outlining its proposals and the reasons for its request to the DfE.

Other relevant funding

Funding may also be received from a LA in respect of statements of SEN for pupils. The academy must ensure that provision detailed in statements of SEN is provided for such pupils.

▩ Financial and accounting requirements

The academy must abide by the requirements set out in the *Academies Financial Handbook*.

COMMENT

Nick MacKenzie, Partner at Browne Jacobson:

'It is important that the funding agreement is read in conjunction with the *Academies Financial Handbook*. The funding agreement specifically states that the academy trust must abide by the requirements of the Handbook and there are various clauses within the funding agreement which refer back to the detail set out within the *Handbook*. For example, if an academy wishes to write off a debt or make a compensation payment, it will need to refer to the limits set out in the Handbook to check whether the value of the transaction is such that it needs Secretary of State consent to do so.'

The formal budget plan must be approved by the academy each financial year.

The academy must put into place financial and other controls which conform to the requirements both of propriety and of good financial management. Audited accounts must be prepared and filed with Companies House and the Secretary of State for Education. Insurance must be procured in respect of the leasehold/freehold interest of the site upon which the academy is situated.

GAG funding may only be used for the educational charitable purpose of advancing for the public benefit education in the United Kingdom, in particular by establishing, maintaining, carrying on, managing and developing an academy offering a broad and balanced curriculum.

The academy may generally use funds received from private sources or other public sources as it sees fit, though these funds must be separately identified in the balance sheet. Funds from other sources may have restrictions placed on them by the donor (e.g. a fundraising event for a new art room could restrict the funds to being used for the new art room).

Thirty days' prior notice must be given to the Secretary of State of any intention to:

- give any guarantees, indemnities or letters of comfort;
- write off any debts owed to it (above the delegated limit set out in the *Academies Financial Handbook*) or offer to make any *ex gratia* payments;
- make any sale, purchase of, or otherwise dispose of freehold or leasehold property including entering into a contract to dispose of land or granting an option to acquire an interest in land; or
- take up any leasehold or tenancy agreement for a term exceeding three years.

The prior written consent of the Secretary of State must be obtained where such actions relate to publicly funded assets or property.

The academy must balance its budget each year, though it may carry forward surpluses (subject to any limitation set out in the *Academies Financial Handbook* or as notified by the Secretary of State).

The academy must observe the Charity Commission's guidance to charities and charity trustees and in particular the Charity Commission's guidance in Protecting Charities from Harm.

Every academy must appoint an Accounting Officer and notify the Secretary of State of that appointment. The expectation (as set out in the *Academies Financial Handbook*) is that this will be the principal/head teacher or the chief executive officer in a MAT, unless an alternative approach exists which better suits the academy's circumstances.

Chapters 10 and 11 provide more information on this topic.

Borrowing powers

The academy cannot borrow, whether short-term or long-term, without the specific approval of the Secretary of State which will only be granted in limited circumstances.

An overdraft may only be operated to cover irregularities in cash flow and will require the approval of the members in general meeting and in writing by the Secretary of State. Specific advice should be sought regarding the identification of leases and complexities of lease accounting.

Disposal of assets

An academy must give 30 days' written notice to the Secretary of State where it intends to dispose of an asset at a price less than the highest price that can be obtained. The *Academies Financial Handbook* sets out the classes of asset that require specific consent prior to disposal, in particular publicly funded land and buildings. Proceeds of sale of any asset funded by a capital grant from the Secretary of State may need to be repaid in whole or part.

COMMENT

Nick MacKenzie, Partner at Browne Jacobson:

'Where an academy trust is contemplating acquiring or disposing of land, such as entering into a lease or tenancy agreement or selling land, it will need to refer back to the terms of its funding agreement as Secretary of State consent to the arrangement may be required. The terms in the funding agreement are supplemented by the provisions of the *Academies Financial Handbook* which set out further detail as to when Secretary of State consent is required and how to obtain this.'

Termination

Either party may give not less than seven financial years' written notice to terminate the Agreement, such notice to expire on 31 August.

Termination warning notice

The Secretary of State can issue a written notice of his intention to terminate the funding agreement where he/she considers that:

- the conditions and requirements of the agreement are not being met;
- the standards of performance of pupils are unacceptably low;
- there has been a serious breakdown in the way the academy is managed or governed; and
- the safety of pupils or staff is threatened.

The termination warning notice will specify:

- reasons for the termination warning notice;
- the remedial measures required; and
- the date by which the academy must respond to the termination warning notice.

Notice of intention to terminate

Written notice of the Secretary of State's intention to terminate the funding agreement can be given where the chief inspector has found:

- special measures are required to be taken in relation to the academy; or
- the academy requires significant improvement.

The notice will state the time frame in which the academy can respond.

Termination with immediate effect

The funding agreement can be terminated by the Secretary of State to take effect on the date of the notice where the academy has significant financial issues or is insolvent.

The academy must notify the Secretary of State as soon as possible after receiving any petition which may result in an order for the winding up or administration of the academy.

Change of control

The Secretary of State may terminate the funding agreement if there is a change in control of the academy (i.e. an organisation or individual who is able to appoint and remove a majority of the board and is thereby able to control the way that the academy acts). This could potentially occur where there is a change in the identity of the sponsor, although the Secretary of State can choose not to terminate if satisfied that the organisation assuming control is acceptable.

COMMENT

Katie Michelon, Solicitor at Browne Jacobson:

'Like any contract, the funding agreement can be terminated. A common myth is that the funding agreement is only a seven-year contract. In fact, the funding agreement does not have a set "expiry date"; the seven-year period stems from the fact that either the academy trust or the Secretary of State can choose to bring the funding agreement to an end by providing seven years' written notice. In practice, it is difficult to envisage a situation where the ability to terminate with seven years' notice would be exercised by either party. A funding agreement is more likely to be brought to an end due to circumstances requiring more urgent attention, such as slipping standards or financial difficulties. The funding agreement includes terms which enable the Secretary of State to step in and ultimately terminate the funding agreement in situations such as these. For example, if the Secretary of State considers that there has been a breakdown in the way the school is governed, there is a process through which the Secretary of State can issue a Termination Warning Notice and ultimately may terminate the funding agreement, in a similar way to how a local authority can issue a warning notice to a maintained school.'

Effect of termination

If the funding agreement is terminated, the school shall cease to be an academy. Provisions set out any indemnity to be provided by the Secretary of State and the treatment of any capital assets held by the academy at the date of termination.

■ General

Information

The Secretary of State has the right to call for information which the academy shall make available. The Secretary of State shall provide such information as is reasonably required for the running of the academy.

Access by Secretary of State's officers

The academy shall allow access to DfE officials at any reasonable time to its premises and make available all records, files and reports relating to the running of the academy. In advance of such a visit, the academy shall provide papers prepared for board and member meetings. Two DfE officials shall be entitled to attend and to speak at all such meetings.

The academy must make available for inspection by any interested party:

- the agenda for every meeting of the board or any committee with delegated authority;
- the draft minutes of every such meeting, if they have been approved by the person acting as chairman of that meeting;
- the signed minutes of every such meeting; and
- any report, document or other paper considered at any such meeting.

This documentation must also be sent to the Secretary of State upon request.

Any confidential information or references to named staff or pupils can be excluded or redacted.

Notices

Notices or communications should be sent to the address inserted into the agreement and must be in writing (i.e. not by e-mail) and in English.

Any notice or other communication must be:

- delivered by hand;
- sent by pre-paid first-class post; or
- sent by another next working day delivery service.

It will be considered to have been received if delivered by hand, on signature of a delivery receipt or at the time the notice is left at the address or at 9.00am on the second business day after posting.

The provisions do not apply to the service of any proceedings or other documents in any legal action.

Complaints

Complaints which arose prior to conversion and were investigated by the Local Government Ombudsman will continue to apply to the academy as if it were a maintained school. The Secretary of State will also have the power to investigate the matter as if it had taken place after conversion and the academy will be bound by any recommendation.

The Secretary of State can give an order and/or a direction in respect of any matters occurring within the 12 months immediately prior to conversion.

The academy must investigate any complaint made relating to matters arising in whole or in part during the 12 months prior to the opening of the academy.

▨ Annexes to the funding agreement

Various documents form the appendices to the funding agreement:

Annex A – Memorandum and articles of the academy

This is the constitution of the academy and sets out the rules by which it must be governed (see Chapter 4).

Annex B – Admissions requirements

An academy is its own admissions authority and responsible for managing its own admissions process. Academies are required to comply with the Admissions Code and must follow the procedures set out if it wishes to change admission arrangements. A converter academy retains the admission criteria relevant to it as a maintained school (e.g. a selective school can continue to use selective criteria).

Alternative arrangements are sometimes agreed for new free schools, studio schools and UTCs to aid establishment and ensure fair access.

Annex C – Arrangements for pupils with SEN and disabilities

This annex provides specific details relating to admission and support for SEN pupils.

Academies have equivalent SEN obligations to those placed upon the governing bodies of maintained schools by reason of the Education Act 1996 and subsequent regulations.

MATs

In a MAT, the overarching academy enters into a master funding agreement the terms of which apply to all of the schools operated as part of the MAT and which include provisions along the same lines as the single model funding agreement already discussed. Each of the individual schools within the MAT also enters into a supplemental funding agreement with the Secretary of State for Education which sets out the specific requirements in respect of that school.

COMMENT

Nick MacKenzie, Partner at Browne Jacobson:

'In a multi-academy trust (MAT) structure, termination clauses will be set out in each supplemental funding agreement meaning that one academy's supplemental funding agreement can be terminated without the master funding agreement or other supplemental funding agreements being affected. For example, if one academy within a MAT went into special measures, under the terms of the current model funding agreement, the Secretary of State could give notice of his intention to terminate that supplemental funding agreement without the other funding agreements being impacted. Of course, notwithstanding that the other funding agreement would remain in force, where Ofsted and the Secretary of State have deemed one academy operated by that academy trust to be inadequate, there is likely to be a reputational impact across the group.

In a multi-academy trust, the terms of the master funding agreement are likely to require that the academy trust establishes an 'Advisory Body' for each of the academies in its group. The funding agreement may also set out requirements for the constitution of the Advisory Body – most commonly that it must include two parent governors. Where MATs are looking to retain a substantial amount of control centrally, they must have in mind, therefore, that it is still a term of their funding agreement to establish an Advisory Body or Local Governing Body for each academy. If the academy trust believes this extent of local governance is not appropriate, it could look to explore agreeing an amendment to this requirement with the EFA.'

▪ Summary

Funding agreement

- The funding agreement is the contract by which the academy agrees to provide educational services in exchange for funding provided by the DfE. Reference should be made to the contents of the academy's own funding agreement.

Conditions of grant

- The school will be at the heart of its community, promoting community cohesion and sharing facilities with other schools and the wider community.
- Pupils' performance will be assessed in the same way as in maintained schools and pupils will have the opportunity to study for qualifications.
- The admissions policy and arrangements for the school will be in accordance with admissions law, and the DfE Codes of Practice.
- Teachers' levels of pay and conditions of service will be the responsibility of the academy.
- There will be an emphasis on the needs of the individual pupils including SEN pupils.
- There will be no charge in respect of admission to the school and the school will only charge pupils where the law allows maintained schools to charge.
- The academy must be set up in a way that enables receipt and management of donations and it shall use reasonable endeavours to procure donations.
- Enhanced DBS checks must be made for all members of staff, supply staff and directors.
- The planned capacity of the academy is detailed, including the age range and whether there is a sixth form or nursery unit.

- Other than any SEN coordinator or a designated teacher for looked-after children, an academy can employ anyone it deems appropriate as a teacher irrespective of whether they hold qualified teacher status.
- Academies do not have to follow the national curriculum, but they must provide a 'broad and balanced' curriculum for pupils up to the age of 16, including English, mathematics and science in mainstream academies.
- The academy must make provision for the teaching of religious education and for a daily act of collective worship in both faith and non-faith academies.
- The academy can determine the duration of the school day, term dates and year.

Grants to be paid by the Secretary of State

- Specific prior written agreement by the Secretary of State must be obtained prior to incurring any capital expenditure on which capital grant payments are sought.
- General annual grant will be paid to cover the normal running costs of the academy which will be equivalent to that which would be received by a maintained school with similar characteristics together with an additional element in respect of functions which would be carried out by the LA if the academy were a maintained school.
- Earmarked annual grant may be paid in respect of either recurrent expenditure or capital expenditure for such specific purposes as have been agreed between the Secretary of State and the academy and which may only be spent in accordance with the scope, terms and conditions of the grant set out in the relevant funding letter.
- Funding may also be received from a LA in respect of statements of SEN for pupils.

Financial and accounting requirements

- The academy must abide by the requirements set out in the *Academies Financial Handbook* and must put into place financial and other controls which conform to the requirements both of propriety and of good financial management. Audited accounts must be prepared and filed.
- Notice must be given to the Secretary of State in respect of any guarantees, writing off any debts, *ex gratia* payments, the sale, purchase or granting of an option over land, or taking up a leasehold or tenancy agreement for a term greater than three years.
- The academy must balance its budget each year, though it may carry forward surpluses.
- Every academy must appoint an accounting officer.

Termination

- Either party may give not less than seven financial years' written notice to terminate the Agreement, such notice to expire on 31 August.
- The Secretary of State can terminate the funding agreement, either on notice or with immediate effect, in circumstances set out in the agreement. The agreement may also be terminated if there is a change in control of the academy.

Annexes to the funding agreement

- Annex A – Memorandum and Articles of the academy.
- Annex B – Admissions requirements.
- Annex C – Arrangements for pupils with SEN and disabilities.

MATs

- The overarching academy enters into a master funding agreement and each of the individual schools enters into a supplemental funding agreement. Annex A to the master funding agreement will be the academy trust's Memorandum and Articles and Annex B will set out the arrangements for pupils with SEN and disabilities. The admissions requirements for each academy will be set out in Annex 1 to each supplemental funding agreement.

4 Memorandum and Articles of Association

▦ In this chapter

This chapter looks at the constitution and rules contained within the Memorandum and Articles of Association, considering the specific clauses covering:

- the structure and internal management including the objects, members and directors and delegation to committees and others;
- decision-making by members and directors and indemnity for those involved in the management of the academy;
- requirements for external reporting in respect of the annual return and annual accounts; and
- the limitations on appointing 'Local Authority Associated Persons'.

Appended to the funding agreement are the Memorandum and Articles of Association which are the constitution of the company and set out the rules by which the company must operate.

▦ Memorandum of Association

The Memorandum of Association is a simple document setting out the name of the academy and providing details of the three 'subscribers' who wish to form the academy and become its members under the Companies Act 2006.

▦ Articles of Association

The Articles of Association prescribe the internal management, decision making and running of the academy trust and its liability.

The Department for Education (DfE) has model documentation which schools are expected to adopt. This has changed over time, most notably in December 2012 and January 2013 when new versions were introduced. Furthermore, additional models have been introduced for use with new governance structures (e.g. the MAT Model allowing Church of England VC (Minority) schools to join together with non-Church of England schools which was agreed in August 2013).

The DfE does not generally expect schools to make changes to the model Memorandum and Articles of Association. However, in some instances, academies have negotiated and had amendments cleared by the DfE. It is essential to refer in detail to the version adopted by the academy.

The DfE has indicated its willingness to consider granting approval to academies who wish to change their Articles to the latest version.

Objects

This standard clause states the purpose and range of activities that the academy is set up to carry on. In particular, the primary object contained within the current model articles is to 'advance for the public benefit education in the United Kingdom'.

The clause goes on to set out the various powers that may be exercised in furtherance of its object.

COMMENT

Julia Green, Partner at Browne Jacobson:

'The Academy Trust as a limited company has to record its purpose. In company law this is known as the "objects" and they are recorded in the Articles of Association. The Articles of Association are the corporate record of how the Academy Trust governs itself. The objects of an Academy Trust are prescribed by the Secretary of State and specifically require the Company Directors and Members of the Academy Trust to establish, maintain, carry on, manage and develop education through a broad and balanced curriculum for the benefit of the children attending the named school or schools, in the case of a Multi-Academy Trust.

When considering whether a proposed action by the Academy Trust is appropriate (e.g. offering the use of sporting facilities to the wider community), it is vital that the Directors first look at their objects and decide whether the activity would fall within the objects or not. If it does not, then the Academy Trust needs to consider an alternative approach which could include amending the Articles to reflect the proposed activity. Such an approach would require the Members of the Trust to vote and agree the amendment.'

Members

Sets out details regarding the appointment of members and the removal or termination of their membership (see Chapter 6).

COMMENT

Julia Green, Partner at Browne Jacobson:

'The Academy Trust is a company. In order for the company to be formed it has to be created by a number of individuals known as founding members. These are the signatories of the Memorandum that brings the company into existence. In an Academy Trust there must be a minimum of three Members but there can be more, either at the outset or subsequently if agreed by the existing Members. The Members then go on to appoint Directors up to the number set out in the Articles of Association.

Governors of maintained schools converting to Academy status often find the concept of Members difficult. Common questions are around their role and whether they are more important than Directors or Trustees. The role of the Member is to act as a "guardian" of the company, ensuring that it is operating in accordance with the rules (the Articles of Association) and that it is financially healthy. It is the Members that sign off the accounts each year and who have a financial liability if the company fails; usually £10 per person. Whilst the figure is deliberately not burdensome in order that volunteers are not put off taking on the role, it underlines the significance of the responsibility that the Members have in keeping an overview of the performance of the company.'

General meetings (members' meetings)

The provisions relating to calling of general meetings and notice thereof, proceedings at meetings, voting by members and the appointment of proxies is detailed (see Chapter 6).

Directors/governors

Sets out the number of directors and the terms of their appointment including co-option, term of office, resignation and removal and disqualification. The provisions cover the appointment of the chair and vice-chair of the directors, the powers of the directors and conflicts of interest (see Chapter 7).

The model Articles of Association set out the requirements regarding the constitution of the board. This should comprise:

- at least two elected parent governors in a single academy; parental representation at board or LGB level which may be by election or appointment; and
- the principal (unless they choose not to be).

The remainder of the board and the LGB may be constituted in whatever way the directors feel appropriate, although they should ensure that the board has the necessary skills and expertise to carry out its functions.

COMMENT

Julia Green, Partner at Browne Jacobson:

'Directors are arguably the most important constitutional element of the Academy Trust. The Directors are responsible for the strategic running of the Trust. This is separate from the day to day running of the school which is the responsibility of the Head teacher and the Senior Leadership Team. A simple way to identify the different roles is to regard the Members as the guardians with the Directors and Senior Leadership Team being responsible for strategy and operational management respectively.

The Directors are also Governors and Trustees. The "Director" label depicts the responsibilities that they have under company law, the "Trustee" label depicts the role that they have under charity law and the "Governor" label depicts the role that they have under education law. These differences often confuse Governors looking to change and it is common for schools to query the relationship between the different designations for some time after conversion. They are the same person but wearing three different hats. To add to the layering, it is also possible that the Members of the company are also Governors, Trustees and Directors.

The maximum number of Directors will be set out in the Articles of Association and can be appointed a number of different ways although the majority are likely to be appointed by Members.'

Chief executive officer
In a MAT, the chief executive officer (CEO) is a director whilst they are in office.

Clerk/secretary to the directors
The directors can appoint a clerk/secretary 'at such remuneration and upon such conditions as they may think fit'. This person need not be the company secretary although there is a certain overlap between the roles (see Chapter 1).

The clerk cannot be either a director or principal. However, the board may appoint a director to act as clerk for the purposes of any meeting where the clerk fails to attend.

COMMENT

Julia Green, Partner at Browne Jacobson:

'The role of the Company Secretary is to submit the Annual Report to Companies House and input to Companies House any changes in the make up of the Trust, including resignations and appointments. They should maintain statutory books and registers and advise the Trust in respect of their governance responsibilities.

The role of the Clerk to the Governing Body is to assist the Chair of Governors in running the Board of the Academy Trust, convening meetings in accordance with the provisions of the Articles, minute keeping, record keeping and acting as correspondent for the Governors.

There is overlap between these two roles in that the purpose of both is to enable the Academy Trust to function smoothly and efficiently.

"Academy Trusts" appoint the two roles in different ways; for some both roles are carried out by the same person (usually the original Clerk to Governors) and sometimes the role of Company Secretary is taken by the Business Manager. Alternatively, the role of Company Secretary can be outsourced. All options are perfectly acceptable and will depend on the confidence and capacity of the individual staff members.'

The minutes

The clerk must draw up minutes of board meetings which should be kept in a book kept for the purpose. Once approved by the board, the minutes shall be signed by the person acting as chair at the same or next subsequent meeting.

Committees

The board can establish any committee and determine the constitution, membership and proceedings that will apply. The establishment, terms of reference, constitution and membership of any committee must be reviewed annually. Persons who are not directors can be appointed to a committee as long as the majority of members are directors. They can also be given voting rights as long as the majority of members of the committee present for any vote are directors.

In a MAT, the directors may appoint separate committees known as local governing bodies (LGBs) for each separate school. The requirements in respect of directors making up the majority of a committee do not apply in the case of LGBs. The functions and proceedings of LGBs are subject to regulations made by the directors from time to time.

Delegation

The board can delegate any power or function to an individual director, committee, the principal or any other holder of an executive office. That person must report to the board when that delegated authority has been exercised and any action taken or decision made. The delegation can be made subject to conditions imposed by the directors and may be revoked or altered.

COMMENT

Julia Green, Partner at Browne Jacobson:

'The Directors are responsible for the strategic direction of the Academy Trust. In order to have sufficient resources to implement the strategy and to understand the intricacies of what is in commercial terms a sophisticated business entity, the Directors can choose to set up committees which will report back to the main Board. Most Governors are used to this principle and have varying ways of dividing the different aspects of running a school. Most usually, committees are made up of a teaching and learning or curriculum committee; a finance committee; a personnel committee and a sites and buildings committee. Each committee will have Directors who have a particular interest or strength in that area of activity. The committee will have written terms of reference which clearly set out what the purpose of the committee is and what it is responsible for. A particular issue may be considered by the committee and a recommendation taken back to the main Board for a decision and vote. The main Board is entitled to rely on the recommendation of the committee but is not automatically expected to accept it favourably, allowing for an additional layer of scrutiny.

Multi Academy Trusts have resulted in a further development of governance and management. The Articles allow for committees to be set up and anticipate that there will be a "Local Governing Body" for each school within a Multi Academy Trust. Given that the emphasis is to make the Board of Governors "lean" and "effective", not every member of an existing governing body can sit on the Board when they join a MAT as this would result in too many numbers of Directors and become unmanageable. A significant number will remain at LGB level. The name is slightly confusing as the LGB has no legal status and is essentially a committee with delegated powers. For a MAT there will be a "Scheme of Delegation" setting out the extent of the authority that has been passed on to them. Where a MAT has schools of different abilities, the delegated authority may vary and can operate on a "sliding scale".'

Principal

The directors appoint the principal and/or CEO in a MAT, to whom they delegate powers and functions necessary 'for the internal organisation, management and control' of the academy.

Meetings of directors/governors

The Articles set out the requirements for board meetings (see Chapter 8).

Patrons and honorary officers

The directors can appoint someone as a 'patron' or to hold an honorary office without the need to appoint them as a member or director. They can agree the period of office that will apply.

The seal

The Articles provide that a seal can be used if authorised by the directors. Historically, a company or common seal was used to stamp an impression on melted wax signifying that the document was the act and deed of the company. However, since 1989, there is no requirement for a seal provided documents are signed by a director and secretary or two directors.

Although not legally required, seals may sometimes still be used which create a raised impression on the paper. Often this is combined with a stick-on wafer which imitates a wax seal and also shows up better on photocopies.

The Articles provide that where the seal is used, it shall also be signed by a director and the clerk or by two directors, or whoever the directors shall determine.

Annual report and accounts

Accounts should be prepared in accordance with the relevant SORP and filed with the DfE by 31 December each year (see Chapter 11).

Annual return

The directors must prepare an annual return to be filed at Companies House (see Chapter 5).

Notices

Any notice, apart from a notice calling a meeting of the directors, should be in writing or given using electronic communications to an address notified to the person giving the notice. Notice given by the academy to a member may be given:

- personally;
- by sending it by post in a prepaid envelope addressed to the member at his/her registered address;
- by hand delivery to their registered address; or
- via electronic communications to an address notified to the academy.

A member based outside the United Kingdom may only receive notices either electronically or to an address within the United Kingdom.

Indemnity

Any director, officer or auditor of the academy is entitled to be indemnified against any liability incurred whilst in that role in connection with any court action. This means that as long as the individual is acting within their capacity, they will be recompensed for any loss.

COMMENT

Julia Green, Partner at Browne Jacobson:

'As a limited company the Academy Trust is the legal entity that has liability when something goes wrong, rather than the individuals that make up the Members and Directors. The Articles of Association specifically provide that the Governors are entitled to be indemnified by the Academy Trust if they incur any costs as a result of successfully defending any proceedings. However, like maintained schools, Governors will be held liable where they have acted beyond their remit and been negligent. In a situation where a Governor has acted recklessly or wilfully against advice and the decision to do so has resulted in a loss, the individual will be held to be personally liable and any indemnity will not apply.

Governors of maintained schools converting to academy status and becoming a Director often get concerned over the possibility of action against them but equally often do not realise that they are in this position already as a Governor. There is also often confusion about the difference between making a wrong decision and making a bad decision. A decision made following appropriate advice and after consideration which turns out to have been the wrong decision is unlikely to lead to personal liability. A decision that has been made recklessly without seeking proper guidance or one that has been made wilfully ignoring advice or guidance is one that could lead to personal liability. In these circumstances, an indemnity may not be relied upon. In short, acting professionally and responsibly will make it very unlikely that there will be personal liability and the indemnity from the Academy Trust will provide protection from expenses.'

Rules

The directors are entitled to make 'such rules or bye laws as they may deem necessary or expedient or convenient for the proper conduct and management of the academy' in connection with matters that are 'commonly the subject matter of company rules' such as in connection with meetings or members.

Avoiding influenced company status

The Articles contain strict limits on the number of 'Local Authority Associated Persons' (LAAPs) that can be involved in the management of the academy. This is to avoid 'influenced company status' (i.e. where the LA has significant influence or power in the running of the company). This, therefore, is closely regulated.

A person is a LAAP if:

- they are a member of the LA;

- they are an officer (i.e. direct employee) of the LA;
- they are both an employee and either a director, manager, secretary or other similar officer of a company which is under the control of the LA; or
- at any time within the preceding four years they have been a member of the LA.

Any person who is an elected councillor will, therefore, be regarded as a LAAP along with anyone who has been a member within the past four years. An officer will be any person who is employed by the LA. This could be someone who is directly employed by the LA as a council officer, administrator, cleaner, etc. It will also apply to any staff employed by a maintained school.

A LA can be:

- a county council;
- a district council (including metropolitan boroughs, non-metropolitan districts/boroughs and unitary authorities);
- a London borough council;
- a parish council; and
- a community council.

The number of votes exercisable by LAAPs must not exceed 19.9% of the total number of votes exercisable by members. The votes of the other members will be increased on a *pro rata* basis to avoid this situation.

LAAPs must make up less than 20% of the total number of directors. On any resolution, the number of votes exercisable by LAAPs must not exceed 19.9% of the total number of votes exercisable by directors. The votes of the other directors will be increased on a *pro rata* basis to avoid this situation.

A LAAP must have their appointment as director authorised by the LA with which they are associated.

If a member or director subsequently becomes a LAAP, they will be 'deemed to have immediately resigned his membership and/or resigned from his office'.

The Articles make reference to s. 69 Local Government and Housing Act 1989 (LGHA 1989) which defines 'companies subject to local authority influence'. However, the effect of the drafting in the Articles makes them much more stringent than the requirements of LGHA.

Interestingly, under LGHA 1989, the relevant percentage limits are only effective where there is a business relationship with the LA. This requirement will be fulfilled where an academy continues to occupy their land and buildings as a tenant of the LA under a 125-year lease.

The limitation does pose logistical difficulties, particularly for academies situated in large conurbations where there may be several LAs relatively closely situated.

COMMENT

Judith Barnes, Partner and Head of Local Government at
DAC Beachcroft LLP:

'The DfE introduced a set of "model" Articles for academies. They contain
strict limits on the number of "Local Authority Associated Persons" (LAAPs)
that can be involved on the board of the academy, in order to avoid it being
a local authority "influenced company" under the Local Government and
Housing Act 1989 and the Local Authorities Companies (England) Order
1995.

A person is a LAAP if:

1. He/she is a member (councillor) of the LA, or
2. He/she is an officer (ie direct employee) of the LA, or
3. He/she is both an employee and either a director, manager, secretary or
   other similar officer of a company which is under the control of the LA, or
4. At any time within the preceding four years he/she has been a member of
   the LA.

It is worth noting that local authority interests, where there is involvement by more than one, including the LAAP, are amalgamated, even where
those personnel are unconnected.

In order to be an influenced company there needs to be both a LAAP of
between 20–50% and a business relationship with a local authority (or more
than one). Business relationships can include the occupation of premises
from a LA at less than the best consideration reasonably obtainable.

To avoid LA influence, where LAAP involvement is equal to 20% or
more there is a mechanism in the model articles to reduce decision-making
and involvement of the LAAP to 19.9%.

Originally the legislation was intended to ensure that where local authorities controlled or had decisive influence over companies it was treated for
financial purposes as the expenditure of the local authority, but this was
dropped when the new prudential financial regime was adopted in 2004.
The only controls that remain are "propriety controls" which require various
steps to be taken such as noting on letterhead when a company is controlled
or influenced; expenses being limited to no more than members' allowances;
no party political publicity; avoiding LA appointees who would be disqualified from being local authority members; and the provision of information to
LAs and their auditors.

The provisions in the model Articles are outdated and no longer necessary, in the context of controls on academies.

The effect of compliance is that it may not always be possible to appoint
otherwise good candidates for the role of Director (e.g. an individual who

has been nominated and voted for in a ballot by the parent body may not be eligible for appointment due to their LA association). This will be the case whether they are associated with the LA in which the academy is situated or not and even if they are employed by the LA in a role which has no educational connection and with no potential for entering into any business relationship with the Academy. The model Articles may therefore have the unintended consequence of reducing effective community involvement.'

Changes to the Articles

Changes can, in theory, be made to the Articles of Association to alter the existing organisational arrangements. However, a formal application must be made to the Secretary of State via the Education Funding Agency (EFA) setting out a business case for the proposed change and seeking approval.

Since 28 January 2014, fast-track significant changes relating to expansions, age-range changes (by up to three years), adding boarding provision and amending admissions arrangements in old-style funding agreements will no longer require a formal business case. Formal approval from the Secretary of State is still required, but requests are likely to be approved where there has been adequate local consultation, financial arrangements are sound and appropriate planning permissions have been secured.

Summary

Memorandum and Articles of Association

- The constitution of the company which sets out the rules by which the company must operate.
- The Memorandum of Association sets out the name of the academy and provides details of the three 'subscribers'.

Articles of Association

- Articles prescribe the internal management, decision making and running of the academy trust and its liability.
- The DfE has model documentation which schools are expected to adopt without changes.
- It is *essential* to refer in detail to the specific documentation adopted by the academy.

Miscellaneous

- **Objects**: the purpose and range of activities that the academy is set up to carry on.

- **Members**: the appointment of members, removal or termination of their Membership.
- **General meetings (members' meetings)**: calling general meetings, notice, proceedings at meetings, voting by members and the appointment of proxies.
- **Directors/governors**: numbers of directors, appointment including co-option, term of office, resignation and removal and disqualification, appointment of the chair and vice-chair of the directors, powers of the directors and conflicts of interest.
- **Chief executive officer**: in a MAT, the CEO is a director whilst they are in office.
- **Clerk/secretary to the directors**: appointment of a clerk/secretary to the board. This person need not be the company secretary and cannot be either a director or principal.
- **The minutes**: the clerk must draw up minutes of board meetings.
- **Committees**: establishment of committees and local governing bodies; terms of reference, constitution and membership must be reviewed annually.
- **Delegation**: delegation of power or function to an individual director, committee, principal or other holder of an executive office who reports to the board when delegated authority has been exercised.
- **Principal**: appointment of principal and delegation of powers and functions.
- **Meetings of directors/governors**: requirements for board meetings.
- **Patrons and honorary officers**: appointment without the need to appoint as a member.
- **The seal**: used if authorised by the directors and signed by a director and the clerk, by two directors, or whoever the directors decide.
- **Annual report and accounts**: prepared in accordance with the relevant SORP and filed with the DfE by 31 December each year.
- **Annual return**: must be prepared and filed at Companies House.
- **Notices**: apart from a notice calling a meeting of the directors, should be in writing or given using electronic communications to an address notified to the person giving the notice.
- **Indemnity**: any director, officer or auditor of the academy is entitled to be indemnified against any liability incurred whilst in that role so long as they were acting within their capacity.
- **Rules**: directors can make rules or bye-laws.
- **Avoiding influenced company status**: limits on number of members and directors that can be connected with a local authority.
- Changes may be made to the Articles subject to approval by the Secretary of State.

5 Statutory registers and Companies House

▨ In this chapter

This chapter looks in detail at the requirements to hold and update company information both in statutory registers and Companies House in particular:

- the range and contents of the registers required by law;
- filing with Companies House in hard copy and WebFiling including protections for users;
- the requirements of the annual return and the annual report and accounts;
- the various filings necessary including detailed guidance on the relevant forms and information to be included and notification of changes to the Articles of Association; and
- potential offences for failure to file and the late filing penalty notice.

▨ Statutory registers

Academies are required by law to keep specific records which collectively are known as statutory registers or the statutory books. The registers record information relating to the academy's operations and structure such as the current directors. Records should be kept up-to-date to reflect any changes that take place.

The registers should be held at the company's registered office and are the official records of the academy (Companies House records are effectively copies).

Statutory registers are generally held in a loose-leaf binder, although it is possible for them to be written, printed or in machine readable form (i.e. a version held on computer would be acceptable).

If a company fails to maintain the statutory registers, an offence is committed by the company and every officer of the company who is in default may be punishable by a fine.

The statutory registers should be maintained and preserved for the life of the academy.

Register of members

A register of members must be kept which should contain (ss.113–128 CA 2006):

- the names and addresses of the members;
- the date on which each person was registered as a member; and
- the date at which any person ceased to be a member.

The register is evidence that the relevant appointments have been made as members are not registered as such at Companies House (see Appendix 1 for example registers).

Register of secretaries

Where a secretary has been formally appointed, details are kept in a register (s. 275 CA 2006) (see Appendix 1).

Register of directors

A register of directors must be kept (ss.162–166 CA 2006) recording the required information for every director. Each director must provide:

- forename and surname and any former name;
- a service address;
- the country or state (or part of the United Kingdom) in which he is usually resident;
- nationality;
- business occupation (if any); and
- date of birth.

Where a director is a corporate body, the following is required:

- the name of the corporate body or firm;
- the registered office address;
- for companies registered within the European Economic Area (EEA) the country/state where the company is registered and its registration number; and
- for non-EEA companies, the legal form of the company or firm, the law by which it is governed and, if applicable, the country/state in which it is registered and its registration number.

The register should also record the date of termination or resignation (see Appendix 1).

The Companies Act allows directors to use a service address so that their private home address is not included in the public records. Generally, the service address will be the registered office of the academy which is often the school site. Although directors can opt not to disclose their private address publicly, it must be declared to the academy and to Companies House.

The register of directors must be open to inspection by any member of the company without charge. It must be made available to any other person under the provisions of the Freedom of Information Act and on payment of any fee required (see Chapter 15).

Register of directors' residential addresses

A register of the directors' residential addresses is also required (s.165 CA 2006). However, this is a confidential register that is not available for public inspection (see Appendix 1).

Register of directors' interests

There is no longer a statutory requirement to maintain a register of directors' interests as was the case under previous legislation. However, it remains good practice to maintain a register noting any interests that the directors hold (see Chapter 12). It is also good practice to extend this requirement to key members of staff who may have delegated authority to act on behalf of the academy and enter into contracts on its behalf.

Directors and key staff should be asked to complete a declaration on appointment which should be updated annually. The individual should provide details of any interests that could possibly conflict with those of the academy. These details should be used to produce the Register which should also be updated annually or on appointment of any new persons.

Declarations should be made in relation to 'persons connected with the director' (ss. 252–254 CA 2006) which will include any spouse, civil partner or person with whom the individual lives as partner in an enduring family relationship, any child or stepchild up to age 18, parents and any company in which they hold a voting interest of 20% or more (see Appendix 1).

Single alternative inspection location (SAIL)

An academy can arrange for a professional firm to provide company secretarial services and maintain all records and registers. In this case, the registers would be kept at a place other than the registered office and it is necessary to formally disclose their location to Companies House (which can be searched by any member of the public).

The location where the company records and registers are kept is known as the single alternative inspection location (SAIL).

Inspection of the registers

Every academy must keep the statutory registers and provide access to them. They must be kept at the registered office or the SAIL notified to Companies House.

The register of members must be available for inspection without payment to any member and to any other person under the provisions of the Freedom of Information Act and on payment of any appropriate fee required (see Chapter 15).

A request must be made to inspect the register or to seek copies which must contain:

- the name and address of the individual making the request;
- the name and address of any individual who is making a request on behalf of an organisation and the name of that organisation;
- the purpose for which the information is to be used; and
- whether the information will be disclosed to any other person, and if so who they are and the purpose for which the information is to be used by that person.

The academy must comply within five working days of receipt of such a request or apply to the court if the request was not made for a 'proper purpose'. Failure to comply is an offence and the academy and any employee in default may be subject to a fine.

In reality, there are rarely requests to view statutory registers. Much of the information they contain is, in any event, also recorded at Companies House and is easily obtainable electronically and by post for a small fee.

Register of gifts, hospitality and entertainments

Directors and key staff should declare any instances where they receive gifts, hospitality or entertainment from any third party (Bribery Act 2010).

It is possible to include the information within the register of directors' interests rather than maintaining an additional register.

All members, directors and staff must be seen to act with complete honesty and integrity. Formal declarations ensure transparency and avoid conflicts of interest which could potentially arise through the acceptance of gifts or hospitality compromising the impartiality of decision making.

A clear gifts, hospitality and entertainments policy should be agreed which will set *de minimis* levels below which declarations need not be made.

Any individual who is found to be involved in bribery, either by offering or accepting a bribe, will be guilty of an offence. However, an academy could also be found to have committed an offence if it, as a corporate body, or an individual acting on its behalf, is involved in bribery. It will be a defence for the academy to show that it has adequate procedures to prevent bribery, so it is extremely important that appropriate procedures, including a register, are put into operation (see Appendix 1).

Companies House

All limited companies, including academies, must be registered at Companies House.

Companies House is an Executive Agency of the Department for Business, Innovation and Skills (BIS) and is the government body tasked with maintaining a register of information on every company. Information must be provided to Companies House which examines and stores it and makes it available to the public.

Basic information must be delivered including details of the directors and company secretary, annual report and accounts and an annual return. Documents may be filed with Companies House either in hard copy form or online via WebFiling.

The main company registry for companies registered in England and Wales is in Cardiff and there is a satellite office in Bloomsbury Street, London. Search, inspection and copying facilities are available at both locations.

The public record

Generally, information filed with Companies House can be inspected by any member of the public. There are some exceptions (s. 1087 CA 2006), most notably:

- directors' residential addresses; and
- documents supporting a proposal to use certain words or expressions in the company name.

Certain administrative correspondence is not put on the public record.

The following basic information about the company is available free of charge:

- name;
- registered number;
- registered office address;
- names and services addresses of directors;
- accounting reference date;
- date last accounts were made up to and when next accounts are due; and
- date last return were made up to and when next return is due.

Other information, as well as copies of specific forms and documents that have been filed are also available subject to a small fee.

Records can be checked online using the WebCHeck facility on the Companies House website. Searches can be carried out on a company either by use of its name or its company registration number.

Some of the information, including certain free information such as the current appointments report showing the most recent details of directors and secretary registered is available but must be 'ordered'. This requires users to register with Companies House and, where necessary, make payment by means of credit or debit card or PayPal. Where a large number of chargeable filings are made, the academy can apply for a credit account so that a monthly invoice is generated.

All documents are delivered electronically and can be downloaded. It is possible to monitor a specific company, receiving e-mail alerts whenever new documents are filed at Companies House.

Companies House now offers a mobile app which is available to download free. No chargeable information is contained so there is no need to register. The app provides easy access to basic company details as well as information on filing history and details of appointments of officers (which needs to be ordered online).

Alternatively, copies of forms and documents filed can be obtained by visiting Companies House in person, or can be ordered by phone for postal delivery.

Filing hard copies

Originally, all filing was done by filling in the relevant forms or providing appropriate documentation which was physically lodged or sent to Companies House. There is a move by Companies House towards electronic filing, but it is not mandatory and certain filings must still be done in hard copy.

Forms can be downloaded free from the Companies House website or purchased from legal stationers.

Certain changes such as amendments to the Articles of Association and the audited annual report and accounts must be filed in hard copy even if the company is registered for WebFiling. In any event, a company can choose for hard copy documentation to be sent by post or delivered by hand. It is worth bearing in mind that documents can be posted into Companies House post boxes right up until midnight (beyond normal office hours) to be regarded as being filed on that day. The Companies House website should be checked to confirm hand delivery options.

A receipt can be obtained for documents sent by post or courier, if a copy of the covering letter is enclosed with a pre-paid addressed return envelope. Companies House will barcode the copy letter with the date of receipt and return it in the envelope provided.

All documents should state the registered name and number of the academy and should be printed on plain white, A4 size paper with a matt finish. The text should be black, clear, legible and of uniform density. Companies House states that failure to follow the following guidelines is likely to result in the document being rejected:

- use black ink or black type;
- use bold lettering (some elegant thin typefaces and pens give poor quality copies);
- do not send a carbon copy;
- do not use a dot matrix printer;
- photocopies can result in a grey shade that will not scan well;
- use A4 size paper with a good margin;
- supply in portrait format (i.e. with the shorter edge across the top); and
- include the company name and number.

The original form or document should be submitted and should generally be signed by an authorised person (i.e. a director or the company secretary).

Most forms contain a checklist of information that should be included.

WebFiling

Whilst it is possible for all filing to be done in hard copy, increasingly use is made of Companies House WebFiling service which can be used for filing:

- the annual return; and
- changes of directors, secretary, company address or name.

A full list of the forms that can be filed by means of the WebFiling service can be found on the Companies House website.

Filing online will generally be quicker and almost immediate confirmation of filing is received in the form of an automatic e-mail acknowledgement. WebFiling is also cost-effective and charges, such as the fee for filing an annual return, are actually cheaper. Payment of any applicable fee must be made prior to the submission of any form or documentation.

Academies must register with Companies House in order to use WebFiling. However, no specific software is necessary to make use of the service. When registering, the user sets up a password which is linked to the particular e-mail address used to log in. An authentication code comprising six alpha-numeric characters is generated by Companies House and sent by letter to the registered office address. Filing can only be done by a user who has a registered e-mail address, a registered password and an authentication code.

When documentation has been filed, an e-mail confirmation is automatically sent to the user's e-mail address; a further e-mail is sent when the document has been accepted or rejected.

Companies registered for WebFiling can sign up to an 'eReminders' service which will send e-mail reminders to up to four addresses that the accounts and the annual return are due. This is a particularly useful service given the increasingly strict approach to the appropriate time limits and may well help to avoid any resultant fines!

PROOF

Companies can choose to take advantage of the PROOF (PROtected Online Filing) service, whereby they commit to filing all documents electronically. Companies House will generally reject any attempt to lodge paper filings of:

- change of registered office address;
- appointment or termination of director or company secretary;
- changes in director's or secretary's details; and
- the annual return.

However, it may be possible to file in hard copy if an accompanying form PR03 is completed with the academy's authentication code.

This gives some protection against fraudulent attempts to change company information or corporate identity theft. This is a huge issue with reportedly around 50–100 cases of corporate identity threat identified by Companies House every month.

Companies must choose to opt into PROOF and agree to the terms and conditions of the scheme. However, it is possible to opt out at any time and the company can then deliver in either electronic or paper formats that will be accepted by Companies House.

Monitor

Companies House also offers the Monitor service which is accessed via WebCHeck. By signing up, registered users are notified by e-mail whenever documents are filed at Companies House. The request is valid for a 12-month period and can be renewed or cancelled. Documents can be downloaded for a small additional fee.

As well as the opportunity to see what other academies are up to, the service can be used to monitor your own academy so that any illegitimate filings will immediately be identified.

Annual return

Every academy must file a completed annual return at Companies House each year (CA 2006, Part 24). This must be lodged within 28 days of:

- the anniversary of the date of incorporation of the academy; or
- the anniversary of the date that the last annual return was completed (the 'made-up' date).

Care should be taken as the date of incorporation may not be the same as the date that the academy converted or commenced 'trading'.

Companies House will send reminder e-mails for academies registered for WebFiling and requesting the eReminder service. Alternatively, a letter will be sent to the registered office.

A fee is payable in respect of the annual return and filing may be done by means of WebFiling. Alternatively, an AR01 form can be completed in hard copy. This can be posted or hand delivered to Companies House. There is a higher fee payable to file an annual return on paper.

The return provides a snapshot of company information which includes:

- the name of the academy;
- its registered number;
- the date to which the annual return is made up;
- the SIC code;

- the principal business activities of the company;
- the type of company (i.e. private);
- the registered office address;
- the address (single alternate inspection location – SAIL) where the company keeps certain company records if not at the registered office, and the records held there;
- company secretary (corporate or individual), where applicable; and
- the company's directors (corporate or individual).

The return must reflect the information that is held at Companies House at the relevant time. Any changes must be made beforehand by WebFiling or the relevant form or document must be delivered at the same time as the annual return.

An annual return which does not include the required information will be rejected. However, Companies House can accept a completed annual return but mark it as inconsistent with the public register if the records do not match what is already held there.

Each return must include a five-digit 'standard industrial classification' ('SIC' code), which can be used to identify a company's business. A list of the various codes is available, although most academies will fall under one or more of the following:

- 85100 Pre-primary education
- 85200 Primary education
- 85310 General secondary education
- 85320 Technical and vocational secondary education.

Many MATs will have more than one SIC code relating to the nature of their business (e.g. a MAT with both primary and secondary schools may have both 85200 Primary education and 85310 General secondary education). However, as more complex multi-academy structures develop, it is possible that further classifications will be created so the SIC code should always be checked.

The return must be signed by a director or the secretary.

The directors and secretary (where applicable) are responsible for ensuring that the annual return is filed on time. Failure to do this is a criminal offence and, as a consequence, Companies House may prosecute the company and its officers.

Annual report and accounts

Under the CA 2006, the annual report and accounts must be filed with Companies House each year (see Chapter 11).

The deadlines for filing are initially set by the incorporation date of the company; this may not correlate with either the date of conversion, or the date when the academy commenced operations. For the first period, accounts may be prepared for a period of more than 12 months. These must be delivered to Companies House:

- within 21 months of the date of incorporation; or
- three months from the accounting reference date, whichever is longer.

In subsequent years, academies must submit accounts to the registrar of companies within nine months of the date to which the accounts are made up. The accounting reference date (ARD) for all academies is 31 August, meaning that accounts must be submitted by 31 May each year (although the accounts must be submitted to the EFA by 31 December). Filing may be done through the Companies House e-filing service or through submission of a paper filing.

Filing deadlines are calculated to the exact day and cannot be extended except in exceptional circumstances. Failure to submit the annual accounts on time will trigger an automatic late filing penalty.

With respect to signatories when filing, the copies of the accounts must contain the following:

- the copy of the balance sheet must be signed by a director;
- the copy of the balance sheet must show the printed name of the director who signed it on behalf of the board even if the signature is legible;
- the copy of the directors' report must include the printed name of the director or company secretary who signed the report on behalf of the board; and
- the auditor's report must state the auditor's name. Where the auditor is a firm, the report must state the name of the auditor and the name of the person who signed it as senior statutory auditor on behalf of the firm.

Change to the accounting reference date

When a new company is incorporated or set up, the first accounting reference date (ARD) will automatically default to the anniversary of the last day of the month in which it was incorporated (e.g. a company incorporated on 17 April 2014 will have a first ARD of 30 April 2015). Subsequent ARDs automatically fall on the anniversary each year.

Academies, however, are required to have an ARD of 31 August which brings the financial year into line with the academic year. This means that after conversion, the records at Companies House must be amended; no resolution by the directors is necessary to facilitate this. In any event, the change of ARD must be made before the filing deadline of the accounts.

The change may be made via WebFiling or using Form AA01 'Change of Accounting Reference Date'. There is no charge for making the change.

The following must be provided:

- company number;
- company name;
- current date of accounting reference period; and
- the new end date for the accounting period, either:
  - extending the accounting reference period, or
  - shortening the accounting reference period.

The change to the ARD should be made immediately the academy goes live.

It is not possible to extend the accounting reference period so that it lasts more than 18 months from the start date of the accounting period. Academies should note that this is calculated including the date of incorporation as the first day of the accounting period. For many academies, the date of incorporation will, in fact, pre-date the date of conversion, so advice should be sought from a relevant professional.

Change of registered office address

The registered office address can be changed. The registered office is the official address of the academy and need not be in a school location (e.g. this might happen in a MAT where the central services move out from a school base and into separate offices). It may also be possible for the academy's registered office to be that of a firm of solicitors or accountants which provides ongoing professional support and is the address for service.

The change may be made via WebFiling or using Form AD01 'Change of Registered Office Address'. The new registered office will not take effect until it has been formally registered by Companies House. There is no charge for making the change.

The following must be provided:

■ Company number
■ Company name
■ New registered office address (including postcode).

The Post Office address database is used to verify addresses.

Appointing a director

When a new director has been appointed, by whatever means, the change must be notified to Companies House within 14 days (see Chapter 7).

The change may be made via WebFiling or using Form AP01 'Appointment of Director' or Form AP02 'Appointment of Corporate Director'. There is no charge for making the change.

The following must be provided when an individual is appointed as director:

■ company number;
■ company name;
■ date of director's appointment;
■ new director's details including any former names;
■ new director's service address; and
■ new director's usual residential address.

If the director is a corporate body such as a company or charitable organisation, the following must be provided:

- company number;
- company name;
- date of corporate director's appointment;
- new corporate director's details;
- registration details for EEA companies; and
- details for non-EEA companies.

Directors will generally use the academy's registered office address as their service address instead of their private home address.

Appointment of a company secretary

Academies do not need to formally appoint a company secretary (see Chapter 1). However, when one has been appointed, the change must be notified to Companies House within 14 days via WebFiling or using Form AP03 'Appointment of Secretary' or Form AP04 'Appointment of Corporate Secretary'. There is no charge for making the change.

The following must be provided:

- company number;
- company name;
- date of secretary's appointment;
- new secretary's details; and
- the service address of the new secretary.

Further details in respect of EEA companies or non-EEA companies must be given if the appointment is a corporate secretary.

Change of director's or secretary's details

Changes can be made to the information registered via WebFiling or by submission of Form CH01 in respect of a change of director's details, CH02 for a corporate director, CH03 for the secretary and CH04 for a corporate secretary. There is no charge for making the change which must be made within 14 days.

The following must be provided:

- company number;
- company name;
- current details;
- date of change of details; and
- details of change:
    - name
    - service address
    - usual residential address
    - other change.

Termination of appointment of director or secretary

Generally, appointments are made to the board for a fixed period of time. However, at the end of the relevant term of office, the details held at Companies House do not automatically expire. It is necessary to terminate the appointment via WebFiling or by submission of Form TM01 'Termination of Appointment of Director' or TM02 'Termination of Appointment of Secretary' within 14 days. There is no charge for making the change.

The following must be provided:

- company number;
- company name;
- current details; and
- termination date.

Notification of single alternative inspection location (SAIL)

Every academy must maintain company records and registers (see Chapter 5) and directors must disclose where these are held. An academy can arrange for a firm of solicitors or accountants or other professional firm to keep and maintain all such records and registers. In this case, the SAIL is the location where the company records and registers are kept. A company may only have one SAIL so that it is not possible for certain records to be kept in different locations.

For initial notification of a SAIL, either WebFiling or use of Form AD02 'Notification of Single Alternative Inspection Location' is required and the following must be provided:

- company number;
- company name; and
- address of the SAIL.

Notification that relevant documents have relocated to the SAIL address are made on Form AD03 or, where they have moved back to the registered office, on Form AD04.

The SAIL must be included in the annual return together with a full list of the records kept there.

Removal of auditor

An auditor can be removed at any time during their term of office (see Chapter 11). Within 14 days of the resolution being passed at a general meeting of members Form AA03 'Notice of Resolution Removing Auditors from Office' must be filed at Companies House.

The following must be provided:

- company number;
- company name;
- date of resolution;
- auditor's details; and
- date of removal.

Special resolutions

Any special resolutions passed by the members, whether in general meeting or by means of a written resolution which amend the constitution, must be filed with Companies House within 15 days. This means that any appointment of a new member made by a special resolution should be notified to Companies House.

COMMENT

Nick MacKenzie, Partner at Browne Jacobson:

Sections 29–30 Companies Act 2006 state that any special resolution must be filed with the Registrar within 15 days.

Article 16 of the latest DfE models for both single and multi-academy trusts stipulate that a Member must be appointed by special resolution. Strictly speaking, the Trust must then satisfy the filing requirements and a failure to do so is an offence by the Trust and every officer in default (s. 30(2) CA 2006) with a potential level 3 penalty fine.

It is important to note, however, that the DfE model articles have changed over time and, additionally, they can be varied. So there is every chance that academies may have an altered Article 16 which does not stipulate a 'special resolution' but, perhaps, 'unanimous agreement' which is different and does not invoke the filing requirements.

Subject to the prior approval of the Secretary of State, members may pass a special resolution to amend the Articles and change the academy's constitution (see Chapter 4). If so, the academy must file a copy of the amended Articles within 15 days of the amendment taking place (s. 26 CA 2006).

The following must be filed with Companies House:

- the amended Articles, clearly stating that they are 'amended' on the front page and showing all amendments made; and
- the resolution signed by a director or company secretary.

EXAMPLE OF A MEMBERS' SPECIAL RESOLUTION

Company number: 7990029

Company name: Presdales School Academy Trust

SPECIAL RESOLUTION

At the Annual General Meeting of the Members of the above-named company duly convened and held on Tuesday 1 October 2013 at the registered office of the company, Hoe Lane, Ware SG12 9NX, the following resolution was duly passed:

In accordance with the provisions of the Companies Act 2006, that the requirement to hold an Annual General Meeting of the Members is removed from the Articles of Association and that Article 19 be deleted and Articles 21, 40 and 41 be amended accordingly.

(Signed)   *Katie Paxton-Doggett*

Company Secretary

(Date)   3 October 2013

Powers and duties of Companies House

Forms and documents lodged at Companies House are examined to ensure that they meet the requirements relating to form, manner of delivery and authentication of documents (CA 2006, Part 35). Companies House has set out clear guidance about what is expected irrespective of whether documents are submitted in hard copy or electronically. Failure to comply with these requirements will mean that the document or form is not 'properly delivered' and will be rejected. Companies House will notify the academy of the rejection and what needs to be done to correct it.

Where a submitted document is either incomplete or has inconsistencies within it, Companies House can request that it is corrected. However, although Companies House does have some powers to remove 'unnecessary material' or resolve inconsistencies, correcting information may be difficult to do – best to get it right first time!

Late filing

Failure to file information within the specified time limits is an offence, potentially resulting in prosecution and fines. Any 'officer' of the company will commit such an offence if she/he 'authorises or permits, participates in, or fails to take all reasonable steps to prevent, the contravention'. An 'officer' can be any director, shadow or *de facto* director, manager or secretary (s. 112 CA 2006).

If the annual accounts are not filed by the deadline, Companies House will automatically issue a late filing penalty notice levying a fine. The penalty reflects the importance that is attributed to making the information available for the public record. The deadline cannot be extended or waived even by a day except in 'exceptional circumstances'. If there is a special reason why the accounts might be filed late, an application to extend the period for filing can be made prior to the deadline. Companies House will usually only extend the period if the reasons really are 'exceptional'.

Academies must file their audited accounts within nine months of the end of the accounting period (i.e. no later than 31 May (s. 442(2a) CA 2006). The first accounts following incorporation, if made up for a period of more than 12 months, must be filed within 21 months of incorporation, or within three months of the end of the accounting period, whichever is later (s. 442(3) CA 2006). Again, care must be taken as the date of incorporation may not correlate with the date of conversion to academy status.

Accounts should, as far as possible, be delivered in advance of the last date for delivery. If accounts are delivered within the deadline, but are subsequently returned due to omissions or errors which require amendment, the corrected accounts must be delivered within the relevant period to avoid a late filing penalty.

As the accounts are audited in accordance with the requirements of the EFA in the Funding Agreement, they must be submitted in hard copy and cannot be submitted online or via WebFiling.

If the deadline is missed, the initial fine will be £150 with penalties on a rising scale if the accounts continue to be late. Penalties will be doubled if a company files accounts late in two successive financial years.

Filing reminders in respect of the annual accounts are sent to the registered office address and it is flagged whenever WebFiling is accessed in the period up to the deadline.

There are no filing penalties for other company documents, although it is obviously good practice for them to be filed as soon as possible and certainly within any relevant period (usually 14 days).

Directors are responsible for filing of annual accounts. Any failure to do so is a criminal offence and the directors may find themselves personally liable. There is no late filing penalty for annual returns but, again, directors could potentially find themselves liable.

Summary

Statutory registers

- Academies are required by law to keep specific records known as 'statutory registers'. These must be maintained and preserved for the life of the academy.
- If the registers are not maintained an offence is committed by the company and every officer of the company who is in default and may be punishable by a fine.
- The statutory registers are: register of members; register of secretaries; register of directors; and register of the directors' residential addresses.
- It is good practice to maintain a register of directors' interests.
- The registers can be kept at a single alternative inspection location (SAIL).
- The academy must provide access to the registers when a request has been made in accordance with the legislation.
- A register of any instances where directors or key staff have received gifts, hospitality or entertainment from any third party must be kept.

Companies House

- All limited companies must be registered at Companies House and, generally, information filed can be inspected by any member of the public.
- Certain changes such as amendments to the Articles of Association and the audited annual report and accounts must always be filed in hard copy.
- All documents and forms should comply with Companies House print requirements and quality of documentation.
- The original form or document should be submitted, generally signed by an authorised person (i.e. a director or company secretary).

WebFiling

- WebFiling can be used for filing annual returns, changes of directors, secretary, company address or name forms.
- An 'eReminders' service is available which will send e-mail reminders to up to four addresses that accounts and annual returns are due.
- Academies can commit to filing documents electronically to take advantage of the PROOF service and get notifications via Monitor whenever documents are filed.

Annual return

- A completed annual return must be filed within 28 days of the anniversary of the date of incorporation of the academy or the anniversary of the date of the last annual.

Annual report and accounts

- For the first period, accounts may be prepared for a period of more than 12 months and delivered to Companies House within 21 months of the date of incorporation, or three months from the accounting reference date, whichever is longer.
- In subsequent years, academies must submit accounts to the registrar of companies within nine months of the date to which accounts are made up, which will be 31 May.
- Failure to submit the annual accounts on time will trigger an automatic late filing penalty.
- The following filings must be made, free of charge, within 14 days by WebFiling or lodging the relevant form:

Change to accounting reference date	Form AA0 'Change of accounting reference date'	ARD must be 31 August. Change as soon as possible and, in any event, before the filing deadline of the accounts.
Change of registered office address	Form AD01 'Change of registered office address'	The new registered office will not take effect until it has been formally registered.
Appointment of director	Form AP01 'Appointment of Director' Form AP02 'Appointment of corporate director'	Directors generally use the academy's registered office address as their service address.
Appointment of company secretary	Form AP03 'Appointment of Secretary' Form AP04 'Appointment of Corporate Secretary'	
Change of director's or secretary's details	Form CH01 'Change of Director's details' Form CH02 'Change of Corporate Director's Details' Form CH03 'Change of Secretary's Details' Form CH04 'Change of Corporate Secretary's Details'	

Termination of appointment of director or secretary	Form TM01 'Termination of Appointment of Director' TM02 'Termination of Appointment of Secretary'	Appointments do not automatically expire.
Notification of single alternative inspection location (SAIL)	Form AD02 'Notification of Single Alternative Inspection Location' Form AD03 to notify that documents have relocated to SAIL Form AD04 where documents have moved back to Registered Office	
Removal of auditor	Form AA03 'Notice of Resolution Removing Auditors from Office'	

- A copy of the amended Articles and special resolution making the change must be filed within 15 days of the amendment taking place.
- Companies House can reject any document or form that is not 'properly delivered'.
- Failure to file information within the specified time limits is an offence, potentially resulting in prosecution and fines for any officer of the company.
- A late filing penalty notice will be issued automatically if the annual accounts are not filed by the deadline.

6 Members

▦ In this chapter

This chapter looks at the members of the academy, in particular:

- appointment and cessation of membership;
- the responsibilities, rights and remedies available to members;
- procedures and requirements for general meetings including the annual general meeting; and
- decision making by resolutions at general meetings as well as written resolutions.

The academy is set up as a charitable trust limited by guarantee. Consequently, it has a two-tier management and governance structure. The members are responsible for strategic oversight with the directors responsible for the day-to-day management of the company.

Figure 6.1: Two-tier management system

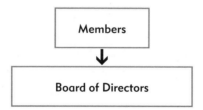

The members are akin to the 'shareholders' in a company limited by shares. However, the members in an academy do not have shareholdings but offer a guarantee which is limited to £10. The amount of the guarantee is fixed when the academy was incorporated and cannot subsequently be increased. The members will only be liable for the maximum amount they have guaranteed (i.e. £10) if the company goes into insolvent liquidation. In practical terms, this is unlikely ever to happen as the DfE will have stepped in long before the £10 becomes payable!

Appointment of members

Upon incorporation, the Memorandum is signed by the 'subscribers' who confirm that they wish to form a company and have agreed to become the first members. Subsequently, the number of members can be increased and members are appointed when their name is entered into the company's register of members.

It is possible to be both a member and a director and many of the early single academy converters had a flat governance structure where all directors were also appointed as members. This is not feasible with Mark 1 sponsored academies or with the MAT or umbrella structures. The Education Funding Agency's (EFA) current preference is for a small number of members.

Reference should be made to the specific requirements of the Articles. However, in addition to the original subscribers, members will be:

- appointed by the sponsor or other foundation body;
- chair of the board of directors; and
- appointed by the members.

Members can be either natural persons (i.e. humans!) or corporate bodies. As the academy is a charitable company, members are not eligible to participate in any profit of the company. This is particularly relevant for companies or other for-profit organisations appointed as members as they should not profit from that involvement.

In a sponsored academy, the majority, if not all, of the members are appointed by the sponsor. For non-sponsored academies, there may also be provision for a trust or foundation associated with it to make appointments. Commonly, the local Diocese will be appointed as a corporate member of an academy involving church schools, whether as a single or multi academy. In the more collaborative arrangements, in practice it is often the directors who identify and recommend suitable candidates to be appointed.

When new members are being appointed by the existing members, the Articles require that this be done by means of passing a special resolution either by means of a 75% majority in a meeting or by means of a written resolution. Any such appointment should be 'in the interests of the Academy Trust'.

A person nominated to be a new member either signs a written consent to become a member or signs the register of members which signifies consent.

COMMENT

Graham Burns, Partner with Stone King:

Appointment of members

The starting point to determine who appoints the members is to check the academy trust's Articles of Association. The Department for Education's model articles provide the basic outline of the appointment procedure. The current model articles provide it is the existing members' role to appoint (and remove) members, provided that such appointment or removal is in the interests of the academy trust.

Depending on the individual requirements of the academy trust, the Articles may be amended to provide for appointment rights to organisations or third parties (such as a foundation, religious group or Diocese). In cases where the academy trust has a corporate member, an individual of the corporate member's choice will be nominated to attend members' meetings.

Responsibilities, rights and remedies

Members' responsibilities

One of the most important functions of the members is the appointment of directors apart from *ex officio* or elected directors.

In addition, the Articles permit the members to remove any directors that they have appointed. In order to do so, members pass a special resolution and then give written notice to the clerk that the director is thereby removed. This simple provision means that a considerable amount of control is retained by the members.

Although the members theoretically have strategic oversight of the academy, in most cases the general power to manage the academy is vested in the directors. The level to which the vision and strategic direction is set by the members will depend very much on the organisational structure and will be greater in sponsored academies.

However, ultimately, only the members (subject to approval by the Secretary of State) have the power to amend the Articles and change the academy's constitution. In order to do this, the members must pass a special resolution in accordance with s. 21(1) CA 2006 (see Chapter 4).

Members' rights

Company law gives members certain rights:

- to receive a copy of the Memorandum and Articles of Association;
- to receive notices of meeting, proposed written resolutions and audited accounts and annual report;
- to attend, speak and vote at general meetings;
- to require the directors to call a general meeting;
- to remove a director from office;
- to remove an auditor;
- to appoint proxies to vote at general meetings; and
- to inspect the register of members on reasonable notice during normal office hours.

Protection against 'unfair prejudice'

A member may petition the court for a remedy where the company's affairs are being, have been, or are likely to be 'conducted in a manner that is unfairly prejudicial to the interests of members generally or of some part of its members (including at least him/herself)' (s. 994 CA 2006). The member would have to show that:

- *The prejudice was unfair*. An objective approach is taken so that it is not necessary to show that the prejudice was intentional or that anyone acted in bad faith, but that a hypothetical reasonable bystander would regard it as unfair.
- *The rights/interests of the member have been prejudiced*. This relates to rights or interests of the member in his/her capacity as member and not arising as a consequence of any other relationship that he/she has with the academy such as director or employee. However, the courts have interpreted this widely so consideration is likely to be given to legitimate expectations that the member may have but which are not included in the Articles of Association.

Occasions when recourse to this protection will be made are likely to be extremely rare. However, this is powerful protection for members. Examples might be:

- being excluded from the management of the academy where there is a legitimate expectation of participation; and
- abuses of power and breaches of the Articles such as delaying accounts and depriving members of the right to know the state of the academy's affairs.

If a petition is successful, the court can make any order it thinks fit and this will often be to require the academy to do, or to refrain from doing, the act complained of (s. 996 CA 2006).

Derivative claims

Members are also able to bring an action on behalf of the academy against a director, former director or shadow director. A derivative claim can be brought in respect of a cause of action arising from an actual or proposed act or omission by a director involving:

- negligence;
- default – the failure to perform a legally obligated act;
- breach of duty – including 'general duties' (see Chapter 7) or any other duty; and
- breach of trust.

Negligence is ratifiable, so that if a negligent action is subsequently confirmed or sanctioned by the academy any derivative claim would be barred.

It remains to be seen how derivative claims might arise in the context of academies; in a wider context the number of derivative claims made remains low with the majority refused permission to continue to full trial. Possible situations might be financial mismanagement, acting outside the company's powers and applying academy money to an object not in the academy's Articles. The courts have adopted a strict application of the tests which need to be satisfied to grant a derivative claim, so any such course of action will need careful consideration and preparation.

CASE STUDY

In July 2013, Greg Wallace, Executive Principal of Best Start Federation schools, was suspended during an investigation into the award of an IT contract to his boyfriend's company. He subsequently resigned.

However, if Mr Wallace had been a director of the academy and the contract, awarded otherwise than on the basis of the merits of the supplier, had caused the academy a loss because of his acting in a conflict of interest, that could well have been grounds for a derivative claim.

Of course, a derivative claim allows members to sue individual directors on behalf of the academy. This means that any resultant award is due to the academy rather than the member themselves. Further, bringing a claim is a time-consuming and expensive process and members must be convinced that the director against whom action is to be taken is able to fund any potential award.

Ceasing to be a member

Termination of membership

Membership will terminate automatically if a member:

- in the case of a corporate entity, ceases to exist and is not replaced by a successor institution;
- in the case of an individual, dies or becomes incapable by reason of illness or injury of managing and administering his own affairs; or
- becomes insolvent or makes any arrangement or composition with that member's creditors generally.

Removal of a member

Those who are entitled to appoint members, such as a sponsor or foundation body, can remove any member appointed by them by delivering written notice to the academy's registered office.

The subscribers to the Memorandum can be removed where the remaining members 'agree unanimously in writing' to remove them. Additional members appointed by the members may be removed if the members pass a special resolution in writing.

All such removals must be 'in the interests of the academy trust'.

Resignation

Any member may resign provided that three members remain in office. Resignation is effected by lodging a notice in writing signed by the person or persons entitled to remove him/her.

General meetings

Meetings of the members are known as general meetings. Apart from any specific requirement to call an Annual General Meeting, the Articles contain no specific obligations with regard to holding general meetings. This means that it is feasible for long periods of time to pass without any meetings being held since all resolutions are passed using the written resolution method!

Members' meetings are closely regulated and the Companies Act 2006 has a whole chapter (Part 13, Chapter 3) dedicated to the requirements. This can be contrasted with board meetings which have very little in the way of formal requirements.

It is extremely important that members' meetings and board meetings are kept separate both in terms of managing the work and in preparing minutes. This is particularly an issue where there is a flat governance structure and all directors are also members, or when the members are a sub-section of the board. In these circumstances, there may be a temptation for a members' decision to be taken in the course of the board meeting. This is not legally permitted. If a decision is required before the board meeting can continue, then the meeting must be adjourned, the members' meeting held (on short notice if necessary) and the board meeting subsequently reconvened.

Directors, who are not also a member, are entitled to attend and speak at any general meeting, although they will not have a vote.

When general meetings are held, it is important that all procedural requirements are met in order that resolutions passed are legally valid.

Convening a general meeting

Members' meetings will generally be called by the directors. However, the directors must call a general meeting if it is requested by members holding at least 5% of the total voting rights of all the members able to vote at general meetings.

Members must state the general nature of the business to be conducted when they make the request and can provide any resolution which they wish to be considered. A request may be made in hard copy or electronic form, and must be authenticated by the member/s making it.

Where a request is properly made, the directors must, within 21 days, call a meeting for a date not more than 28 days after the date of the notice calling the meeting. Where a request included the text of a proposed resolution, this must be included in the notice signifying whether it is a special resolution. Any such resolution will become part of the business that can be conducted at the meeting.

If the directors do not comply with a valid request to convene a general meeting, members representing over half of the members' total voting rights may call a general meeting within three months of the date on which the directors became subject to the requirement to call a meeting. Such a meeting should be called in a similar manner to that in which it would have been had the directors called it.

Notice

The model articles provide that the notice of members' meetings must be given with 14 clear days' notice. This period of notice is dictated by s. 307(1) CA 2006 and cannot be shortened (although a longer period could be specified in the articles if desired).

Giving notice is more than simply notifying members that a meeting is taking place – there is a legal requirement for a formal notice containing details of the business to be circulated. It is a technicality, but it does need to be recognised so that there can be no future challenge to any decisions taken at the meeting.

When calculating the correct day on which, or before which, the notice should be provided, the period is calculated excluding the day on which the notice is given and the day of the meeting. Therefore, notice must be given on Monday of week one for a meeting on Tuesday of week three (to comply with a requirement for fourteen *clear* days' notice).

It is possible to call a meeting on short notice if a majority of the members holding at least 90% of the voting rights agree.

The notice must be sent to every:

- member
- director
- auditor.

It must be given:

- in hard copy form;
- in electronic form;
- by means of a website; or
- partly by one such means and partly by another.

The articles do, however, provide that the process will not be invalidated where any individual entitled to receive notice has not done so 'due to accidental omission or non-receipt'.

The notice must state:

- date;
- time;

- place;
- the general nature of business to be dealt with; and
- that members are entitled to appoint a proxy.

Where practicable, the details of any special resolution intended to be passed should be contained within the notice.

On a practical level, it is often more straightforward to include the agenda with, or within, the formal notice.

Quorum

The quorum is the minimum number of persons required to validly conduct business at a meeting. For a general meeting, only individual members or a representative of a corporate member (such as the sponsor or foundation body) count towards the quorum. Any other persons present, such as observers or advisors, even if they are there legitimately, will not count. The exception to this is where there are validly appointed proxies.

The model articles provide that the quorum for general meetings will be two members.

If there are insufficient members present, the meeting is inquorate and any business transacted will be invalid. If the meeting is not quorate within half an hour of the notified start time, or if member/s leave the meeting causing it to be inquorate, the meeting will be adjourned. It will be automatically rescheduled to the same day in the next week at the same time and place or to such time and place as the directors decide.

Chair

The chair of the board will generally chair general meetings of members. In the absence of the chair, the directors may nominate another member of the board.

If neither the chair nor any other director nominated and willing to act as chair are present at the general meeting within 15 minutes of its notified start time, then directors present will elect one of them to be the chair. If there is no director present or willing to act as chair, the members can vote to choose one of the members to be chair.

Adjournment

If a majority of members at a quorate meeting agree, the chair may adjourn the meeting to a later time and place. No business other than that included in the agenda for the original meeting may be transacted at the adjourned meeting.

If the meeting is adjourned for 14 days or more, a fresh notice must be sent out giving at least seven clear days' notice.

Decision making at general meetings

Resolutions

A resolution is a formal decision taken by a meeting. When a resolution is passed, the academy and members are bound by it irrespective of whether they personally voted in favour of it.

Great care should be taken in the drafting of resolutions and reference should be made to Companies House for guidance. If in doubt, always seek professional help when framing the wording to ensure that the resolution achieves the desired aim. The effective date of any resolution should be made clear so that rather than simply approving a resolution, it could state:

> IT WAS RESOLVED THAT the name of the academy *be and they are hereby* changed from AN ACADEMY to ANOTHER ACADEMY.

The inclusion of the word 'hereby' indicates that the change is to take place with immediate effect. Alternatively:

> IT WAS RESOLVED THAT the name of the academy be changed from AN ACADEMY to ANOTHER ACADEMY on 1 September 2014.

This will be more appropriate where the change is to take place on a stated future date or on the occurrence of a stated event.

SPECIAL RESOLUTION ON CHANGE OF NAME
Company number: 123456789

Existing company name: _____

At an Annual General Meeting*/General meeting* of the members of the above named company, duly convened and held at:_____

On the _____ day of _____ 20 _____ .

That the name of the company be changed to:

New name: _____

Signed: _____

*Director/secretary on behalf of the company.

(*delete as appropriate)

Voting

Most resolutions, known as ordinary resolutions, require a simple majority (i.e. at least 50% plus one of the votes cast).

Special resolutions require a 75% majority. Special resolutions relate to changes to the constitution or more important decisions affecting the future of the academy:

- changes to the Articles;
- change of name of the academy;
- any resolution required by the Articles to be a special resolution; and
- the appointment of members.

In addition, changes to the Articles will require approval by the Secretary of State for Education.

If the Articles do not specify that an item should be passed by a special resolution, then only an ordinary resolution is necessary. Where the Companies Act specifies that a special resolution is required (e.g. when changing the name of the academy) this cannot be overridden by changing the Articles.

Each member will have one vote, whether a decision is taken on a show of hands or by poll. No member can vote at any general meeting if they owe any money to the academy.

Voting will be decided on a show of hands and the chair will declare that the resolution is carried in order to pass it. The number of votes for, against and abstentions need not be counted and should not be included in the minutes. The entry in the minutes that a resolution has been passed will be conclusive evidence of the fact without the proportion or number of votes cast.

However, a poll can be demanded by:

- the chair;
- at least two members having the right to vote at the meeting; and
- a member or members representing not less than one-tenth of the total voting rights of all the members having the right to vote at the meeting.

A poll is simply a written vote. In an academy, there is no difference in voting power for individual members between a vote on a show of hands and a poll; each member has one vote.

A poll can be demanded before a vote or on the declaration of the result of the show of hands. However, withdrawal of a demand for a poll may only be done with the consent of the chair. Any result of a show of hands previously declared will still be valid.

The chair shall determine the time, date and place for declaring the results of a poll which will, nevertheless, be regarded as a resolution taken at the general meeting where it was demanded. Any poll on the election of chair or on a question of adjournment must be taken immediately. A poll must be taken not more than 30 days after the poll is demanded. Notice does not need to be given of a poll not taken immediately if the time, date and place at which it is to be taken are announced at the meeting. Otherwise, at least seven clear days' notice shall be given specifying the time, date and place at which the poll is to be taken.

Any member who is absent but who has not appointed a proxy will not count in any vote whether on a show of hands or on a poll.

Proxies

Members are entitled to appoint another person to attend the general meeting in their place and exercise their right to speak and vote. The person authorised to act for the member must be appointed by a formal document signed by or on behalf of the member appointing the proxy which is delivered:

- at the office or at such other place within the United Kingdom specified in the notice convening the meeting or in any instrument of proxy sent out, not less than 48 hours before the meeting;
- not less than 24 hours before the time appointed for taking of a poll, where the poll is taken more than 48 hours after it is demanded; or
- at the meeting at which the poll was demanded (to the chair, clerk or any director) where the poll is taken not more than 48 hours after it was demanded.

The proxy can either be appointed simply to attend, speak and vote in the member's name and on their behalf (i.e. voting in favour or against resolutions as they wish) or they can be appointed giving specific instruction on how the proxy should act and the votes to cast in respect of resolutions. The specific wording for both forms of appointment is set out in the Articles and should be followed.

Annual general meeting

It is no longer a requirement for private companies to hold an AGM and various versions of the model articles have no specific requirement to do so. However, care should be taken to take note of the provisions of the academy's Articles to see if it is necessary to hold an AGM; in particular, many MATs are required to do so.

For the majority of converter academies, the members are not a group entirely independent of the board. This means that requirements for an AGM can sometimes seem somewhat superfluous, as every individual has a platform for raising concerns and an opportunity to consider the details provided at an AGM by virtue of their position as director.

The annual reports and accounts are prepared and formally approved by the board of directors. They are also presented to the members (historically this was done at the AGM). Where academies do not hold an AGM, the accounts must be sent to all members by the time they are due to be filed with the registrar of companies.

It is feasible for the Articles of Association to be amended so that documentation including accounts can be provided to members by means of publication on a website. This is a provision more generally used by large companies with great numbers of members and is unlikely to be required by most academies. In any event, members will retain the right to request paper copies.

Despite the requirements, members are not required to approve the annual report and accounts and do not have any recourse if they do have issues apart from removing members of the board of directors!

Some schools see the AGM as an opportunity to showcase its activities over the previous year and will invite along the wider local community and press.

EXAMPLE NOTICE OF AN AGM

This notice is sent to all members, governors and the external auditors as required by the Articles of Association.

Please note that only *members* i.e. the appointed representative of The Schools of King Edward the Sixth in Birmingham (Foundation), the Chairman of the Foundation Board, the Deputy Chairman of the Foundation Board and the Chairman of Governors of King Edward VI Five Ways School need to attend the AGM and that only these members are allowed to vote. Therefore the reference to proxy voting is only relevant to a *member* who is unable to attend.

Other governors may attend the AGM (it will take place during the governing body meeting) if they wish, but do not need to and should be aware that they cannot vote. It is envisaged that the AGM will take approximately 15 minutes.

Notice of an Annual General Meeting

Notice is hereby given that the Annual General Meeting of King Edward VI Five Ways School Academy Trust (Company) will be held at the Foundation Office on 17 December 2012 during the Governing Body meeting (which starts at 5.00pm) for the following purposes:

1. to receive the annual accounts of the Company for the financial period ended 31 August 2012; and
2. to reappoint Baker Tilly LLP as auditors of the Company and to authorise the directors to agree the remuneration of Baker Tilly LLP.

By order of the Board

Philippa Cole
King Edward VI Five Ways School
Scotland Lane
Bartley Green
Birmingham
B32 4BT   3 December 2012

NOTES to the Notice of Annual General Meeting:

1. A member entitled to attend and vote at the meeting convened by the notice set out above is entitled to appoint a proxy to attend and, on a poll, to vote in his place. A proxy need not be a member of the company.
2. A form of proxy is enclosed (for members only). To be effective, it must be deposited at the office of the company's registered office so as to be received not later than 48 hours before the time appointed for holding the annual general meeting. Completion of the proxy does not preclude a member from subsequently attending and voting at the meeting in person if he or she so wishes.

Drafting the minutes of general meetings

Minutes of all general meetings and Annual General Meetings should be prepared and stored. The basic principles relating to preparation of robust board minutes (see Chapter 9) are equally applicable to general meetings.

Heading

Minutes should be headed with the practical details about the meeting:

- Name of the academy.
- Company registered number. Consider use of the academy's usual headed paper which includes the company number.
- Date, time and location.
- Names of members present.
- Names of proxies present and details of the instrument which appointed them including the member that they are replacing.
- Names of those 'in attendance' including directors.
- Apologies. Names of those not present who have informed the meeting beforehand that they would not be able to attend and the apologies have been accepted.
- Absent. Where apologies are not given or they have not been accepted.
- Identify who is chairing the meeting.
- Confirmation that the meeting was quorate. If a meeting is not quorate, no valid decision making can take place.

It is good practice to note the actual time that the meeting started.

Participants may be identified in the body of the minutes using their full name, title and surname, or by initials which are identified after the individual's full name in the heading. Whichever approach is selected should be used throughout the minutes.

Written resolutions

Members can also make decisions using the written resolution procedure and, for many academies, this will be the way that most decision making by members will be done in practice.

Written resolutions cannot be used to dismiss a director or to remove an auditor before the end of their term of office.

A copy of the proposed resolution must be sent to every member.

The resolution will be passed if the required majority is met as set out in the Companies Act 2006 unless the Articles contain other specific provisions. Ordinary resolutions require a simple majority of those eligible to vote (i.e. half plus one of all appointed directors with a vote). Special resolutions, such as a change of name or an amendment to the Articles, require at least 75% of those eligible to vote.

Consent to, or acceptance of, the resolution may be by way of several instruments in like form each agreed by one or more members. This means that the resolution could be returned signed or agreed to by each member individually and still be valid.

A member signifies his agreement by providing an 'authenticated document' which can be in hard copy and signed or electronically sent indicating agreement. A member may not revoke their agreement once it has been signified in this way.

Copies of any written resolutions must be kept for 10 years from the date of the resolution and must be made available for inspection by members on request.

Irrespective of the regular use of written resolutions, members and directors still have the power to demand that a meeting be held.

Companies House filing

A copy of any special resolution or any agreement agreed to by all the members which would otherwise have been a special resolution must be filed at Companies House within 15 days of being passed or made. The resolution should be signed by a director or the secretary on behalf of the members.

Summary

Members

- Members offer a guarantee which is limited to £10.
- The subscribers to the Memorandum are the first members.
- Members can be either natural persons or corporate bodies, but they must not make a profit from their involvement.
- A person signs a written consent or the register of members to become a member.

Responsibilities, rights and remedies

- Members appoint and can remove directors.
- Members (subject to approval by the Secretary of State) have the power to amend the Articles.
- Members have rights in particular to receive notices of meetings, proposed written resolutions and audited accounts and annual report. They can require the directors to call a general meeting, and they can appoint proxies to vote at general meetings.
- A member may take action against the academy where its affairs are 'conducted in a manner that is unfairly prejudicial to the interests of members generally or of some part of its members (including at least him/herself)'.
- Members can bring an action on behalf of the academy against a director, former director or shadow director in respect of a cause of action arising from an actual or proposed act or omission by a director involving negligence, default, breach of duty or breach of trust.

Ceasing to be a member

- In certain circumstances (e.g. where a corporate entity ceases to exist or where an individual dies, becomes incapable of managing and administering his/her own affairs or becomes insolvent) membership will terminate automatically.
- Those entitled to appoint members can remove any member appointed by them by delivering written notice to the academy's registered office.
- Subscribers to the Memorandum can be removed where remaining members 'agree unanimously in writing' to remove them.
- Additional members appointed by members may be removed if the members pass a special resolution in writing.
- All removals must be 'in the interests of the academy trust'.
- Any member may resign by notice in writing signed by the person entitled to remove them provided that three members remain in office.

General meetings

- Members' meetings and board meetings must be kept separate.
- Directors are entitled to attend and speak at any general meeting but do not have a vote.
- Members' meetings will generally be called by the directors.
- Directors must call a general meeting if it is requested by members holding at least 5% of total voting rights.
- If the directors do not comply with a valid request to convene a general

meeting, members representing over half of the members' total voting rights may call a general meeting.

- Notice must be given with 14 clear days' notice and sent to every member, director and the auditor.
- A meeting can be called on short notice if a majority of the members holding at least 90% of the voting rights agree.
- The model articles provide that the quorum for general meetings is two members.
- If the meeting is not quorate within half an hour of the notified start time, or if member/s leave the meeting causing it to be inquorate, the meeting will be adjourned.
- The chair of the board will generally chair general meetings of members.
- A majority of members at a quorate meeting may agree to adjourn the meeting to a later time and place.

Decision making at general meetings

- Ordinary resolutions require a simple majority (i.e. at least 50% plus one of the votes cast).
- Special resolutions require a 75% majority.
- Special resolutions relate to changes to the constitution or more important decisions affecting the future of the academy such as changes to the Articles or name of the academy, or appointment of members.
- Each member has one vote, whether a decision is taken on a show of hands or by poll.
- Voting is decided on a show of hands unless a poll is demanded.
- A proxy may be appointed by a formal document signed by or on behalf of the member.

Annual general meeting

- Although no longer a statutory requirement, an AGM may be required by the Articles.
- The annual reports and accounts are presented and the auditors appointed for the next financial year.

Written resolutions

- Written resolutions cannot be used to dismiss a director or to remove an auditor before the end of their term of office.
- A copy of the proposed resolution must be sent to every member which will be passed if the required majority of votes is met.
- Consent to the resolution may be done by individual documents signed or authenticated by members.

- Copies of any written resolutions must be kept for 10 years and made available for inspection by members.

Companies House filing

- A copy of any special resolution must be filed at Companies House within 15 days.

7 Directors, governors and trustees

▧ In this chapter

This chapter looks at the tri-partite nature of the role of director/governor/trustee looking in turn at the three aspects:

- the role of directors, appointment and termination, duties and liabilities and the restrictions on eligibility to be appointed including LAAPs;
- governors as 'critical friend' providing solid governance to support improvement; and
- trustees upholding the charitable principles of the company and ensuring that the academy is run for the purpose that it was intended.

The management of an academy is the responsibility of the board. The members of the board have a tri-partite role as:

- directors of the charitable company for the purposes of company law;
- governors of the academy; and
- trustees for the purposes of charity law.

This is largely a technical distinction which makes little difference to the day-to-day role of the individuals concerned.

However, the language is confusing and an academy should adopt a title and stick with it rather than using the terms interchangeably.

According to the funding agreement, the priorities for the governing body of the academy are:

- to set the vision of the school;
- to hold the head teacher to account for educational performance; and
- to ensure that the academy's money is well spent.

▧ Directors

As a company, an academy's corporate structure is dictated by company law. An individual academy's particular structure is dictated by the Articles of Association.

An academy has a two-part governance structure made up of members and directors. These directors are the equivalent of governors in a maintained school (and generally in a single academy will be called governors).

Multi-academies are more complex corporate structures but the directors sit on the main board which retains the legal responsibility for running the overall organisation. 'Governors' sitting on local governing bodies of the separate schools are more like committee members.

The Companies Act 2006 does not contain a definition of a director as such although it does state that: 'A director can be a natural or legal person.'

The majority of directors on an academy board will be 'natural persons' or a real human being. However, there may be corporate membership of the board where a company, charity or other organisation is appointed as a director. Care must be taken to ensure that such appointments are in accordance with the Articles of Association.

The board of directors is responsible for the management of the school, although they can delegate functions to committees, individual directors or the head teacher. The head teacher will be delegated the responsibility to run the school on a day-to-day basis implementing the strategic vision and acting within the agreed framework though they will report to the board and provide such information, advice and recommendations as required. However, the board remains ultimately responsible.

EXPERIENCE

John Swift, the Business Manager at The Knights Templar School explained:

'Academy status has changed the landscape for school governance significantly. In the absence of local authority support, governors are being asked to assume greater responsibility and accountability, yet remain unpaid volunteers. We are very lucky to have such supportive governors whose efforts underpin much of our success.'

The size and make-up of the board will be dictated by the Articles of Association. However, it may include:

- appointments by the members;
- appointments by the sponsor/foundation;
- elected parent governors;
- staff;
- head teacher; and
- co-opted governor.

The DfE requires that an academy must have at least two parent governors. No more than a third of governors can be academy staff, but there no longer needs to be a local authority (LA) governor. The DfE has indicated a move away from the stakeholder model whereby the various different parties involved with the organisation have some form of representation at governing body/board level so that the interests of those groups are given due regard. Moving forward, there will be a greater emphasis on making the right appointments to the board rather than that they are drawn from specific sectors of the community.

Irrespective of the way that appointments are made, careful consideration should be given to ensure that the board has a balance of skills and experience and is truly able to provide effective direction and governance.

Any directors elected from the staff body as well as directors elected from the parents of current pupils help to ensure that the focus of the board always remains on the pupils themselves and on providing the best possible education.

The directors are a central part of the leadership of the school, deciding on the strategic direction and overall conduct as well as overseeing policies and finances. They are there to support the head teacher and senior leadership team in realising the vision and ethos of the school. They are also there to provide challenge so that the school is continually improving. This relationship between the directors and the school – the so-called 'critical friend' – is fundamental to good governance. This much has not changed from the position as a maintained school; as the DfE points out 'the principles of governance are the same in academies as in maintained schools'.

However, academies are independent of LA control which means that the governing body has greater autonomy – but they also have greater responsibility.

The board of directors works as a team and is a 'corporate entity'. This means that directors are bound by decisions made by the board and are loyal to them even if they did not vote for them.

COMMENT

Graham Burns, Partner with Stone King:

Appointment of directors

The DfE's model articles provide that academy trusts must have at least three directors, but there is no prescribed maximum number. In reality most schools will convert with a similar number of governors to that which they had prior to conversion.

There are some prescribed rules regarding the composition of the governors: firstly it is DfE policy for at least two of the governors to be elected parent governors (i.e. parents of pupils attending the academy). Secondly, the total number of governors who are also employed by the academy trust must be less than one third of the total number of governors including the principal. Finally, the principal is not required but is 'expected' to be a director of the academy trust.

Provided the requirements regarding the composition of the governing body are satisfied the exact powers of appointment will depend upon the individual requirements of the academy trust. For instance the articles may provide provision for a foundation or sponsor body to have certain appointment rights.

It will also be likely that the articles will provide a power for the governors to 'co-opt' the appointment of further governors. This provides the current governors with the power to appoint governors themselves; this can be useful if particular expertise are required, for example co-opting a governor with a background in construction would be beneficial if the academy trust was proposing to undertake a new building project.

Eligibility for directorship

Under company law, there are some restrictions on who can be appointed as a director. However, the Articles should be consulted as there may be specific provisions in relation to some of the appointments:

- Directors must be aged 18 or over at the date of election or appointment. No current pupil of the academy can become a director.
- Both real and corporate persons can be directors although there must be at least one real person on every board.
- A person cannot be a director during a period of disqualification whether in the UK or in an overseas jurisdiction.
- A person cannot be a director during any period s/he is an undischarged bankrupt (without the permission of the court).
- The academy's auditor cannot be a director.

Directors' duties

However, as directors of a charitable company, there are legal duties and responsibilities to observe. Directors have a fiduciary duty to the academy (i.e. they must act with the 'utmost good faith'). They also have a responsibility to ensure that the academy complies with charity law requirements.

The Companies Act 2006 sets out 'general duties' that apply to directors (ss. 170–177 CA 2006). They have a duty to:

- act within powers – acting in accordance with the academy's constitution and only exercising powers for the purposes for which they were conferred;
- promote the success of the academy;
- exercise independent judgement;

- exercise reasonable care, skill and diligence;
- avoid conflicts of interest;
- not accept benefits from third parties; and
- declare an interest in any proposed transaction or arrangement.

Appointment of directors

The method of appointment will depend on the category of director and the terms of the Articles. However, there must be at least two parent governors and no more than a third of directors, including the head teacher, can be academy staff. Directors are generally appointed for a term of four years.

Parent directors

A single academy, special academy or an alternative provision academy will typically be required to appoint a certain number of parents to the board and the model articles provide that such individuals 'shall be elected by parents of registered pupils' at the academy. They must be a parent of a pupil at the academy at the time when they are elected, although they will not be required to terminate their position if they no longer have a pupil at the school. The board is responsible for making all necessary arrangements for an election which should be held by secret ballot if it is contested.

If the election process brings forward insufficient nominees to fill the vacancies, the board can appoint a person who is the parent of a registered pupil at the academy or if this is not reasonably practical, a person who is the parent of a child of compulsory school age.

Staff directors

There is often a requirement for elected staff directors.

Member appointments

The majority of director appointments will be made by the members through such process as they may determine. It is wise to set up a selection process by which the skills and experience of suitable individuals can be considered against the current requirements or weaknesses on the board.

Member appointments may be made in a general meeting. The minuted resolution should reflect the requirements of the Articles, for example:

'It was unanimously agreed that Mr J Smith be appointed as a Director of the Academy Trust for a term of four years with effect from [date].'

If the appointment is to be made immediately, this would read:

'It was unanimously agreed that Mr J Smith be and hereby is appointed as a Director of the Academy Trust for a term of four years.'

Often, however, it is easier for a written resolution to appoint a director to avoid the requirement for holding a meeting. This is a mechanism regularly used by Presdales School Academy Trust, a single academy based in Ware, Hertfordshire.

EXAMPLE

Company number: 7990029

Company name: Presdales School Academy Trust

ORDINARY WRITTEN RESOLUTION

This written resolution is proposed and made under the procedure set out in Chapter 2, Part 13 of the Companies Act 2006. Upon acceptance of this resolution by an ordinary majority of the Company's Members it shall be as valid and effective as if it had been passed at a properly called and constituted general meeting. This ordinary resolution may comprise more than one document in this form, each signed by one or more Member.

IT IS RESOLVED:

That Mr Michael Robinson be appointed as Governor of the Academy Trust for a term of office commencing on 24 March 2013 and expiring on 23 March 2017.

By signing this document I acknowledge that I have accepted and agreed this resolution:

(Print Name)
(Signed)
(Date)

Director appointments

The directors may be able to appoint co-opted directors. Resolutions passed at a board meeting should follow similar terms to those of member appointments. The most recent version of the Articles also permits directors to make decisions via the written resolution procedure. Any co-option of an employee of the academy must not exceed the limit on staff directors of one third of the total number of directors (including the head teacher).

Sponsor/foundation appointments

A certain number of director positions may be retained for appointments made by the sponsor or foundation.

Finding the right director

The DfE have indicated a move away from the stakeholder model of representation on the board. This means that, increasingly, academies will have a level of control over who is appointed.

It is good practice to undertake a regular skills audit; the information gathered can be used to identify the right individuals for appointment. Recognition of the gaps in skills or experience on the board will enable a focused search and appointment. Gone are the days of appointing someone just because they were keen and available!

EXPERIENCE

Dave Gardner, Chair of Governors at Royal Wootton Bassett Academy:

'We undertook a skills audit. Subsequently when we sent out the papers for parent governor elections we suggested the types of skills that we were looking for. Surprisingly it seemed to elicit more volunteers than usual. We had seven nominations for three vacancies where previously we would just fill the vacancies.

For community governors, we usually use our own local network and stretch out to where the current governors have links. If we need an HR professional or a lawyer, for example, we can usually find someone. I have been going out to talk to Rotary Clubs and Chambers of Commerce so that we have a wide range of people to tap into for any specific needs.'

Generally, the first port of call for academies looking for governors is the connections of those already on the board. However, if particular skills have been identified, it may be possible to contact a relevant professional body, many of whom will be extremely helpful in the search for a new governor. Alternatively, SGOSS, the School Governors' One-Stop Shop, offers a free 'match-making' service which connects prospective governors with schools and academies. Their aim is to 'ensure that every school in England has access to volunteers with transferable business skills'.

Certainly, more needs to be done to raise the profile of governors who play a vital role in the running of academies! They are required to make a commitment and accept the responsibility and accountability of running a publicly funded organisation despite being volunteers.

EXPERIENCE

Rosemary Bolton, Chair of Governors of Presdales School Academy Trust:

'The Board of Directors of the new Academy consists of competent and capable professionals from a wide range of fields. A skills audit taken at the time of conversion revealed a need for certain experts and these were then targeted and invited to join the Board. The current process is for new Directors to be approached via personal recommendation, contact with the LA Governance team or using the SGOSS (School Governor One Stop Shop) or other professional bodies, they are invited to meet with the Chair, Vice Chair and Head teacher and their CVs together with recommendations are put to the full Board for a discussion and vote.

A Board of 21 Directors is often considered large and unwieldy, however all our Directors are busy professionals with various other commitments and many are unable to commit as much time to the Academy as often as others, but all of their skills are useful at different times. Each Director sits on at least one of the committees and has a link within the school, either with a department or a particular role. Teleconferencing facilities are available at meetings if required. There are five committees in addition to the Board, Achievement & Curriculum, Finance, Personnel and Premises and also a Strategic Group consisting of the Chairs of the other four committees, the Chair, Vice Chair and the Head teacher. There is a separate audit committee. All the committees report back to the Board every half term. There is also a panel which deals with Disciplinary, Exclusions and Appeals if required.'

Skills audits and analysis of training needs

A review of board skills and experience should be undertaken periodically. As well as identifying any gaps on the board, it will also assist in developing an ongoing programme of training for directors to expand and update their existing knowledge and skills.

For some useful documents, please see Appendix 2.

Induction and training

A structured process should be developed to familiarise newly appointed directors with the academy and their role. The programme should aim to provide a full grounding as often directors have no previous experience of a corporate environment and/or the educational world. Whilst induction must convey sufficient

Figure 7.1: The process for recruiting and appointing new community governors

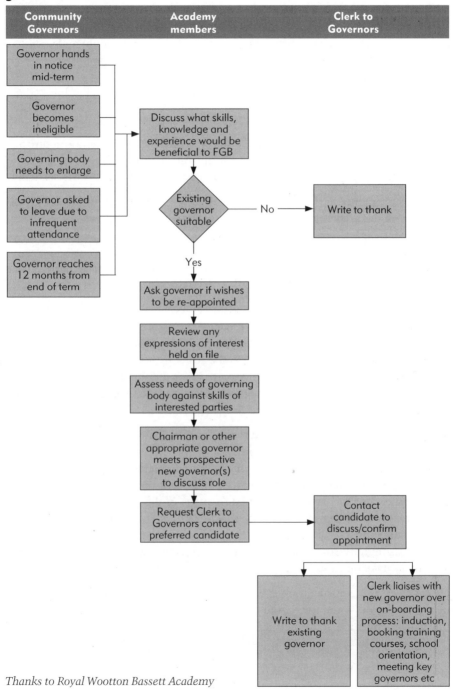

Thanks to Royal Wootton Bassett Academy

information and support to enable the director to become effective as quickly as possible, it must be remembered that directors remain volunteers and will generally have other demands on their time which may prevent their attendance.

Despite tight funding, consideration should be given to setting a budget for governance training and support. The demands on a director should not be underestimated and appropriate training and professional development will assist individuals to feel confident in their role.

Payment of directors

An academy is an exempt charity and subject to charity law. Generally a director or member is not permitted to make a profit from their role. However, there are some limited circumstances when academy directors can be paid by the academy:

- reimbursement of reasonable expenses properly incurred when acting on behalf of the academy (at the discretion of the board);
- payment for services provided outside the role of director (subject to strict rules); and
- payment of salary to staff directors or the headteacher/executive headteacher in their capacity as an employee and not as a director.

Care should be taken by members and directors when entering into a trading relationship with the academy. The model Articles of Association provide that members who are not also directors may be paid reasonable and proper remuneration for any goods or services supplied to the academy.

A director is entitled to enter into a contract for the supply of goods or services to the academy, other than for acting as a director, as long as certain conditions are fulfilled:

- remuneration or other sums paid to the director do not exceed an amount that is reasonable in all the circumstances;
- the director is absent from the part of any meeting discussing such relationship, must not vote on any such matter and is not counted in the quorum;
- the other directors must be satisfied that it is in the interests of the academy to employ or to contract with that director rather than with someone who is not a director;
- the reason for the directors' decision is recorded in the minute book; and
- a majority of directors then in office have received no such payments or benefit.

However, greater consideration is being given to permitting remuneration, particularly in relation to the role of the chair. FASNA have called for remuneration of the chair of governors to be 'neither mandatory nor banned'.

Termination of office

Generally, directors are appointed for a fixed term of office, which in the model articles is set at four years. A director may resign by giving written notice to the clerk at any time, although the articles provide that this will only be valid if there are at least three directors remaining in office when the notice of resignation is to take effect.

The Companies Act 2006 provides that a 'company may by ordinary resolution at a meeting remove a director before the expiration of his period of office, notwithstanding anything in any agreement between it and him'. This very wide provision is slightly tempered by the model articles which state that directors can generally be removed from office by the person or persons who appointed them. This means that where directors are appointed by the members they can be removed from office, following a member resolution, by written notice to the clerk. Elected directors cannot be removed in this way.

Disqualification of directors

The Company Directors' Disqualification Act 1986 grants the court the power to make an order disqualifying a person from promoting, forming or taking part in the management of a company without the leave of the court. There are numerous grounds for disqualification and the model articles set out specific instances which will be regarded as disqualification, where a director:

- becomes incapable by reason of illness or injury of managing or administering his own affairs;
- is absent without the permission of the directors from all their meetings held within a period of six months and the directors resolve that his office be vacated;
- has his estate sequestrated and the sequestration has not been discharged, annulled or reduced; or he is the subject of a bankruptcy restrictions order or an interim order;
- is subject to a disqualification order or a disqualification undertaking under the Company Directors' Disqualification Act 1986 or to an order made under s. 429(2)(b) of the Insolvency Act 1986;
- ceases to be a director by virtue of any provision in the Companies Act 2006 or is disqualified from acting as a trustee by virtue of s. 178 of the Charities Act 2011;
- has been removed from the office of charity trustee or trustee for a charity by an order made by the Charity Commission or the High Court on the grounds of any misconduct or mismanagement in the administration of the charity for which he was responsible or to which he was privy, or which he by his conduct contributed to or facilitated;
- has, at any time, been convicted of any criminal offence, excluding any that have been spent under the Rehabilitation of Offenders Act 1974 as amended,

and excluding any offence for which the maximum sentence is a fine or a lesser sentence except where a person has been convicted of any offence which falls under s. 178 Charities Act 2011; and

■ has not provided to the chair of the board a disclosure and barring service check at an enhanced disclosure level under s. 113B Police Act 1997. In the event that the certificate discloses any information which would, in the opinion of either the chairman or the principal, confirm their unsuitability to work with children that person shall be disqualified.

Where a person becomes disqualified from holding, or continuing to hold office as a director, the Articles require that he should give written notice of that fact to the clerk. The disqualification provisions also apply to any member of any committee of the directors even if they are not themselves a director.

▧ Shadow and *de facto* directors

The Companies Act 2006 provides that a director 'includes any person occupying the position of director, by whatever name called'.

This is a broad definition which will include all those who have been validly appointed as a director as well as anyone who, although not appointed, may act as a director. This means that boards can no longer appoint an 'associate governor' as any such individual would be regarded as a director irrespective of whether they have been appointed as such. These *de facto* (meaning 'in fact') directors will be subject to the same general duties and other legal responsibilities as a properly appointed director.

A shadow director is 'a person in accordance with whose directions or instructions the directors of the company are accustomed to act' except when advice is given in a professional capacity. Shadow directors are those who have a real influence over an element of the company's business affairs. It is a wide definition and it can be difficult to identify a shadow director. Consequently, case law has identified factors to take into account in ascertaining whether an individual is a shadow director:

■ communications were either a 'direction or instruction';
■ it is not necessary for a shadow director to give directions or instructions over all areas of the company's activities;
■ advice of a non-professional nature can constitute a direction or instruction;
■ it is not necessary to show that the board acted in a subservient manner;
■ the majority of the board were accustomed to following the directions and instructions and not only a number of individuals;
■ it must be shown that the directors act on directions or instructions; the mere giving of them is insufficient evidence; and
■ a person can be a shadow director if s/he is involved in the internal management of the company.

A shadow director could be a legal person (i.e. a company, charity or other organisation) which gives directions or instructions that are acted upon by the board.

Although neither *de facto* nor shadow directors are formally appointed to the board and will not be registered as such at Companies House, they may acquire liabilities and, depending on the terms of cover, may not be covered by insurance provision. The general duties contained in the Companies Act 2006 apply to *de facto* and shadow directors against whom a disqualification order could also be made by a court.

Liability

Responsibilities also bring potential liabilities, although these should not generally be a threat to a director who is acting in good faith. In an extreme situation, a director who is found to be acting fraudulently could be charged under criminal law and receive a prison sentence of up to ten years. Directors could also find themselves disqualified from acting as a director of a UK company for a period of up to 15 years as well as being subject to a fine.

Directors are responsible for fulfilling the company secretarial requirements of the academy, although they may choose to do so by delegation to an individual. There is an automatic late filing penalty if the Annual Accounts are delivered late which is on an increasing scale. It is also a criminal offence and directors could find themselves personally liable. The annual return does not have a late filing penalty as such but directors could also find themselves potentially liable, as well as for failures to file other information at Companies House when necessary.

Members can bring an action on behalf of the academy against a director in respect of a cause of action arising from an actual or proposed act or omission by a director involving:

- negligence;
- default – the failure to perform a legally obligated act;
- breach of duty – including the 'general duties' or any other duty; and
- breach of trust.

This means that if a director is not fulfilling their duties under company law, they expose themselves to the risk of legal action. It is, nevertheless, possible for the board to ratify or formally approve the director's action if it was performed negligently, so that any derivative claim would be barred.

In most cases where a director is acting both within powers and in the best interests of the academy, any claim arising as a result of their actions or omissions should be covered by directors' liability insurance.

LAAPs

The Articles contain strict limits on the number of 'Local Authority Associated Persons' (LAAPs) that can be appointed as directors of an academy (see Chapter 4):

- LAAPs must make up less than 20% of the total number of directors. On any resolution, the number of number of votes exercisable by LAAPs must not exceed 19.9% of the total number of votes exercisable by directors. The votes of the other directors will be increased on a pro-rata basis to avoid this situation;
- a LAAP must have their appointment as director authorised by the LA with which they are associated; and
- if a director subsequently becomes a LAAP, he/she will be 'deemed to have immediately resigned his membership and/or resigned from his office'.

The limitation poses logistical difficulties particularly for academies situated in large conurbations where there may be several LAs relatively closely situated. The effect is that it may not always be possible to appoint otherwise good candidates for the role of director.

EXPERIENCE

Rosemary Bolton, Chair of the Board of Directors at Presdales School Academy Trust explains:

'Prior to conversion the Governing Body had consisted of 21 Governors including Staff, Parent and Parent Association Governors, Community and Local Authority Governors; a third of the membership were considered to be LAAPs (Local Authority Associated Persons) according to the DfE guidance, despite the fact that some of them worked in roles unrelated to education and for other Local Authorities and also included a retired ex Councillor. At the time the rules were that LAAPs could constitute no more that 19.9% of the Board of an Academy. Post conversion the Board was made up of 21 Directors, including Community, Parent and Staff Representatives; the LAAP issue has hindered recruitment of experienced and professional people, including democratically elected parents who could not be appointed due to them being regarded as LAAPs.

Presdales is situated in an area where unemployment is very low and, according to census information, one fifth of residents are employed in public services. There is a significant commuter population with many people travelling into London or to other large conurbations.

Directors currently regarded as LAAPs include two who work for London Boroughs which have no relationship with the Academy. Both are employed in roles which have no potential for entering into any business relationship with the Academy.'

Governors

Since the Education (No. 2) Act 1986, governing bodies have been responsible for the strategic management of their schools, supervising the budget and appointing the head teacher. This was further expanded in 1988 with many of the administrative and business functions formerly undertaken by local authorities delegated to individual schools. Governors found themselves responsible for the school budget, appointing and dismissing staff, fixing pay, dealing with complaints, maintaining and extending buildings and overseeing catering arrangements.

Governors were already well used to a significant level of responsibility. However, the transition to academy status is another big step and increased responsibility brings with it an increased risk of liability.

As with maintained schools, governors have three key roles of providing strategic management, ensuring accountability and acting as a 'critical friend' by providing support and challenge to the school's leadership team.

School governors make up the single largest group of volunteers in the country. However, 'academisation' has increased the need to professionalise the quality of governors and governance. Being a volunteer does not mean that governors can be amateurs!

In stand alone academies, there is huge overlap between the roles of 'governors' and 'directors' which cannot really be separated. However, in a MAT, the governance function may be delegated to the LGB where the day-to-day governorship is conducted.

Ofsted's *Annual Report* published in December 2013 stated:

'Good governance is crucial to tackling underperformance and supporting improvement. Governance that is weak does not challenge the school about its performance or press the school to increase its aspirations.'

In fact, the report goes on to say:

'School leaders and governors are primarily responsible for tackling the decline in teaching and standards that usually lead to a school being judged inadequate.'

This is an onerous responsibility.

Link governors

Many schools operate a 'link governor' programme which connects individual governors with a particular department or year group. They can build relationships with key individuals and gain a deeper understanding and insight into a particular area.

EXPERIENCE

Dave Gardner, Chair of Governors at Royal Wootton Bassett Academy:

'To provide points of contact on specific issues and to ensure all governors have lead roles, we also operate a Link Governor process with links to curriculum subject areas. This facilitates some contact direct with key staff or heads of department that can humanise governors in the eyes of staff (we have nearly 200 staff in a school of our size). I am not keen on governor classroom visits (other than for induction of new governors) as we have a rigorous system of observations undertaken by lead teacher practitioners and peers. On each FGB agenda there is an item: "News from the Links"'.

Trustees

As a charitable company, directors are also trustees for charity law purposes. In essence this means ensuring that the academy is run for the purpose that it was intended, is operated in accordance with its Articles and any applicable laws and that funds are appropriately spent.

However, the terminology is, without doubt, confusing. There is no legal trust in an academy and the pupils are not 'beneficiaries'. Furthermore, particularly in church schools, there will be other trusts relating to the land and buildings with their own trustees!

It is helpful for board members to bear the trustee role in mind when making decisions so that the focus remains on the stated object of the academy (i.e. to advance education).

A person cannot be a trustee if they have an unspent conviction for an offence involving dishonesty or deception, are an undischarged bankrupt subject to bankruptcy restrictions or an interim order, have an individual voluntary arrangement with creditors, have been removed as a trustee by the Charity Commission or High Court due to misconduct or mismanagement or have been disqualified as a director (s.178 Charities Act 2011).

Just like payment for services to directors, it is generally forbidden to make payments for an individual's service as a trustee except in accordance with the specific circumstances set out in the Articles. The Charity Commission regard the voluntary nature of trusteeship as a strength: 'The concept of unpaid trusteeship has been one of the defining characteristics of the charitable sector, contributing greatly to public confidence in charities.'

In a MAT, where powers are delegated to a local governing body appointed for each school, the LGB is not a charity. The members of an LGB will typically be known as 'governors' although they will not be directors, governors or trustees of the MAT. Interestingly, this means that the restrictions on payments to trustees do not literally apply. It would still be necessary to consider whether any such payment would be in the best interests of the charity and it will always be best practice that they remain independent and unpaid.

Summary

Directors, governors and trustees

- The management of an academy is the responsibility of persons with a tri-partite role as:
  - governors of the academy;
  - directors of the charitable company for the purposes of company law; and
  - trustees for the purposes of charity law.

Directors

- A director can be a person or a corporate body.
- The board of directors is responsible for the management of the school, but can delegate functions to committees, individual directors or the head teacher.
- There must be at least two parent governors and no more than a third of governors can be academy staff. The exact proportions and appointments will be dictated by the Articles.
- The directors are part of the leadership of the school and decide the strategic direction.
- The board works as a team and is a 'corporate entity'; directors are bound by decisions made by the board and are loyal to them even if they did not vote for them.

Eligibility for directorship

- Directors must be aged 18 or over.
- No current pupil of the academy can become a director.
- Both real and corporate persons can be directors although there must be at least one real person on every board.
- A person cannot be a director during a period of disqualification.

- A person cannot be a director if they are an undischarged bankrupt (without the permission of the court).
- The academy's auditor cannot be a director.

Directors' duties

- Directors have a fiduciary duty to the academy and must act with 'utmost good faith'.
- They have a responsibility to ensure that the academy complies with charity law requirements.
- The Companies Act 2006 sets out 'general duties' which directors must observe.

Appointment of directors

- There must be at least two parent governors and no more than one-third of directors, including the principal/head teacher/chief executive, can be academy staff.
- Directors are generally appointed for a term of four years.
- There may be a requirement for elected parent and staff directors. However, in MATs it may be possible to select and appoint suitable candidates.
- The majority of director appointments will be made by the members.
- Directors may be able to appoint co-opted directors.
- Some director positions may be retained for appointments made by the sponsor or foundation.
- Skills audits should be undertaken regularly and efforts made to recruit appropriate directors to fill the gaps.
- SGOSS, the School Governors' One-Stop Shop, offers a free 'match-making' service connecting prospective governors with schools and academies.
- Skills audits will also assist in developing an ongoing programme of training for directors to expand and update their existing knowledge and skills.
- There should be a structured induction process for new directors.

Payment of directors

- Generally a director cannot be paid except for:
    - reimbursement of reasonable expenses;
    - payment for services provided outside the role of director; and
    - payment of salary to staff in their capacity as an employee.

Termination of office

- Directors are usually appointed for a fixed term of four years.
- A director may resign at any time if there will then be at least three directors remaining in office.
- Directors can generally be removed from office by the person/s who appointed them.
- Directors may be disqualified from being involved in the management of an academy.

Shadow and *de facto* directors

- A director will be anyone who acts as a director whether they are formally appointed as such.
- An 'associate governor' could be regarded as a director.

Liability

- A director who acts fraudulently could be charged under criminal law and receive a prison sentence of up to ten years.
- Directors can be disqualified from acting as a director for up to 15 years as well as subject to a fine.
- Directors can be personally liable for the failure to file information at Companies House.
- Members can bring an action on behalf of the academy against a director where they have been negligent, in default or in breach of duty or breach of trust.

LAAPs

- Local Authority Associated Persons must be less than 20% of the total number of directors. The total number of votes exercisable by LAAPs must not exceed 19.9% of the total.
- A LAAP must have their appointment as director authorised by the LA with which they are associated.
- A director who subsequently becomes a LAAP is deemed to have immediately resigned.

Governors

- Governors have three key roles: providing strategic management, ensuring accountability and providing support and challenge to the school's leadership team.
- In a MAT, the governance function may be delegated to the LGB where day-to-day governorship is conducted.

Trustees

- Directors are trustees for charity law purposes.
- Trustees must ensure that the academy is run for the purpose that it was intended, is operated in accordance with its Articles and any applicable laws and that funds are appropriately spent.

8 Board meetings and director decision making

In this chapter

This chapter explains the decision-making process for directors with regard to:

- the procedures to follow when arranging a directors' meeting including preparation of notice, agenda and dealing with supporting documentation;
- managing the meeting by briefing the chair, the role of chair and clerk, quorum requirements, adjournments and conferencing;
- the ICSA Code for Good Boardroom Practice; and
- using the written resolution procedure for decision-making.

Calling board meetings

Formal meetings of the directors are known as board meetings.

The directors are given a certain degree of flexibility in the way that they conduct board meetings as they 'may regulate their proceedings as they think fit' subject to compliance with the rules set out in the Articles of Association.

There must be 'at least three meetings in every school year'. However, the board may decide to meet more frequently to ensure that they are complying with their duties to the company and exercising their duty of care.

Board meetings are called or 'convened' by the clerk who will generally follow the directions of the board. Alternatively, instructions may be given by the chair – or if there is no chair the vice-chair – as long as the direction is not inconsistent with any direction given by the board.

It is also possible for three directors to requisition a board meeting. This is done by 'notice in writing given to the clerk' who must then convene such a meeting as soon as is reasonably practicable.

On a practical level, it is useful to set dates for meetings prior to the start of the academic year to cover the whole period. Dates should take account of important milestones in the calendar that will require board consideration such as pupil performance data, budget setting or the annual accounts. Ideally, a schedule of dates for committees should also be set to ensure that there is sufficient time for detailed consideration of matters by the committee and preparation of minutes to support the report back to the board.

Attendance

There is no legal requirement for directors to attend board meetings. However, directors are expected to do so and the annual report that is filed with the accounts is required to set out how many meetings each director did, in fact, attend (see Chapter 11). Regular attendance demonstrates that a director is diligently fulfilling their role and meeting their statutory duties. Board meetings are central to a robust corporate governance structure. Non-attendance by a director for a period of at least six months without the permission of the board can be grounds for removal.

Only the directors themselves have a right to attend board meetings. There may be other senior staff (e.g. a school business manager) who are accustomed to attending. However, their role is as an advisor to the board and they have no automatic right to attend. Care should be taken to ensure that additional parties who habitually attend remain advisors to the board and do not inadvertently find themselves regarded as a *de facto* director (see Chapter 7).

Notice

In order to be properly convened, a valid notice and agenda of a meeting must be circulated. Without this, decisions may be invalid.

It does not matter whether the directors were aware of the date and time of the meeting; specific formal notice must be sent prior to each meeting.

The model articles provide for notice of meetings to be called by at least seven clear days' notice, although earlier versions included the requirement for 14 clear days' notice. The period is calculated excluding the day on which the notice is given and the day of the meeting. Therefore, notice must be given on Monday of week one for a meeting on Tuesday of week two (where seven days' notice is required) or Tuesday of week three (where 14 days' notice is required).

It is possible to call meetings on short notice (i.e. where it is less than the period required in the Articles) where the chair (or if there is no chair or they are absent) the vice-chair, determines that there are 'matters demanding urgent consideration'.

The notice must specify the date and time of the meeting and where it is to take place. The Articles specify that the notice should be in writing and 'signed by the clerk'.

The notice should be sent to each director at the address given by them. On a practical level, notices are now often circulated by e-mail. Even if a director has informed the clerk that they will be unable to attend the meeting and given apologies, the notice must still be sent to them. Directors should read the reports and documentation to keep themselves informed irrespective of whether they can attend every meeting.

There is no required format for the notice which could be along the lines of:

EXAMPLE NOTICE OF MEETING

Our Ref: GSGM/4-6
26 February 2013

To: All Governors of King Edward VI Camp Hill School for Girls

Dear Governor
You are requested to attend a Meeting of the Governors of King Edward VI Camp Hill School for Girls at 6.00pm on Tuesday 5 March 2013 at the School in Vicarage Road.
Yours sincerely

Philippa Cole
Clerk to the School Governors

The notice should be given to each director, although the Articles provide that the process will not be invalidated if any individual has not received the notice or agenda. Not only is it good practice to make every effort to ensure that the notice is given to all directors but it also assists in the efficiency and effectiveness of board meetings which are central to corporate governance.

Agenda

The Articles also require that a copy of the agenda for the meeting is circulated with the notice. The agenda sets out the headings for the matters of business to be discussed at the meeting.

Both the contents and order of the items to be included should be carefully considered and organised. As well as setting out a schedule of the business to be discussed, a good agenda enables all participants to focus on the aims of the meeting.

Whilst it is important that items are self-explanatory, confidential items to be discussed should be described at a high level (e.g. 'Personnel issues' to discuss a staffing reorganisation).

A clear, well-thought-through agenda helps to direct the business and the order will help with the flow of the meeting. Items of greatest importance should be placed near the beginning after the formalities where it will be given maximum focus. However, the agenda is also invaluable to the clerk who is preparing the minutes and gives an easy structure for note-taking!

A typical agenda may include:

- Welcome
- Apologies
- Declarations of interest
- Review of the minutes of the previous meeting
- Any matters arising
- Old business or open issues
- New business such as specific points to be discussed
- Reports from:
  - Head teacher
  - Chair
  - Committees
- Governor visits and training
- Any other business as notified to the chair prior to the meeting
- Items for next meeting.

It is useful to set time limits for individual items to avoid wasting time. It will be for the chair to ascertain whether a guillotine should be imposed at the end of that time period and directors asked to vote, or whether further time is necessary to fully consider the issue.

A meeting cannot decide to rescind (i.e. repeal or withdraw) a decision of a previous board meeting or to vary it, unless it is specifically included as an item of business on the agenda for that meeting.

Opinion is split about including a general 'Any Other Business' heading. Clearly it is poor practice to give an open invitation for anyone to raise any issue. However, there will be times when items arise after the agenda has been circulated which will need to be noted formally by the board. Requiring directors to notify the chair of AOB items prior to the meeting is generally an acceptable middle course.

EXPERIENCE

Presdales School Academy Trust includes Any Other Business on its agendas. As well as items that have arisen subsequent to the circulation of the agenda, Directors note successes enjoyed by the school and pupils such as sporting achievements, successes in inter-house competitions and other outstanding achievements by the girls. At the end of the meeting it is good evidence of the progress of the school and the impact of strong leadership and management.

The agenda to accompany the notice provided previously:

EXAMPLE AGENDA

BUSINESS

1. Welcome to Mr M Clark, newly elected Parent Governor, congratulations to Mrs H Singleton on her reappointment as a Foundation Governor and farewell to Mrs P Raghuram, Foundation Co-opted Parent Governor
2. Appointment of Clerk
3. Apologies
4. Minutes*
5. Matters Arising from the Minutes
6. Head's Report*
7. King Edward's Consortium (Initial Teacher Training – presentation by Ms F Child)
8. Widening Accessibility*
9. Composition of Committees*
10. Terms of Reference: Budget Committee*
11. Business Interests
12. Recommending Body included in Head's Report
13. School Development Plan Review included in Head's Report
14. Link Governors
15. Staff Appointments
16. Approval of Educational Visits
    (a) Approvals by Chairman since last meeting
    (b) Approvals required
17. Reports of Committees
    (a) Curriculum Liaison Committee
        The Committee has met once since the last Governors' Meeting 26 February 2013. An oral report will be given of the February meeting.
    (b) Pupil Welfare and Discipline Committee*
        The Committee has met once since the last Governors' Meeting on 29 January 2013. Minutes are enclosed.
    (c) Health & Safety Committee*
        The Committee has met once since the last Governors' Meeting on 29 January 2013. Minutes are enclosed.
    (d) Budget Committee*
        The Committee has met four times since the last Governors' Meeting, on 9 October, 13 November, 4 December and 18 December 2012. Minutes of the October, November and December meetings are enclosed.

18. Income and Expenditure Accounts to 31 December 2012*
    MOVE: That the Income and Expenditure Accounts to 31 December 2012 be approved.
19. Condition Survey Summary*
20. Capital Projects Update*
21. Appointment of Auditors
    MOVE: That Baker Tilly be appointed Auditors for the period ending 31 August 2013.
    MOVE: That a tender process be undertaken for the 2013/2014 academic/financial year.
22. Admissions Policy*
23. Charging and Remission Policy*
24. Best Value Statement*
    MOVE: That the Policies and Best Value Statement be approved.
25. Political Developments/Report from Foundation Grammar Schools' Committee
26. Dates of Next Meetings (Suggested dates: Tuesday 18 June 2013; Tuesday 8 October 2013 at 6.00pm at the School)

* = Note enclosed

EXAMPLE OF A NOTICE INCORPORATING THE AGENDA

Company Number: 1234567
NOTICE is hereby given that a Meeting of the Governors
will be held on Tuesday 1st October 2013 at 6.00pm

1. Declarations of interest
2. Election of Chair and Vice Chair
3. Apologies for absence
4. Matters to be raised under AOB
5. Approval of the minutes of the Governors' Meeting held on 3rd July 2013 (attached)
6. Matters arising
7. Governor vacancies
8. Governor Self Evaluation
9. Chair's Report
10. Headmistress' Report (attached)
11. SEF/School Development Plan
12. Admissions
13. Reports from:
    (i)   Finance Committee
    (ii) Personnel Committee

      (iii) Premises Committee
      (iv) Curriculum Committee
14. Governors' visits
15. Governor training
16. Policies
      (i) Appraisal policy
      (ii) Pay policy
17. Correspondence
18. Items for agenda of next meeting of the Governing Body
19. Any other business

By order of the board

K Paxton-Doggett

Katie Paxton-Doggett

Company Secretary

DATE ISSUED: 23 September 2013

Reports and other documentation

All papers to be discussed at the meeting should be attached when the notice and agenda are circulated. Clearly, the meeting should be used to discuss issues rather than the directors being presented with documentation that they will need time to read and digest.

Where there are a significant number of documents it is useful to cross-reference the paper with the agenda items to which they relate.

The person responsible for the report will generally 'speak to the report' (i.e. they will comment on the contents and outline the issues). They should not summarise the report. A well-run meeting will not spend time outlining the contents of a previously circulated document which directors will be assumed to have read. Discussion of the item should be limited to questions relating to the content of the report or discussion of issues arising or decisions to be made.

Unfortunately there may be occasions where it is not possible to provide a written report ahead of the meeting. In this instance, a short synopsis should be given. However, decision making requires directors to be fully informed and conversant with the matter at hand and great care should be taken when making decisions without the opportunity to fully consider any implications.

Annual schedule of business

It is good practice to draft an annual schedule of business for board consideration in the same way that maintained schools would set up a year planner for their full governing body. The schedule timetables issues for consideration and decision over the course of the academic year. This ensures:

- all items are considered on a timely basis to meet applicable deadlines; and
- the work of the board is spread across the course of the year.

Naturally, unforeseen circumstances occur which may impact on the schedule and additional items arise for consideration, but modifications can be made across the year to meet the requirements of the company and the board.

▦ Managing the meeting

Briefing the chair

The chair is key to ensuring the productivity and smooth running of any board meeting as it is their job to ensure that each item of business on the agenda is addressed and that discussions and decisions are conducted in an orderly way. Where there is decision to be made, the chair will formally propose a resolution to the meeting, take a vote and then declare the result (i.e. that the resolution is carried or defeated).

The chair may not have experience of conducting a meeting under the specific requirements of academy administration. The procedure is more formal than that required under the maintained system, so it is good practice for the clerk to brief the chair prior to the meeting. A good relationship between the clerk and the chair is essential for the smooth running of a meeting and it is essential to discuss what level of support is required as many chairs will not want a formal briefing. Some may find a series of notes helpful or may wish to talk through the main items of business prior to the meeting. Nevertheless, the clerk will be required to provide support and advice as required throughout the meeting.

A briefing document or 'script' provides all the information that the chair will need, although few chairs will rely on the document word for word. In particular, the briefing should contain information on the elements of the meeting that are required under statute and set out the wording of any proposed resolutions.

EXAMPLE   10 June 2013 – A Meeting of the Governors of King Edward VI Handsworth School

PRESENT: Mrs S Roberts, Chairman

Mr G Andronov	Mr A Patel
Mr J Cammish	Dr T Purewal
Rev P Challis	Miss K Reid
Mr P Cotterill	Mr GP Thomas
Ms A Lloyd	Mrs E Wager
Mr R A Mansell	Mr P Williams
Mrs U Minchin	Mrs J Wilson

Mr J Collins, Secretary, Mrs P Cole, Clerk and Mrs S Soni will attend.

1. **FAREWELL TO REV P CHALLIS**

2. **APOLOGIES**
   Apologies have been received from Mr A Crampton, Professor T Norris

3. **MINUTES**
   Copies of the Minutes of the Meeting held on 25 February 2013 have been circulated to Members of the Governing Body.
   MOVE: that the Chairman be authorised to sign the Minutes.

4. **MATTERS ARISING FROM THE MINUTES**

5. **HEAD'S REPORT**
   The Head has circulated a written report.

6. **BUSINESS INTERESTS**
   In accordance with Sections 177 and 182 of the Companies Act 2006, Governors are required to declare their interest in Directorships, Shareholdings, and other appointments of influence within organisations that may have dealings with the School, or declare there are no such interests. Governors are reminded of their obligations to note ongoing conflicts of interest under Articles 98 & 99 of the Articles of Association. The register of business interests is a public document available for inspection. Governors are asked to check the details in it are accurate and, where appropriate, to complete a new form and give it to the Clerk. Please sign the 'date reviewed' on the second sheet as well as initialling the first page to indicate no changes.

7. **FIVE-YEAR FINANCIAL PLAN**
   The Director of Finance will comment and this item will be taken together with item 8 Threats and Challenges Paper.

8. **THREATS AND CHALLENGES DISCUSSION PAPER**
   A Note has been circulated to Members of the Governing Body

MOVE: that, in principle, the recommendation to increase the Published Admissions Number for Year 7 from 128 to 150 for September 2014 be accepted subject to the following:

(i) the Budget Committee gives further consideration to strategies to address the impact of funding cuts; such consideration to be coordinated with an assessment of the impact of cuts by the Curriculum Committee and to include consideration of the increase to the Published Admissions Number for Year 7 from 128 to 150 for September 2014;

(ii) the Committees report back to the Governing Body in the autumn term with recommendations either at the next scheduled meeting (2 October) or at a Special Meeting arranged specifically to consider such recommendations;

(iii) such consultation and approvals as may be required by the Foundation Board.

Quorum

The quorum is the minimum number of persons required to validly conduct business at a meeting. Only directors will count towards the quorum and any other persons present at a meeting such as observers or advisors, even if they are there legitimately cannot be included.

The quorum for a board meeting is set out in the Articles as the greater of:

- three directors; or
- one-third (rounded up to a whole number) of the total number of directors holding office at the date of the meeting.

The quorum must be present, either in person or via telephone/video conferencing, so that a meeting can take place.

It is important that the quorum remains present throughout a meeting. Great care must be taken to note if any director leaves the meeting, even if only for a few moments, or where any director has a conflict of interest (meaning that they cannot participate in the consideration of an issue) as they will not be counted in the quorum.

If the number drops below the quorum then the meeting cannot continue and it will be 'terminated forthwith' or immediately brought to a close. If all business on the agenda has not been covered, the clerk must call another meeting as soon 'as is reasonably practicable' but this must be within seven days of the original date of the meeting.

Any decision taken when the quorum is not present will not be valid and can be challenged.

If at any time the total number of directors appointed is less than the quorum, then the remaining directors may act 'only for the purpose of filling vacancies or of calling a general meeting' (i.e. a members' meeting where further directors can be appointed). Such a situation is only likely to occur in the event of a mass resignation by directors leaving less than three in office!

The role of the chair

The chair is the cornerstone in the corporate governance structure and the success of the board. Whilst their ability to chair meetings effectively is important, their role is much wider and demands a talented individual.

There is, of course, no simple formula for what makes a good chair and it will differ from school to school, but the main attributes may be:

- the ability to build effective teams;
- a good working relationship with the chief executive/head teacher;
- willingness to have the 'difficult' conversations;
- PR champion;
- credible public speaker;
- understanding of the educational environment and current changes;

- excellent knowledge of the academy and key staff;
- ability to delegate;
- effective chairing of meetings; and
- the ability to recognise the skills that the team has and to use them effectively.

CASE STUDY

Bob Wintringham is chair of the Faringdon Academy of Schools, a multi-academy trust which has recently expanded from three to eight schools. It is a ground-breaking arrangement which includes infant, junior and primary schools alongside the secondary school. Most importantly it is one of the first to have Church of England schools in a multi-academy trust with community schools. Bob has been extremely successful in his roles; he has chaired five Independent Examinations Boards and has been Chair of Faringdon Community College for over 20 years.

'I build teams' he explained. 'I build teams that are prepared to put in the work to achieve results.'

With a team largely composed of unpaid volunteers this is no mean feat. But Bob does create remarkably cohesive teams who work well together.

Bob also feels the Chair's relationship with the head teacher is key to effectiveness in the role. But this is not some cosy, symbiotic relationship which does little to challenge the head teacher or the organisation. In fact, quite the reverse.

> 'The Chair must be able to have those difficult conversations. Sometimes there is no option but for the Headteacher to leave and the Chair must be able to recognise this and tell them.'

In fact, what Bob says really sums up the 'support and challenge' or 'critical friend' role that is at the heart of good governance.

What is more, Bob is a charismatic speaker and fantastic PR champion for the MAT. Although he is relatively softly spoken, he conveys an authority so that others stop to listen when he speaks. He has a credibility that comes from a deeply held conviction that the actions of the board, led by the chair, can really make a difference to the children.

Experienced chairs of governors can apply to become National Leaders of Governance (NLGs) through a programme developed by the National College for Teaching and Learning. They must demonstrate a proven track record of contributing to school improvement through the effective leadership of a governing body.

NLGs use their skills and experience to increase the leadership capacity of other chairs to help raise standards so that improvements can be sustained.

Voting

Decisions made by the board, known as 'resolutions', are passed by a majority of the votes cast by the directors present at a meeting.

Every director has a right to be heard on a subject, so adequate time should be given for consideration of a proposal before it is put to the vote. Every board will operate in its own way, but the chair should ensure that all get an opportunity to speak if they so wish.

Each director has one vote, although if the number of votes cast for and against a resolution are equal, the chair will have a casting vote in addition to his/her normal vote. However, this will not apply if the chair is not eligible to be counted in the quorum for the purposes of the particular decision.

Only the directors have a vote and any others present, albeit invited in an advisory role such as the school business manager, do not have a vote.

It is for the directors to decide on the best way to facilitate voting, but generally it will be on a show of hands with the chair declaring that the resolution is carried. In accordance with the collective responsibility that the board has for decisions, the number of votes for, against and abstentions should not be included in the minutes.

Once a resolution is passed, it is binding on all directors irrespective of whether they personally voted in favour of it.

There are occasions when it is preferable to conduct a secret ballot. This could be where a resolution is contentious or where directors may not wish to publicly declare their vote (e.g. in a situation where a staff director may wish to vote contrary to the wishes of the head teacher!).

Conducting a secret ballot need not cause administrative difficulties. Each director is given a piece of paper on which to identify their choice. This could be a blank piece of paper on which the director can indicate acceptance or rejection. In a situation such as a contested election for chair, the names of the nominees can be printed on the paper with the director indicating which one gets their vote. The clerk will then collect and count the votes.

Conflicts of interest

It is essential that a fair and just process is applied at all times in directors' meetings and all should be diligent to note any conflict of interest that arises. If any director has other interests which could possibly influence or corrupt their motivation or decision making – or could be seen to do so – then these should be declared (see Chapter 12).

Such a conflict could occur from a 'direct' personal interest or an 'indirect' interest arising through a relative such as where the spouse of a director runs a business that is offering services to the academy.

The director must declare any interest and will be excluded from the discussion. They will not be eligible to vote on any resolution in which they have an interest.

Clerk to the board

The DfE recognises that the clerk to the board has an important part to play in the organisation of a governing body's work, irrespective of the governance structure of the school and it states:

> It is helpful if the clerk is able to offer information and advice to the governing body, particularly on matters involving the law and procedures to be followed at meetings.

Clerks are appointed by the board of directors but they report to the chair of the board. Where the role of the clerk is undertaken by the school secretary, bursar or other member of staff, the individual concerned should be clear that clerking the governing body is outside their normal reporting arrangements. The value of a professional, independent clerk is increasingly recognised. As well as being able to offer appropriate legal and regulatory guidance when applicable, they bring an unbiased view.

It will be for the board to decide if the clerk should be appointed to a particular committee.

The clerk cannot be a director or the head teacher. They cannot vote at board meetings (although a director who acts as clerk for a meeting if the clerk fails to attend may take part in discussions and vote).

Depending on the conditions of service on which the clerk is engaged, the board may have the power to remove them from office.

The importance of the role should not be underestimated. The minutes prepared by the clerk are among the first documentation viewed by Ofsted inspectors and other external bodies in assessing the effectiveness of a school.

Telephone/Video conferencing

The Articles include a provision that directors can participate in board meetings 'by telephone or video conference'. This very practical provision allows those directors who may be unable to be physically present to attend meetings. Teleconferencing is now used as a matter of course for many organisations and the majority of directors working in professional or business roles outside of education have considerable experience of it.

The director must give at least 48 hours' notice and suitable equipment must be accessible; if reasonable efforts do not enable access to the 'appropriate equipment' to facilitate participation by telephone or video conference, then the meeting may still proceed provided it is quorate despite the absence of the director.

HELPFUL HINTS

Here are some guidelines for directors to bear in mind:

1. Be careful of your surroundings. Consider confidentiality and sensitivity of information and do not conduct your conversation in a place where you will be overheard. NEVER take part in a meeting if you are travelling on a train – apart from inadvertently sharing information, it is extremely annoying to other passengers!
2. Pay attention! It will very quickly become clear to everyone if a person is not listening to the proceedings, particularly if they are asked for their vote. Focus on the matters being discussed and do not try to multi-task by reading e-mails or watching TV.
3. Conferencing enables directors to 'participate in meetings'. This does not mean that they simply dial in for the items on the agenda that they are interested in!
4. Identify yourself if you speak. This is more relevant for the people in the meeting room. Whilst everyone present can see who they are the person on the other end of a telephone line can't.
5. Be respectful. This should, of course, apply to all meetings of directors but it is more pronounced where some attendance is via conferencing. Try not to interrupt or overtalk – it is confusing and ultimately wastes time.

Adjournments

The directors can decide to adjourn a meeting before all items on the agenda have been dealt with. If so, they must set the date and time that a further meeting will take place for considering the outstanding items. The clerk will be directed to formally convene such a meeting.

■ ICSA Code for Good Boardroom Practice

The Institute of Chartered Secretaries and Administrators (ICSA) has formulated a code for directors and company secretaries setting out matters which it believes 'should be addressed and, wherever applicable, accepted formally by boards of directors in recognition of a commitment to adhere to an overall concept of best practice'.

Although it is accepted that there will be differences in style of boardroom management between organisations – even between academies – ICSA has identified basic principles of good boardroom practice which are 'universally applicable'.

Appropriate boardroom procedures should be implemented as well as being made subject to periodic review.

1. The board should establish written procedures for the conduct of its business which should include the matters covered in this code. A copy of these written procedures should be given to each director. Compliance should be monitored, preferably by an audit committee of the board, and breaches of the procedures should be reported to the board.

2. The board should ensure that each director is given on appointment sufficient information to enable him/her to perform his/her duties. In particular, guidance for non-executive directors should cover the procedures:

   ■ for obtaining information concerning the company; and
   ■ for requisitioning a meeting of the board.

3. In the conduct of board business, two fundamental concepts should be observed:

   ■ each director should receive the same information at the same time; and
   ■ each director should be given sufficient time in which to consider any such information.

4. The board should identify matters which require the prior approval of the board and lay down procedures to be followed when, exceptionally, a decision is required before its next meeting on any matter not required by law to be considered at board level.

5. As a basic principle, all material contracts, and especially those not in the ordinary course of business, should be referred to the board for decision prior to the commitment of the company.

6. The board should approve definitions of the terms 'material' and 'not in the ordinary course of business' and these definitions should be brought to the attention of all relevant persons.

7. Where there is any uncertainty regarding the materiality or nature of a contract, it should normally be assumed that the contract should be brought before the board.

8. Decisions regarding the content of the agenda for individual meetings of the board and concerning the presentation of agenda items should be taken by the chair in consultation with the company secretary.

9. The company secretary should be responsible to the chair for the proper administration of the meetings of the company, the board and any committees thereof. To carry out this responsibility the company secretary should be entitled to be present at (or represented at) and prepare (or arrange for the preparation of) minutes of the proceedings of all such meetings.

10. The minutes of meetings should record the decisions taken and provide sufficient background to those decisions. All papers presented at the

meeting should be clearly identified in the minutes and retained for reference. Procedures for the approval and circulation of minutes should be established.

11. Where the Articles of Association allow the board to delegate any of its powers to a committee, the board should give its prior approval to:

   - the membership and quorum of any such committee;
   - its term of reference; and
   - the extent of any powers delegated to it.

12. The minutes of all meetings of committees of the board (or a written summary thereof) should be circulated to the board prior to its next meeting and the opportunity should be given at that meeting for any member of the board to ask questions thereon.

13. Notwithstanding the absence of a formal agenda item, the chair should permit any director or the company secretary to raise at any board meeting any matter concerning the company's compliance with this Code of Practice, with the company's Memorandum and Articles of Association and with any other legal or regulatory requirement.

Written resolutions

The most recent version of the Articles permits directors to make decisions using the written resolution procedure. This may be applied to full board or committee decisions.

The usual rules regarding conflicts of interest apply so that any directors with an interest are not eligible to vote in favour of a written resolution (see Chapter 12). If the number of directors excluded from voting due to a conflict of interest means that the quorum requirements are not satisfied, then it is not possible to pass a written resolution.

A copy of the proposed resolution must be sent to every director entitled to receive notice of a board or committee meeting, as appropriate. The resolution will only be passed if there is a unanimous vote in favour, with each director signing the resolution. This may be difficult to achieve not least on a practical level to secure the relevant paperwork!

Consent to or acceptance of the resolution may be by way of several 'instruments in like form' (i.e. identical copies of the same document) each agreed by one or more directors. This means that a copy of the resolution could be returned signed by each director individually yet the resolution would be valid.

The resolution is passed only when all directors have signed and returned the written resolution.

Copies of each of the signed written resolutions must be kept in the minute book.

Although written resolutions are useful on occasion, they cannot replace regular board meetings.

■ Summary

- The directors have some flexibility in conducting board meetings but must comply with the rules set out in their own Articles.

Calling a meeting

- There must be at least three meetings in every school year.
- The clerk calls board meetings following the directions of the board. It is also possible for three directors to requisition a board meeting.
- Only directors have a right to attend board meetings.
- A valid notice and agenda must be circulated at least seven (or 14) clear days before the date of the meeting. Meetings can be called on 'short notice' if there are urgent matters to consider.
- All papers to be discussed at the meeting should be attached when the notice and agenda are circulated.
- It is good practice to draft an annual schedule of business for board consideration.

Managing the meeting

- A briefing document or 'script' provides all information that the chair will need for the meeting.
- The quorum for a board meeting is the greater of either three directors or one third (rounded up to a whole number) of the total number of directors holding office at the date of the meeting.
- Only directors count towards the quorum but they may be present either in person or via telephone/video conferencing.
- The quorum must be maintained throughout or the meeting will automatically terminate.
- Decisions or 'resolutions' made by the board are passed by a majority of the votes cast by directors present at a meeting.
- Each director has one vote, although the chair will have a casting vote in the event that the number of votes cast for and against a resolution are equal.
- The director must declare any conflict of interest and will be excluded from any discussion and vote in connection with the interest.
- The clerk reports to the chair and provides information and advice involving the law and procedures to be followed at meetings.
- Directors can participate in board meetings by telephone or video conference, where appropriate equipment is available.
- The directors can adjourn a meeting.

ICSA Code for Good Boardroom Practice

- On appointment, directors must be given information and guidance to enable him/her to perform his/her duties.
- When conducting board business, each director should receive the same information at the same time and be given sufficient time in which to consider it.
- The board should set out procedures for making decisions between meetings and delegation of such decision making.
- All material contracts should be referred to the board for decision prior to the commitment of the company. The board should outline what is likely to require prior board approval but in the case of uncertainty it is assumed that the contract should be brought before the board.
- The chair (in consultation with the company secretary) decides on the content and presentation of the agenda.
- The company secretary is responsible to the chair for the proper administration of board and committee meetings.
- The minutes of meetings should record the decisions taken, providing sufficient background to those decisions. All papers presented at the meeting should be clearly identified in the minutes and retained for reference. Procedures for the approval and circulation of minutes should be established.
- The board should give prior approval of membership and quorum of committees, terms of reference and the extent of delegated powers.
- The minutes of all meetings of board committees should be circulated to the board prior to its next meeting and board members given an opportunity to ask questions about it.
- The chair should permit any director or the company secretary to raise at any board meeting any matter concerning the company's compliance with the Code of Practice, the Memorandum and Articles of Association and any other legal or regulatory requirement.

Written resolutions

- Directors can use the written resolution procedure to make decisions for full board or committee decisions.
- Any director with a conflict of interest is not eligible to vote on a written resolution.
- There must be a unanimous vote in favour to pass a written resolution.
- Each director must sign the resolution but this may be achieved through duplicate copies of the document.

9 Minutes of directors' meetings

■ **In this chapter**

This chapter considers the need for minutes for board meetings, in particular:

- the practical considerations when preparing minutes;
- detailed guidance on drafting the minutes with suggested examples of items considered;
- preparation of confidential minutes;
- practical steps to take after the meeting; and
- storage of minutes and requirements for making documents available for inspection.

A formal record of proceedings at board meetings must be taken (CA 2006, s. 248).

These requirements are also contained within the model articles which state that minutes 'shall be drawn up and entered into a book kept for the purpose'. Once approved by the directors, the minutes are signed 'at the same or next subsequent meeting by the person acting as chairman thereof'.

Once approved and signed by the chair at the next directors' meeting, minutes are evidence of the proceedings at the meeting. Minutes also act as evidence that directors are complying with their duties in running the company and have a central role in the leadership and management of the academy in terms of Ofsted. In some limited situations, directors can be personally liable (see Chapter 7) so great attention should be given when drafting minutes to reflect the consideration given by directors.

Minutes are also a very useful practical tool for everyone involved in the board meeting to recognise decisions made, delegation of authority and any subsequent actions for which they may be responsible.

Given the importance of accurate minutes, drafting, as well as subsequent checking and approval, should be undertaken with care. Inaccuracies should always be corrected prior to approval.

▦ Practical considerations

There are no specific rules regarding the way in which minutes must be written. However, there is generally a 'house style' in drafting minutes and a clerk should endeavour to mirror this approach when appropriate. Minutes can follow a fairly traditional style with directors referred to by their title and surname (e.g. Mrs Bolton) or a more modern approach where initials, previously set out against names in the heading, are used. Despite any efforts to modernise minutes, they remain a legally required document and should not be overly informal. Whatever approach is adopted it should be consistent across all board minutes.

In essence, the minutes provide an explanation of the issue, the reasoning behind any decision made and any resultant actions.

- Minutes should be written in the past tense.
- Minutes must always be written in the third person (i.e. 'he', 'she', 'it' and 'they').
- Number paragraphs. It is useful to use a reference system that can be carried forward into other minutes (e.g. a simple increasing numeric system or a system indicating the calendar year such as 01/14 for the first item in the first meeting of 2014).
- Use plain English and avoid acronyms where possible (if they are unavoidable, make sure they are defined).
- Use short sentences and paragraphs to make the minutes reader-friendly.
- Layout should encourage accessibility and easy reading of the content. Action points and resolutions should be easy to identify.
- Make reference to supporting documentation but do not replicate information.
- Any legal or procedural advice given by the clerk should be recorded.

It is useful to identify the individuals participating in a board meeting – signing-in or attendance sheet can be used to evidence who was present. Name cards are helpful, particularly with larger boards where directors may have difficulty in remembering newer members. In addition, the clerk can ask for everyone to introduce themselves and can prepare a simple diagram of the meeting and attendees. This is a good reference tool when noting when individuals leave the room or when actions are delegated.

The board has a collective responsibility for decision making. Once a decision is passed it is binding on all, whether or not they voted for it. Furthermore, minutes should provide a subject-based record so that it is the nature of the discussion that is important rather than who said what. Individual directors will not generally be identified in the minutes except where they:

- have been tasked with a particular action;
- have requested that their objection to a decision is noted; or
- are being thanked for their efforts.

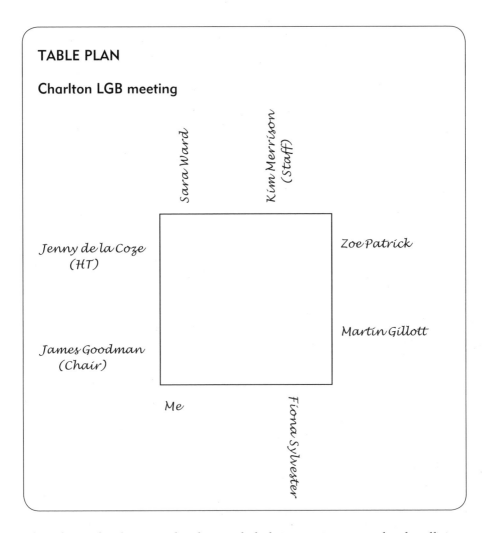

TABLE PLAN

Charlton LGB meeting

Sara Ward

Kim Merrison
(Staff)

Jenny de la Coze
(HT)

Zoe Patrick

Martin Gillott

James Goodman
(Chair)

Me

Fiona Sylvester

The relationship between the chair and clerk is very important for the efficient and effective running of a meeting. Whilst the chair leads the meeting, making sure that the items on the agenda are covered, decisions made and actions delegated, the clerk provides practical support with carefully organised documentation, and appropriate legal and procedural guidance when necessary. The clerk is, in fact, one of the most important individuals present at a meeting, responsible for preparing the legal record of what has happened. The clerk should always sit next to the chair in meetings as they are effectively the management team running the meeting.

Board minutes and members' meetings

It is extremely important to ensure that board minutes remain just that! There may be a temptation where the members are present, for a necessary decision to be taken in the course of the board meeting. This is not legally permitted. If a decision is required before the board meeting can continue, then the meeting must be adjourned and subsequently reconvened. Obviously this is only likely to be an issue either where there is a flat governance structure and all directors are also members, or when the members are a sub-section of the board.

> It was agreed that the meeting be adjourned to enable a members' meeting on short notice and immediately thereafter reconvened.

Drafting the minutes

Heading
Minutes should be headed with the practical details about the meeting:

- Name of the academy.
- Company registered number. (It may be easier and look more professional to use headed paper, which would include the company number.)
- Date, time and location.
- Names of those present. If any director is not physically present (i.e. attending by other means such as telephone conferencing) this should be noted.
- Names of those 'In attendance'. Other persons present in a role as observer or advisor to the meeting should also be noted.
- Apologies. Names of those not present who have informed the meeting beforehand that they would not be able to attend and the apologies have been accepted.
- Absent. Where apologies are not given or they have not been accepted.
- Name of the chair.
- Confirmation that the meeting was quorate. If a meeting is not quorate, no valid decision making can take place.

Modern minute style tends to list the various names in columns, although some academies prefer to list in a paragraph. Whichever way, it is best to avoid any hierarchical order to the list apart from the chair who should be identified first. The board acts as a body and individuals are present as directors rather than as representatives of a particular body or group.

It is possible to refer to participants by their:

- full name – Katie Paxton-Doggett;
- title and surname – Mrs Paxton-Doggett; or
- by initials – KPD. The initials to be used should be identified after the individual's full name in the heading.

Whichever approach is selected should be used throughout the minutes.

It is good practice to note the actual time that the meeting started.

EXAMPLE MINUTES OF MEETING

Company Number: 07977368

MINUTES of a Meeting of the Directors
held on Thursday 17 October 2013
at Faringdon Community College at 7.00pm

Present:
Bob Wintringham – Community (**BW**)
  CHAIR
Alex Bond – Parent FCC (**ABo**)
Heather Hambridge – Head FIS (**HH**)
Liz Holmes – Chair FCC (**LH**)
Peter McGurk – Parent FIS (**PM**)
Mark Mobey – Chair FJS (**MM**)
Lisa Proctor – Community (**LP**)
Paul Turner – Head FJS (**PT**)
Alun Williams – Community (**AW**)

Apologies:
Alex Bannister – FJS parent (**ABa**)
Roger Cox – Chair FIS (**RC**)
Rachel Kenyon – Staff (**RK**)
David Wilson – Head FCC (**DW**)

Absent:
Dan Read – FIS parent (**DR**)

In attendance:
John Banbrook – Business Manager
  (**JB**)
Kathryn Hall (**KH**)
Katie Paxton-Doggett – Clerk (**KPD**)
Ian Wright – Chair Watchfield (**IW**)

The meeting was quorate and commenced at 7.15pm

Please see Appendix 3 for useful minute-taking checklists for before, during and after a meeting.

Quorum

The meeting cannot take place unless a quorum is present. The Articles state that the quorum is the greater of:

- three directors; or
- one third (rounded up to a whole number) of the total number of directors holding office at the date of the meeting.

Directors attending by telephone or video conferencing count towards the quorum. However, any other persons present at a meeting, such as observers or advisors, do not count.

The quorum must be maintained throughout any meeting. Therefore, if any director leaves the meeting, even if only for a few moments, it should be noted. If a director has a conflict of interest and cannot participate in the consideration of an issue, they will not be counted in the quorum.

When any director joins or leaves the meeting this should be noted and the quorum confirmed.

> 4.15pm   RA left the meeting
>   The clerk confirmed that the meeting was quorate.

Introduction/chair's welcome

Although the agenda may have an introductory item or welcome by the chair, often this will not appear on the minutes. One exception is where faith schools use the opportunity to open the meeting in prayer. In such cases, the introduction is included in the minutes as an indication that the board have the faith aspects of the school uppermost in their minds. It is also useful evidence where an inspection takes place in accordance with s. 48 of the Education Act 2005.

> *Welcome and opening prayers*
> KW welcomed everyone and AW opened the meeting with prayer.

Apologies

Apologies should be considered in respect of each director individually. It is for the meeting to decide whether apologies should be accepted and give consent. Failure to give apologies, or for apologies not to be accepted, will be relevant when a director has been 'absent without the permission of the directors' from all meetings within a six-month period. In this case, the directors can resolve that their office be vacated.

> *Apologies*
> Apologies were received and accepted from ABa, RC, RK and DW. PM would be late.

Declaration of interests

It is good practice for directors to complete a declaration of interests form annually and for the Register of Interests to be updated accordingly (see Chapter 5). The Register of Interests should be laid before each board meeting for reference and updating.

In addition, at the beginning of each meeting, directors should be asked whether they have any particular interest in any item on the agenda. Interests need not be pecuniary (i.e. financial) but could be any wider business interest that could affect their decision and lead to a conflict of interest.

Where an interest is declared in a particular item, the individual should be asked to leave the room during the discussion and will not be able to participate in any vote. They will not count towards the quorum during the part of the meeting where the item is to be discussed.

Declarations of interest
The Register recording governors' interests was laid on the table. No new interests were declared.

Appointment of chair and vice chair

The model articles require that the board elect a chair and a vice-chair of the board annually. All directors, with the exception of staff, are eligible to stand.

It is good practice to ask the nominees to leave the room to enable a full and frank discussion and to take a vote, even when individuals are standing uncontested. It is also good practice to conduct a secret ballot.

Election of chair and vice-chair
Nominations had been received for JG for Chair and for SW for Vice chair. JG and SW left the room.

The clerk conducted a secret ballot and confirmed that JG was duly elected as chair and SW as vice chair for the academic year 2013–14.

Minutes of the last meeting

The minutes of the last meeting are formally approved and signed by the chair on behalf of the board. Until this point, minutes are technically 'draft' even though they might have been approved by the chair. Where minutes are in loose-leaf, which is currently the norm, the chair should sign and date each page. This is to prevent any subsequent (potentially fraudulent) changes to a page or pages of the minutes.

Approval indicates that the minutes are accurate as to fact. Any errors should be amended by hand on the copy of the minutes that is subsequently signed by the chair with the amendment initialled. The amendment is also noted in the minutes of the meeting:

Approval of the minutes of the Governors' Meeting held 5 July 2012
The minutes were amended to show that apologies had been received from
Dr J Downs.

The minutes were then accepted as an accurate record, approved by the
governors and signed by the chair.

Directors should have read the minutes prior to the meeting. The content and
any updates are not discussed at this point in the meeting, nor should individuals be reporting back in relation to specific actions. The chair should sign the
minutes on each page to signify that they are an accurate version of events that
has been approved by the meeting.

Approved minutes are evidence that:

- the meeting was duly held and convened;
- proceedings of the meeting are deemed to have taken place; and
- appointments at the meeting are deemed valid.

The minutes cannot be changed after approval unless they are challenged on the
basis of proof of inaccuracy of a fact or proof of bad faith which can be proved.

The minutes provide an audit trail of what has happened and that it was done
appropriately. The minutes are amongst the first documents to be available to
Ofsted inspectors or other external bodies looking at an academy. It is absolutely
essential that minutes reflect the meeting but also demonstrate that the directors are doing their job of strategic oversight, considering progress and providing
appropriate challenge to the head teacher and senior leadership team.

Minutes of the board meeting held on 17 October 2013
The minutes were agreed as an accurate record of the meeting and signed
by BW.

Matters arising from the minutes

Brief updates can be given of any items discussed and minuted from the last
meeting. Each action point should be reviewed to establish whether it has been
completed and, if it has not, when it will be done. Any issues that have arisen in
connection with an outstanding matter can be raised. The minutes provide an
audit trail on action taken in relation to items discussed at a board meeting; as
the board should have a strategic focus, these actions should be fundamental to
the future direction of the academy. However, in general, board minutes will have
fewer action points and greater focus on delegation of duties to progress matters.

It is sometimes possible to identify items that will be covered under 'Matters arising' (e.g. where there is an action point to find out specific information to be reported back to the board). In this case it is useful, particularly for the chair, to include that item as a sub-heading. Any matters which are likely to require significant feedback or necessitate a discussion should be given a dedicated place on the agenda and action points related to that item should be reviewed and discussed at that time.

Reports

Directors can delegate authority to an individual or committee (see Chapter 12). The board minutes should clearly record any delegation and the terms on which it was made. It should be evident who is able to make decisions and what is required to be brought back to the main board. When any delegated authority is exercised 'in respect of any action taken or decision made with respect to the exercise of that power or function', the party should report back to the board at their next meeting.

Reports should, therefore, be provided by any individuals whether a director such as the chief executive or a member of the executive such as the school business manager, or committees with delegated authority.

A significant amount of the work done by directors is conducted through committees. Minutes of committee meetings should be circulated with the agenda prior to the board meeting.

The directors can require the head teacher or chief executive to report to meetings providing such information that they require. Again, a written report should be provided prior to the meeting for circulation with the agenda.

Any reports required should be circulated with the agenda. The assumption at the meeting is that reports have been read and the person presenting it should be asked only whether they have anything to add or highlight. The agenda item will allow questions to be put to the party responsible for the report and discussion confined to areas that require further debate or formal decision making.

The minutes should confirm that a report was circulated:

> *Finance committee*
> The minutes of the meeting held on 25 September 2012 had been circulated.

Sometimes it is not possible to circulate a report or paper, but it is important that it is seen by the directors and considered at the meeting. In such a case the document is handed out at the meeting and this should be specifically noted in the minutes:

> Copies of the full School Development Plan were tabled.

All reports and documentation put before the meeting are filed with the minutes and must be made available for public inspection.

Items of business and resolutions

The minutes should record a summary of the items of business. No attempt should be made to recreate a verbatim record of conversations or debate, but they should set out the issue or situation being considered, any decision and the basis on which it was made as well as any action points. Minutes should make sense to anyone who was not present at the meeting!

'Resolutions' are decisions made by a meeting and must be recorded in full using the exact words used. The minutes will then indicate whether the resolution was passed.

> **1089. School term dates**
> The Head sought a change to the provisionally agreed end of term date for summer term 2014. It was proposed that Friday 18 July 2014 should be the last day of term, rather than the following Monday.
>
> RESOLVED: that the School year 2014 ends on Friday 18 July 2014

Directors have a collective responsibility and, therefore, the actual number of votes cast in favour, against and abstaining should not be recorded. In some cases, a board will have a 'proposer' and 'seconder' in connection with formal resolutions.

> *Appointment of Responsible Officer*
> Directors RESOLVED that JM be appointed as Responsible Officer, proposed by RC and seconded by DR.

Correspondence

Communications received such as from the DfE, LA or Diocese could be reported to the board either in a specific agenda item or as part of any report from the chair.

Any other business

The chair should ensure that the item remains focused on matters of strategic importance. Generally, items for 'any other business' should be submitted to the chair in advance of the meeting to avoid discussion without sufficient preparation. Items should be urgent matters that have arisen after the agenda has been drawn up. It may be necessary for the chair to adjourn any such matter to the next meeting or delegate it for further consideration to a committee or working party.

EXAMPLE AOB

Presdales School often has an 'and finally' feel to AOB which informs governors of the outstanding achievements of pupils which are their focus:

16/13	**Any other business**
	The PE department had enjoyed a number of fantastic achievements including the regional finals for table tennis, cross country and football. A gold medal had been won at a national diving event by a pupil and another pupil had been selected for the England under-16 squad for rounders.
	Two pupils had qualified in the European maths championship.
	There would be a celebratory assembly held on 15 April at 9am at which presentations would be made. All pupils from years 7–13 attend which gives a sense of cohesion.

Next meeting

It is good practice for the board to set dates for full board and committee meetings for the year. In any event, directors should not leave a board meeting without having a date for the next meeting identified.

Action points

It is important to for any actions to be clearly defined and the individual or group responsible to be identified. A clear format is extremely useful so that actions and the person or group responsible are easily identified even on skimming. The clearest layout is a dedicated action column.

55/13	*Governor self-evaluation* All were encouraged to complete the form for consideration at the next board meeting. Although it was not a skills audit, it could help in appointments to link governorship or committees. The committee list would be circulated and reviewed at the next meeting.	**ALL** **KPD**

Alternatively, the action can be identified at the end of the section to which it applies.

> 4.2 *Delegation of governor's responsibilities*
> Governors went through the plan of governor's responsibilities and the annual plan showing what to review and when this is necessary. Lisa will update and put onto the Learning Platform. Action: Lisa Smith.

Where there are a lot of action points arising, it can be useful for a schedule to be prepared and appended to the minutes.

Minute reference	*Action point*	*Person responsible*
6.1	Pupil Premium statement to be sent to all governors	**AR**
8	Computer Science Development Project – Phase 2 /Lecture Theatre implementation	**AR/HH**
9.1	Access to Blue Sky	**AH/relevant governors**
9.2	Training session for governors on Blue Sky	**AH/Clerk**
10	Updating and dissemination of school policies	**Clerk**
11(a)	Reports on the examination outcomes and the university destinations of leavers to be circulated to all governors	**SN/Clerk/TH**
11(b)	Offer of free influenza vaccinations to the staff	**AH/SB**
11(d)	Amendment to Property Committee minutes	**Clerk**
13	Chair to write to Mary Chaplin	**PCHM**

Close of meeting

The closing time of the meeting can be included as part of the heading. However, it is generally easier to note at the very bottom of the minutes. The starting and closing time for the meeting will indicate the length of meetings. If board meetings regularly go on for more than three hours, consideration should be given to whether more meetings should be scheduled. Productivity will dip in long meetings, particularly when there is no break. If meetings are too long, consideration should also be given by the board as to whether their focus is truly strategic or whether they are getting too closely embroiled in the day-to-day.

Very short meetings can seem to be a bonus, particularly to the clerk! However, although the board can delegate its powers and authority, it retains overall responsibility for running the academy. If meetings are regularly short, then it must be queried whether the board is effectively overseeing the delegated responsibility and whether it has a proactive strategy that it is progressing.

▨ Confidential items

Items requiring confidential discussion should be listed on the agenda in general terms so that the details are not provided. Commonly, confidential items are put at the end of the agenda to enable any person who cannot be present for the discussion to leave.

The minutes will contain a simple reference to the confidential item:

> 07/14   A confidential staffing matter was discussed.

Separate confidential minutes are prepared and headed up in exactly the same way as the main minutes. The confidential item is outlined and referenced with the same number taken from the main minutes:

> 07/14   A disciplinary hearing had been held and allegations deemed to have merit. As a result a member of staff had been dismissed. They had now lodged an appeal which would be heard before Christmas.

Great care should be taken when discussing confidential items, particularly when they relate to ongoing complaints, disciplinary or capability hearings. Panels are, initially, drawn from directors appointed to the board. It is important that they are not given too much information, which could be construed as removing their impartiality and disqualifying them from taking part on a panel.

It is always important to remember that discussion of individuals in a meeting situation will constitute 'publication' for the purposes of defamation and any false derogatory comments will be 'slander'. These will be 'libel' if they are repeated in the minutes.

It is usual practice to print confidential minutes on pink paper so that they are easily identifiable. Once approved, they should be stored separately from the main board minutes in a lockable filing cabinet which is accessible only to authorised persons.

Preparation of minutes

A first draft of the minutes should be produced as soon as possible after the meeting, ideally the following day. These should be forwarded to the chair to check for accuracy and approval. The chair should not add extra information that was not available at the time of the meeting nor amend the meetings to give a more favourable slant. The chair should, however, check the contents of the minutes, amending errors or making changes to clarify the proceedings.

When the approved minutes are returned from the chair they should be circulated to all board members and anyone else who receives a copy.

Storing minutes

Minutes must be kept for at least ten years from the date of the meeting. Failure to comply with the requirements for producing and storing minutes will mean that every officer of the company who is in default (which could potentially be every director and the secretary) commits an offence. Anyone found guilty could be liable to payment of a fine.

The funding agreement provides that the academy must make various documents 'available for inspection by any interested party at the academy':

- the agenda for every board meeting or any committee meeting which has delegated power;
- the draft minutes of every such meeting when approved by the person acting as chair of that meeting;
- the signed minutes; and
- any report, document or other paper considered at any such meeting.

The funding agreement also requires copies of this documentation to be sent to the Secretary of State 'as soon as is reasonably practicable'. However, in practice, the EFA will specify if the school is to forward the documentation in accordance with these measures. Instead, the academy should ensure secure storage of documentation at the school and make available to the Secretary of State and his officers as required.

The signed minutes must be kept securely together with the notice and agenda for the meeting and supporting documentation provided for consideration at the meeting. Documentation is generally filed in a dedicated minute book which is usually in the form of a loose-leaf binder to which additional pages can be added easily.

Summary

Minutes of directors' meetings

- A formal record of proceedings at board meetings must be taken.
- Once approved and signed by the chair, minutes are evidence of the proceedings.

Practical considerations

- Minutes provide an explanation of the issue, the reasoning behind any decision made and any resultant actions.
- Minutes should be written in the past tense.
- Minutes must always be written in the third person (i.e. 'he', 'she', 'it' and 'they').
- Number paragraphs.
- Use plain English and avoid acronyms.
- Use short sentences and paragraphs.
- Clear layout with action points and resolutions easily identified.
- Make reference to supporting documentation.
- Any legal or procedural advice given by the clerk should be recorded.
- Individual directors will not generally be identified.
- Board minutes and minutes of members' meetings must be kept separate.

Drafting the minutes

- The heading should contain:
  - Name of the academy.
  - Company registered number.
  - Date, time and location.
  - Names of those present, in attendance, apologies and absent.
  - Who is chairing the meeting.
  - Confirmation that the meeting was quorate.
  - The actual starting time.
- The meeting cannot take place unless a quorum is present which is the greater of:
  - three directors; or

- – one-third (rounded up to a whole number) of the total number of directors holding office at the date of the meeting.
- It is for the meeting to decide whether apologies should be accepted.
- Directors should declare any interest in any item on the agenda.
- The board elects a chair and a vice-chair annually.
- Minutes of the last meeting are formally approved and signed by the chair.
- Brief updates can be given of any items discussed and minuted from the last meeting under 'Matters Arising'.
- Reports should be circulated with the agenda and are taken 'as read'.
- It should be noted if a document is tabled.
- Reports and documentation put before the meeting are filed with the minutes.
- Resolutions or decisions considered must be recorded in full with an indication of whether it was passed.
- Items of 'Any Other Business' should be of strategic importance and should be submitted to the chair in advance of the meeting.
- The date of the next meeting should be agreed.
- Action points should be clearly defined and easily identified on the page.
- The closing time should be noted.

Confidential items

- Listed on the agenda in general terms.
- The board minutes contain a simple reference to the confidential item.
- Separate confidential minutes are prepared and headed up in the same way as the main minutes.
- The confidential item is outlined and referenced with the same number taken from the main minutes.

Preparation of minutes

- The first draft minutes should be produced as soon as possible after the meeting.
- Draft minutes are sent to the chair to check for accuracy and approval.
- Checked minutes are circulated to all who are entitled to a copy.
- Minutes will be formally approved at the next board meeting.

Storing minutes

- Minutes must be kept for at least ten years from the date of the meeting.
- Failure to produce and store minutes will mean that every officer of the company could be liable to a fine.

- ■ Various documents must be made 'available for inspection by any interested party at the academy':
    - the agenda for every board meeting or any committee meeting which has delegated power;
    - the draft minutes of every such meeting when approved by the person acting as chair of that meeting;
    - the signed minutes; and
    - any report, document or other paper considered at any such meeting.

10 Financial management

In this chapter

This chapter considers the obligations on academies to ensure a system of financial accountability, including:

- the accounting reference date and accounting officer;
- the implications of exempt charity status, subsidiary trading companies, gift aid and tax relief and VAT;
- procurement rules;
- financial monitoring, internal controls, the audit committee and responsible officer; and
- financial management and governance self-assessment.

Accounting reference date

The financial year for an academy will run from 1 September to 31 August so that, unlike maintained schools, the academic year and the financial year will be brought into line. The date of the financial year-end is known as the accounting reference date (ARD). This is also the date that determines when accounts are due to be delivered to Companies House.

COMMENT

Martin Wyatt, Partner with Witley Stimpson LLP, explains:

The date to which accounts are prepared is referred to as the accounting reference date. This is a formal registered date and recorded at Companies House.

Academies must have the date of 31 August as their accounting reference date.

Academies must ensure that their accounting reference date is registered as 31 August at Companies House to correspond with the date required under their Funding Agreement. When the academy is first formed the accounting reference date will automatically be set by Companies House to the last day of the month in which the Academy incorporates. For example, if the academy was incorporated on 10 May 2013, its first accounting reference date would be 31 May 2014, and unless amended, 31 May for every year thereafter.

After incorporation the academy must ensure it changes its accounting reference date at Companies House to 31 August.

Immediately after setting up an academy by whichever means, it is necessary to change the ARD at Companies House. As this is a requirement of the funding agreement, no resolution of the directors is required to facilitate this. The change must be formally notified to Companies House (see Chapter 5).

Accounting officer

The funding agreement requires every academy to appoint an accounting officer and notify the Secretary of State of that appointment.

The *Academies Financial Handbook* states that the accounting officer should be a 'fit and suitable person' for the role. In a single academy, the accounting officer should be the principal/head teacher, and in a MAT it should be the chief executive or executive principal/head teacher.

The accounting officer has a personal responsibility for:

- regularity (i.e. that all items of expenditure and receipts are dealt with in accordance with the appropriate legislation);
- propriety (i.e. that expenditure and receipts are dealt with in accordance with Parliament's intentions);
- value for money (i.e. that resources are utilised economically, efficiently and prudently and avoiding waste and extravagance).

The accounting officer also has responsibility for ensuring that proper financial records and accounts are kept.

Of course, whilst the accounting officer has overall responsibility and is accountable for the academy's financial affairs, in practice the role will be fulfilled by a finance director or school business manager.

Exempt charity status

Academies are charitable companies limited by guarantee. However, they are exempt charities, which means that they do not need to register with the Charity Commission. The Secretary of State for Education is the principal regulator for schools which means that the DfE is responsible for overseeing the compliance by academies with charity law.

As well as not being required to submit their accounts to the Charity Commission, there are other advantages of exempt charity status:

- exemption from corporation tax; and
- business rate relief – 80% compulsory and 20% at the discretion of the local authority.

Subsidiary trading companies

As a charity, an academy is not permitted to trade and make a profit. It is, however, possible to set up a subsidiary trading company which can sell products or services and Gift Aid profits back to the academy.

EXPERIENCE

Sujata McNab, Chief Operating Officer of the Cabot Learning Federation:

'CLF owns houses which were part of the leasehold that we were granted from the foundation. The houses are rented out and the income goes through a trading company, John Cabot Ventures. This company receives any commercial income such as fees for consultancy work or any charged-for courses that we put on.

Having a separate trading company helps CLF to manage corporation tax issues and the whole profit is gifted to CLF at the end of the year.'

Gift Aid and tax relief

The funding agreement provides that 'the Academy will establish an appropriate mechanism for the receipt and management of donations and shall use reasonable endeavours to procure donations through that mechanism for the purpose of the objects specified in the Articles'. The presumption is that donations will be encouraged and maximised to further the interests of the academy.

It is possible to 'gift aid' donations to increase the sum by way of tax relief. The academy does not need to register with HMRC for the purposes of gift aid but will need to apply formally to HMRC for recognition as a charity. Tax on the 'gross' equivalent of any donation (i.e. their value before basic rate tax was deducted) can be reclaimed.

As of 6 April 2013, the Gift Aid Small Donations Scheme (GASDS) has meant that gift aid can also be claimed on 'bucket collections' up to a total of £5,000 in a tax year provided that donations are cash of £20 or less, (i.e. in bank notes or coins). The academy must have:

- existed for at least the last two complete tax years (6 April–5 April);
- made a successful gift aid claim in at least two out of the last four tax years, without a gap of two or more tax years between those gift aid claims or since the last claim made; and
- not incurred a penalty on a gift aid or GASDS claim made in the current or previous tax year.

In addition, academies can claim tax back on income received on which tax has already been paid, such as bank or building society interest.

Investment policies

In due course, academies should set out their strategy for investment and enshrine this in a formal investment policy. However, whilst interest rates are low, many see little real need for this to be done as it costs more in terms of man hours to shuffle funds between accounts than would ever be achieved in interest.

EXPERIENCE

John Swift, the Business Manager at The Knights Templar School explained:

> There is no formal investment policy in place and business rates of interest for school cash deposits are very low presently. We continue to consider the merits of placing deposits for greater financial reward.

John Banbrook, Business and Finance Director at the Faringdon Academy of Schools agrees:

> With interest rates so low it has not been worth the staff time to make use of the provisions suggested by the bank. We also do not wish to risk losing our free banking!

As interest rates rise, there will be a greater need to take advantage of investment opportunities. However, in the meantime, there is a need to establish a policy which reflects risk, return and the liquidity challenges of the organisation. Following the example of the failed Icelandic banks, academies should avoid holding amounts greater than £85,000 in any one account. (This is the amount covered by the Financial Services Compensation Scheme (FSCS).)

CASE STUDY

Mike Lawes, Finance Director at Bartholomew School, Eynsham:

Whilst interest rates have been at a historical low level for a considerable period of time, we are generating in excess of £7,000 from our investment, which is four times what our bank account earns annually. As such, it should not be ignored.

The following is taken from our investment policy.

AIMS

The School aims to manage its cash balances to provide for the day-to-day working capital requirements of its operations, whilst protecting the real long-term value of any surplus cash balances against inflation. In addition, the School aims to invest surplus cash funds to optimise returns, but ensuring the investment instruments are such that there is no risk to the loss of these cash funds.

The School does not consider the investment of surplus funds as a primary activity, rather it is the result of good stewardship as and when circumstances allow.

OBJECTIVES

- To ensure adequate cash balances are maintained in the current account to cover day-to-day working capital requirements.
- To ensure there is no risk of loss in the capital value of any cash funds invested.
- To protect the capital value of any invested funds against inflation.
- To optimise returns on invested funds.

IMPLEMENTATION

The School will construct such budgets and cash-flow forecasts as are required by legislation to ensure the viability and sustainability of the activities of the School and to ensure there are adequate liquid funds to meet all payroll related commitments and outstanding supply creditors that are due for payment.

From time to time, operational and strategic decisions will result in substantial cash balances at the bank over a sustained period.

Where the cash flow identifies a base level of cash funds that will be surplus to requirements these may be invested only in the following:

- Interest bearing deposit accounts with any of the following banks only:
  - Lloyds TSB
  - Barclays

- RBS
- HSBC
- Treasury deposits, with maturity dates which do not result in the cash funds being unavailable for longer than eight weeks.

Prior to investing funds, the head teacher must satisfy himself that the cash flow predictions provided by the Finance Director and Finance Officer are accurate and that the amount/time period of the investment will not compromise the viability and sustainability of the activities of the School.

In making decisions regarding where and how any surplus funds should be invested, due regard will be given to the 'Risk that the return on investments is not being maximised' and 'Risk that trustees are not acting in accordance with their Investment Policy' (e.g. investing in high risk investments which are not in the best interests of the School).

▨ Value Added Tax

VAT is a tax charged on the supply of goods and services and will apply to most business transactions. There are currently three rates of VAT depending on the goods or services provided, as well as limited exemptions.

Companies including academies can register for VAT purposes; this means that they can generally reclaim any VAT that they have paid. Companies that are not VAT-registered may reclaim VAT paid on goods and services through the submission of Form 126, although they cannot charge VAT and to do so could be construed as fraud.

A threshold based on turnover is set, above which it is compulsory to register for VAT. However, academies may find it advantageous to voluntarily register for VAT and specific advice should be sought from a relevant professional.

COMMENT

Martin Wyatt, Partner with Whitley Stimpson LLP:

'The mere mention of the three letters, VAT, sends shudders down many a well-qualified and experienced accountant. For the school business manager VAT is a totally alien tax. A tax that prior to conversion to an academy has been administered for them by the local authority.

With the application of certain VAT rules by academies remaining unclear and a loud silence in lieu of any guidance from HMRC on academies, VAT in the academy sector is a financial accident waiting to happen.'

Background
Provision of education by a state school is not regarded for VAT purposes as a business activity. Normally VAT incurred on costs would not be

recoverable. However s. 33 VAT Act provides for certain bodies [i.e. local authorities] to reclaim VAT on costs.

From 1 April 2011, academy schools became an entity recognised as a Section 33 body. Their inclusion, however, was under a new section, section 33B, specifically for academies.

Academies can therefore claim back VAT on costs incurred in providing state-funded education. This is done either via a VAT registration or VAT126 claim.

Registration

Always take professional advice when reviewing the impact of VAT on the academy and whether or not to register for VAT with HMRC.

VAT registration involves an initial formal application to HMRC. VAT is then reclaimed via the completion and submission of VAT returns to HMRC.

If the academy does not formally register for VAT, it can still reclaim any VAT incurred by the completion and submission of form VAT126.

If an academy's 'taxable turnover' exceeds the VAT registration threshold then it is obliged to register for VAT. At the time of writing, the threshold is £79,000.

The golden rule is always seek professional advice to carry out a review of the activities of the academy to ascertain if the registration principles and limit applies. With advantages and disadvantages to both registration and VAT126, ensure the route opted for is right for your academy.

A VAT-registered academy will be able to submit either monthly or quarterly VAT returns. Form 126 claims may be made monthly, quarterly or any combination of whole calendar months.

The priority for the academy must be to recover as soon as possible VAT incurred on its costs. My advice to all my academy clients is to do a monthly return or VAT126 reclaim.

I am currently seeing academies' VAT126 repayments being handled swiftly and without challenge by HMRC. But VAT and academies are new bedfellows and it will not be long before HMRC will begin to review, challenge and then visit academies to inspect the records being maintained to support the reclaims.

Some of the more frequent encountered activities that may generate income and need close review for the application of VAT are:

- Catering
- Letting of buildings and rooms
- Sports facilities
- Use of transport
- Provision of staff to other schools.

▦ Capital grant funding

Academies Capital Maintenance Fund

Academies can apply to the EFA for additional funding from the Academies Capital Maintenance Fund (ACMF) to improve the condition of their school buildings and expand their facilities. Academies must apply within specific time-scales. Great care should be taken that applications conform with the detailed requirements relevant to the programme priorities and assessment criteria. However, the window of opportunity for applications is small and academies should make sure that they are well prepared.

The process is highly competitive with demand exceeding available fund allocation: less than half of applicants were successful in previous rounds. The guidance states:

> Applicants must demonstrate both a strong case for the investment in line with the programme priorities and present an effective, efficient and deliverable project to address the identified issues.

CASE STUDY

John Swift, the Business Manager at The Knights Templar School explained:

'We were recently successful in a bid for capital funding.

We had engaged a consultant who provided good professional advice. We had prepared quite detailed plans and had obtained planning permission. We consider ourselves one of the higher priority schools in the county in terms of needing improved accommodation. We believe that the success of our bid was largely due to the very poor condition of some of our existing buildings.'

Salix funding

Salix Finance is a not-for-profit company funded by the Department of Energy and Climate Change and the Welsh and Scottish Governments which has been set up to remove the upfront capital cost of investing in energy-efficient technologies. Salix provides interest-free loans for projects that fall within its compliance criteria: namely, that returns on investment and carbon savings must be achievable within a stipulated time period.

Salix funding is now the EFA's preferred method to support heating system replacements at academies. Although Salix is loan-based, academies must bid in the same way as ACMF.

Loan repayments can be made for a minimum of four years up to a maximum of eight years, depending on the specific project. Payments are made by direct debit every March and September over the agreed period.

It is hoped that Salix funding will prove to be successful and a 'sustainable initiative' through which all projects will be funded in future.

Procurement

The board is under an obligation to ensure value for money (i.e. that funds are used economically, efficiently and effectively). In any event, good procurement is a means by which financial savings can be made and funds diverted to best benefit the pupils. A number of procurement consortiums now offer access to national contracts and frameworks for commonly purchased categories of goods and services.

However, academies will now be regarded as a 'contracting authority' for the purposes of EU public procurement purposes. Therefore, great care should be taken in respect of procurement, particularly for higher value contracts. There are detailed rules that apply where the value of a contract is above a certain threshold. The thresholds are revised every two years. As at January 2014, the relevant thresholds are €207,000 (around £172,514) for supply and service contracts and €5,186,000 (around £4,322,012) for works contracts.

There are onerous obligations to be followed if these thresholds are exceeded and specialist advice should be obtained where necessary. MATs should take particular heed of the relevant limits.

There are some 'Part B' services which will generally not fall within the procurement rules despite the value of the spending. Relevant services include catering, health and legal services.

Financial monitoring

Academies are under an obligation to ensure that financial operations reflect regularity, propriety and value for money. The accounting officer carries a personal responsibility to ensure that this is achieved.

In order to do this, academies must make sure that financial affairs are properly conducted and accounts are correct on an ongoing basis as well as setting up internal controls to ensure that the academy's money is spent wisely and fraud is avoided.

The *Academies Financial Handbook* requires that finance staff are 'appropriately qualified and/or experienced'. The contrast between a maintained school and an academy is stark with respect to finances and accounting and this is a requirement that academies overlook at their peril!

EXPERIENCE

Catherine Barnes, Business Development Manager of The Propeller Academy Trust:

'As an academy, it is necessary to know a lot more about the finances. Getting involved with the accounting side is a great deal more onerous and involves things that a local authority school doesn't even know exists!

From the moment of conversion, the local authority safety net has gone. We need to work at the highest level and be able to stand up to scrutiny. There is nobody out there to save us. The biggest area of challenge is, without a doubt, the finance and administration side.'

Monitoring and management

The academy is under an obligation to monitor the current and forecast financial position. Bank and control accounts should be reconciled regularly and financial reports should be presented to the board at least termly. It is very important to remember that, unlike maintained schools, academies cannot go into a deficit position and all efforts must be made to ensure this does not happen.

Budget monitoring is essential so that spending can be tracked and controlled. Not only does this ensure that spending is within overall totals, but it also serves to identify any circumstances that may require corrective action.

In addition, forecasting cash flow is key to safeguarding the academy's financial position by making sure that it does not run out of cash. Academies cannot resort to loan funding, even on a short-term basis such as with an overdraft, so running out of cash could have serious implications.

EXPERIENCE

Catherine Barnes, Business Development Manager of The Propeller Academy Trust:

'Budget monitoring is much as it was as a maintained school, though reporting is into the board rather than into the local authority.

Cash flow forecasting will be a bigger challenge, especially in a special school. Personnel take up a much higher proportion of the budget so that there is less flexible income every month. At the most basic level, we need to make sure that there is money in the bank each month for payroll otherwise we won't be able to pay staff!'

Getting the whole school community to understand that even though the budget says that there is money available for something doesn't mean that you can buy it when you want to – the cash flow dictates when in the year you can buy. We are in a stable position now, but it could get more challenging if the budget gets used up and I have to say to someone who wants something that they can't buy it just yet.

The academy must, therefore, carry out regular monitoring checks, usually on a monthly basis.'

COMMENT

Sarah Chambers FCA, School Business Manager and self-employed consultant/advisor on school and academy finance:

The aim of budget monitoring is to look at the actuals (i.e. income and expenditure in the month and more particularly year to date) and compare them to the budget to see how the academy's finances are progressing. Variances need to be investigated and more importantly acted upon. Income from funding generally doesn't change significantly – if it does the assumptions in the budget should be carefully reviewed because this is generally what drives the academy's core activity expenditure. Other income can be more difficult to forecast so assumptions may be need to be updated.

With regard to expenditure, if the payroll is being reconciled each month any variances to budget should be understood. Payroll costs are relatively fixed so if there is an overspend, there needs to be a plan to accommodate this and the governors need to understand how this has happened. If there is an underspend, why? Is the underspend offset by overspends elsewhere (e.g. supply teachers)?

The other areas of expenditure typically account for 20–30% of the budget. If there is an underspend are we happy that we haven't incurred the expense but it still hasn't been invoiced (in which case consider accruing the expense) or is it just that we budgeted an amount that we haven't yet incurred but will still spend (phasing in the budget is different) or have our plans changed and we no longer plan to spend it on this line item (in which case do we want to allocate it to other priorities)? If there is an overspend again, consider whether it is phasing (whether we've spent it all up front but budgeted to spend it over the year) or if there is a real overspend, in which case corrective action will be required. Can a stop be put on further spending? Can other sources of finance be found?

Ideally the academy needs to update the budget/at least have a more up-to-date forecast on a regular basis as the budget is only a plan and plans change. The academy should consider processes around this (i.e. how much governor/director involvement is required in developing and approving an updated budget/forecasts to ensure that governors are up to speed with the latest view and associated plans?).

Cash flow is something that finance staff and governors need to pay attention to and I'd suggest this should be reported on at least monthly. As a maintained school, cash flow is rarely an issue. Academies don't have the local authority to rely on, so need to monitor their cash flow to ensure that they have sufficient funds available at the right point to pay their staff, suppliers, HMRC etc. Insufficient cash flow is a primary cause of business failure. The cash-flow forecast should take into account any major projects (e.g. IT programmes, building works etc) as well as day-to-day expenditure. The forecast will identify whether there are sufficient funds and may drive decisions about the timing of discretionary spend. The academy may even be in the fortunate position of having spare funds. Cash-flow forecasting will enable the academy to make better use of its funds (e.g. by placing what is not immediately required in term deposits) subject to its investment policy.

Sarah has devised a checklist for use at month end to make sure that everything has been covered. (See Appendix 4 for the month-end checklist.)

Internal controls, the audit committee and the responsible officer

Academies are also required to have in place 'sound internal control and risk management processes' and a process for 'independent checking of financial controls, systems, transactions and risks'.

Ideally, the board should appoint an audit committee to review the risks to internal financial control and agree a programme to address any risks identified. However, the *Academies Financial Handbook* sets a limit below which a separate audit committee is not required, although it should be considered by all MATs. For many standalone academies, the function is undertaken by the board's finance committee.

EXPERIENCE

Matthew Hall, Finance Manager at the Diocese of Bristol:

'The Diocesan MAT, Diocese of Bristol Academy Company, originally named a responsible officer to conduct internal audits after it was set up. The EFA then said it was possible to do it another way.

Now the internal audit is run by the Diocesan finance team which is independent of the academy's finance. They have the relevant experience but also have an understanding of the way things work in the Diocese. It ties in the Diocesan advisory role whilst providing a critical eye reporting direct to the board.'

The programme of risk review and internal controls can be carried out in whatever way the board sees fit and the *Handbook* sets out several possible options:

- use of an internal audit service;
- a supplementary programme of work undertaken by the academy's external auditor;
- the work of a 'responsible officer'; and
- use of peer review.

EXPERIENCE

Catherine Barnes, Business Development Manager of The Propeller Academy Trust:

'PAT has an audit committee which is comprised of directors, although their remit and accountability is very different. PAT also currently contracts with the local authority which acts as responsible officer and undertakes audits four times a year. However, in the future I am looking to set up a reciprocal arrangement with another academy. It is a good opportunity to build relationships with other schools which is important as we move forward. It can assist with sharing good practice as well as offering a learning experience for those involved.

The board must decide on the most appropriate method of fulfilling the requirements and must be confident that the financial responsibilities are being discharged in an appropriate way. There is, however, no standard specification as far as the extent of review and sampling necessary, or the approach to be taken.'

COMMENT

Sarah Chambers FCA, School Business Manager and self-employed consultant/advisor on school and academy finance:

Responsible officer tasks.
If you refer to the *Academies Financial Handbook* (pp 33–34) it states, at paragraph 3.5.5 that it is the role of the audit committee to evaluate the risks to the academy and agree a programme of works based on this. The idea is that the audit committee come up with a programme based on their risks and direct the responsible officer to follow/develop that programme.

The risk-based approach is best practice. In practice. I think it is often the case that academies, especially smaller ones, tend to follow a programme of work similar to what was required under FMSiS (Financial Management Standards in Schools) now replaced by FMGS (Financial Management and

Governance Self-Assessment) for academies, which is more self-assessment based.

There is nothing wrong with this except that it may not address risks specific to the academy's circumstances (e.g. rapid expansion, key personnel changes, specific issues that have cropped up (e.g. theft)).

Areas for consideration could include:

- Consideration of internal financial procedures manual – whether the controls described are sufficient and whether they are being applied.
- Reviewing bank reconciliations – checking they have been done promptly, reviewed/authorised by a third party, discrepancies/outstanding items followed up.
- Checking income is promptly banked, reconciled, controls around cash and petty cash.
- Are debts recorded and chased?
- Payroll is checked and authorised prior to payment (usually accounts for 70–80% of school's budget), any issues resolved.
- Controls around change of contracts, leavers, sickness and absence.
- Review of purchasing controls. Is delegated authority followed? How does the academy ensure best value? Are all orders raised on authorised purchase orders? Is budget checked prior to purchase? What are controls around checking (e.g. do we only pay for valid invoices where we have received all the goods that we ordered (match to PO and delivery note?).
- How is the procurement/credit card controlled? Is there a pre-authorisation procedure? Is the card reconciled? Where is it kept? What controls are there around paying invoices, expenses, setting up new suppliers on the system?
- Are capital projects accounted for correctly?
- HMRC – is the academy accounting for VAT, PAYE, NI correctly?
- Review of receipts from EFA – ensure completeness by agreeing to source documentation. Consider availability of additional funding where the academy has to make an additional bid – has anything been missed?
- Review of budget monitoring to see that variances are explained and action taken.
- Review of minutes of governing body.
- Review of policies impacting finance (procedures, remission and charging, investment, pensions, pay ...). Are they up-to-date, appropriate and being applied?
- Review returns to EFA and other bodies – check consistent with under-lying records.

As an academy matures, the needs of the board are likely to be affected. It is important that not only the method and relationship with the individual or organisation fulfilling the internal audit role is reviewed annually, but also the remit and requirements of that audit.

EXPERIENCE

Mike Lawes is Finance Director at Bartholomew School, Eynsham. He supports 14 schools as responsible officer.

'I have developed an audit programme which is broadly based on FMSiS and its replacement, SFVS, that maintained schools had to complete annually and the minimum requirements set out in the original *Academies Financial Handbook*. I go to the academy and prepare a report which identifies any areas of concern and gives recommendations. I give a rating for each of the areas we look at and generally give three months for academies to resolve them. If a serious issue is identified, a shorter deadline will be set, such as recently when I attended an academy where the safe was sitting on the floor!

There is no definition of what is required and it will be down to the board and audit committee to direct the work of the responsible officer. I have noticed a move away from a focus on control systems and transactions to a more risk-based approach.'

Financial management and governance self-assessment

New academies are generally required to complete a Financial Management and Governance Self-Assessment (FMGS) which must be submitted to the EFA within four months of the academy's opening date. Academies may agree to provide an alternative form of assurance that the financial management and governance arrangements are acceptable, particularly if they are joining an existing MAT.

The EFA has published a short self-assessment which covers:

- **Financial oversight:** Whether the directors and managers have the skills, knowledge and experience to run the academy.
- **Financial planning**: Preparation of financial plans to secure the academy's short-term and long-term financial health.
- **Internal control:** Sound internal control and risk management processes must be put in place.
- **Financial monitoring and management**: The board and managers must monitor the current and forecast financial position.
- **Proper and regular use of public funds:** Public funds must be used as intended by Parliament.
- **Audit requirements**: Academies are subject to audit and review to give assurance to Parliament and the public that public funds are being used for the purpose intended.

▨ Summary

Financial management

- The ARD is the financial year-end: 31 August.
- The academy must appoint an accounting officer. In a single academy, this will be the principal/head teacher, and in a MAT the chief executive or executive principal/head teacher.
- The accounting officer has a personal responsibility for ensuring regularity, propriety and value for money.
- As an exempt charity, academies are exempt from corporation tax and are entitled to business rate relief.
- An academy can set up a subsidiary trading company to sell products or services and covenant profits back to the academy.
- Donations can be 'gift aided' and the tax on the 'gross' equivalent of any donation can be reclaimed.
- Academies do not need to register for VAT purposes if turnover is below the relevant threshold, although they may choose to voluntarily register.
- Academies must ensure that all purchasing is value for money. Contracts exceeding relevant thresholds will fall within EU public procurement rules and will be subject to onerous obligations.

Financial monitoring

- Academies must monitor the current and forecast financial position, reconcile bank and control accounts regularly and present termly financial reports to the board.
- Academies cannot go into a deficit position.
- Budget monitoring and cash flow forecasting are key. Monitoring checks will normally be carried out on a monthly basis.

Internal controls, the audit committee and the responsible officer

- Academies must have 'sound internal control and risk management processes' and a process for 'independent checking of financial controls, systems, transactions and risks'.
- A separate audit committee is not required for academies below the turnover threshold, although it is recommended for all MATs.
- The board can select the manner in which risk review and internal controls are carried out, including: use of an internal audit service; a supplementary programme of work undertaken by the academy's external auditor; the work of a 'responsible officer' or use of peer review.

Financial management and governance self-assessment

■ New academies are generally required to complete a Financial Management and Governance Self-Assessment which must be submitted to the EFA within four months of their opening date.

11 Accounts

As charitable companies, academies are required to comply with the Companies Act 2006. As charities, they must comply with the requirements of the Charities Act 2011.

In addition, academies are classified by the Office for National Statistics as 'central government public sector bodies' which means that they are subject to public standards of accountability, involving a higher level of transparency.

The funding agreement requires compliance with the *Academies Financial Handbook* which sets out financial requirements. This states that the EFA expects academies to 'to take full control of their financial affairs'.

At the present time, academies fall under a variety of legislation and accounts direction.

COMMENT

Martin Wyatt, Partner with Whitley Stimpson LLP, states:

'The legislation and regulations governing the accounts reporting process are an amalgam of direction and guidance. With the number of academies increasing, it cannot be long before specific accounting standards and practice are issued for the academy sector.

Care should be taken that guidance is sought to ensure that accounting practice adopted is up-to-date with the latest requirements.'

The *Handbook* is supplemented by the Academies Accounts Direction, which is issued annually and sets out the technical details to fulfil the requirements to:

■ prepare an annual report and financial statements to 31 August;
■ have these 'accounts' audited by an independent auditor;
■ deliver a statement of regularity, propriety and compliance and obtain a regularity assurance report on this statement from the auditor;
■ submit the audited accounts to the EFA by 31 December;
■ file the accounts with Companies House as required under the Companies Act 2006; and
■ arrange an independent audit of regularity and include the auditor's report on regularity as part of the trust's accounts.

The latest version of the Academies Accounts Direction must be referenced when preparing the annual report and accounts as this will change from year to year.

As charitable companies, accounts must be prepared under the Charities' Statement of Recommended Practice (SORP) issued by the Charity Commission. This provides a 'comprehensive framework of recommended practice for charity accounting and reporting'.

Annual report and accounts

It is a condition of the funding agreement that academy accounts must be produced for the 12-month accounting period ending on 31 August.

The annual report and accounts must be filed with Companies House by 31 May and should include the following elements:

Reports:

■ a trustees' report;
■ a governance statement;
■ a statement on regularity, propriety and compliance;
■ a statement of trustees' responsibilities;
■ an independent auditor's report on the financial statements; and
■ an independent auditor's report on regularity.

Financial statements:

■ a statement of financial activities;
■ a balance sheet;
■ a cash-flow statement; and
■ notes which expand on the statements, including a note on the academy trust's accounting policies.

In limited circumstances, an income and expenditure account and a statement of total recognised gains and losses may also be included.

The financial reporting environment is constantly changing, but the Financial Handbook and the Accounts Direction are both essential to understanding the requirements for academies. (The Accounts Direction provides model reports and financial statements which can be used by academies when preparing their own.) Although there is no requirement to have a qualified accountant, the reality is that the accounting standards do need someone with suitable experience to apply them. You will therefore need to review the skills within your team and supplement either through training, recruitment or the use of external advisors.

Reports

Trustees' report

The directors of the academy are responsible for the preparation of a trustees'/ directors' report which supports the financial statements. The report fulfils the requirements for a directors' report as set out in ss. 415–419 CA 2006 as well as a trustees' report under charity law as set out in the Charities' SORP. The main objective is to supplement the financial information with such further information as necessary for a full appreciation of the company's activities.

The report describes what the academy is trying to do and how it is going about it, demonstrates whether and how the academy has achieved its objectives during the year and explains its plans for the future.

The trustees' report should cover the following matters:

- Reference and administrative details:
  - Basic information relating to the directors during the year including their appointment or resignation/expiration of term of office, the senior management team, registered office, auditor, bankers and solicitors.
- Structure, governance and management:
  - constitution;
  - members' liability in the event of the company being wound up;
  - directors' indemnities in respect of qualifying third-party indemnity provisions as required by s. 236 CA 2006;
  - principal activities referring to purposes as set out in the funding agreement and articles of association;
  - method of recruitment and appointment/election of directors including the name of any person or body entitled to nominate or appoint directors;
  - policies and procedures for the induction and training of directors as agreed by the board;
  - organisational structure showing how decisions are made;
  - risk management confirming that the major risks to which the academy is exposed have been reviewed by the directors and systems or procedures have been established to manage those risks; and

- connected organisations including related party relationships including membership of soft federation or other wider network. Details are also required of relationships with related parties and other charities/organisations with which it cooperates in pursuit of charitable activities.
- Objectives and activities: objects and aims, objectives, strategies and activities and public benefit.

Strategic review

Academies are now required to produce a strategic report which must contain a fair review of the academy's business and a description of the principal risks and uncertainties it faces. It will specifically include:

- Achievements and performance:
  - A statement on the academy's ability to continue to operate as a going concern.
  - Analysis against financial or other key performance indicators (KPIs) including information relating to environmental and employee matters.
- Financial review:
  - Financial and risk management objectives and policies.
  - Disclosure of principal risks and uncertainties facing the academy linked to the risk management process. This should include financial risks such as credit, cash flow and liquidity risks. Reference should be made to its defined benefit pension schemes, particularly where there is a deficit.
  - Reserves policy identifying value of free reserves held (income funds that are freely available for general purposes) and information on the policy and other reserves such as restricted general funds. Where material funds have been designated, these should be quantified and the purpose of the designation explained. If any fund is materially in deficit, details of the circumstances giving rise to the deficit and details of the steps being taken to eliminate the deficit must be given.
  - Description and objectives of the investment policy and the extent to which social, environmental or ethical considerations are taken into account.
- Plans for future periods:
  - Aims and key objectives set for future periods together with details of activities planned to achieve them.
- Funds held as custodian trustee on behalf of others:
  - Details of assets and arrangements held on trust by the academy including the name and object of the charity on whose behalf they are being held and how this activity falls within their own objectives.

The directors/trustees must include a clear statement that they are approving the strategic report in their capacity as company directors.

COMMENT

Phil Reynolds, Academies Audit Manager at Reeves & Co LLP, advised:

'The introduction of the Strategic Report does not represent a change to the content of the Trustees Report but a revision in the way in which it is presented. Therefore the introduction of the Report should not be too onerous on academy schools.

Until the EFA release the latest Accounts Direction it will not be clear what format they will require the Strategic Report to take. This stresses the importance of ensuring the latest Accounts Direction is reviewed each year prior to the statutory financial statements being produced to ensure all relevant changes have been included.

The EFA may even choose not to adopt the Charity SORP. The Charity Commission have been consulting about the potential effect the change in UK Generally Accepted Accounting Practice will have, with a new SORP likely to be released for 2015. The EFA will be looking at the currently used Charities SORP and the Further & High Education (F&HE) SORP during this process.

Academies should talk to their auditors in the lead-up to the audit process so that they are aware of the key changes to their sector.'

Governance statement

Academies are recipients of public funding and so must prepare a governance statement which is a requirement by HM Treasury for all public bodies. It must be signed by the chair and accounting officer on behalf of the board.

- *Scope of responsibility*
  - This generic section is applicable to all academies. The wording from the model accounts can be incorporated without alteration unless the principal is not the accounting officer.
  - The trustees acknowledge their overall responsibility for ensuring that effective and appropriate management systems, including both financial monitoring and control systems, are in place.
- *Governance*
  The governance structure is outlined and details of the trustees, changes in composition of the board and number of meetings attended are provided. The committee structure together with membership, the purpose of the committee and details of particular issues dealt with during the year should also be given. An assessment of the board itself can be included together with details of particular challenges encountered.

Part of the section of Reading School's Governance section reads:

The Finance Committee is a sub-committee of the main governing body. Its purpose is to assist the decision making of the governing body, by enabling more detailed consideration to be given to the best means of fulfilling the governing body's responsibility to ensure sound management of the Academy's finances and resources, including proper planning, monitoring and probity and to make appropriate comments and recommendations on such matters to the governing body on a regular basis. Mr D Jubb, who is a qualified accountant, chairs the committee.

■ *The purpose of the system of internal control*
Suggested wording is included in the model accounts which should be tailored to the needs of the individual academy. The statement explains that that system of internal control is designed to manage risk to a reasonable level rather than to eliminate it. The trustees must also confirm that the system of internal control has been in place for the year and up to the date of approval of the accounts.

Reading School:

THE PURPOSE OF THE SYSTEM OF INTERNAL CONTROL

The system of internal control is designed to manage risk to a reasonable level rather than to eliminate all risk of failure to achieve policies, aims and objectives; it can therefore only provide reasonable and not absolute assurance of effectiveness. The system of internal control is based on an on-going process designed to identify and prioritise the risks to the achievement of Reading School's policies, aims and objectives, to evaluate the likelihood of those risks being realised and the impact should they be realised, and to manage them efficiently, effectively and economically. The system of internal control has been in place in Reading School for the year ended 31 August 2012 and up to the date of approval of the Governors' annual report and financial statements.

■ *Capacity to handle risk*
Again, suggested wording is provided which should be tailored to the individual academy. The trustees confirm that operating, financial and compliance controls that have been implemented to mitigate key risks have been in place for the period, on an ongoing basis and are regularly reviewed.

Reading School:

CAPACITY TO HANDLE RISK

The Governing Body has reviewed the key risks to which Reading School is exposed together with the operating, financial and compliance controls that have been implemented to mitigate those risks. The Governing Body is of the view that there is a formal ongoing process for identifying, evaluating and managing the Academy School's significant risks that has been in place for the period ended 31 August 2012 and up to the date of approval of the Governors' Annual Report and financial statements. This process is regularly reviewed by the board of Governors.

■ *Risk and control framework*
This sets out the framework for the risk management process including the segregation of duties and system of delegation and accountability whether by way of Responsible Officer, internal or external auditor or a finance director of another academy by way of peer review.

Reading School:

THE RISK AND CONTROL FRAMEWORK

Reading School's system of internal financial control is based on a framework of regular management information and administrative procedures including the segregation of duties and a system of delegation and accountability. In particular, it includes:

■ comprehensive budgeting and monitoring systems with an annual budget and periodic financial reports which are reviewed and agreed by the Governing Body;
■ regular reviews by the Finance and Property Committees of reports which indicate financial performance against the forecasts and of major purchase plans, capital works and expenditure programmes;
■ setting targets to measure financial and other performance;
■ clearly defined purchasing (asset purchase or capital investment) guidelines, delegation of authority and segregation of duties; and
■ identification and management of risks.

The Governing Body has considered the need for a specific internal audit function and has decided not to appoint an internal auditor. However, the Governors have appointed Mr David Fisher, a governor, as Responsible Officer (RO). The RO's role includes giving advice on financial matters and performing a range of checks on the Reading School's financial systems. The Governors have also appointed Baker Tilly Tax and Accounting Limited to review business processes in the areas of payroll, purchases, income and the accounting system. Over the accounting period no material control weaknesses have been identified.

■ *Review of effectiveness*

The accounting officer is responsible for ensuring that the system of internal control is effective and this section confirms that this is reviewed and gives details of the mechanisms informing the process. Details are also given of any action required to address weaknesses identified and to ensure continuous improvement of the system.

Reading School:

REVIEW OF EFFECTIVENESS

As Accounting Officer, A.M Robson (J.I. Weeds for the period ended 31 August 2012) has responsibility for reviewing the effectiveness of the system of internal control. During the year in question the review has been informed by:

■ The work of the external auditor;
■ The financial management and governance self-assessment process; and
■ The work of the executive managers within the Reading School who have responsibility for the development and maintenance of the internal control framework.

The Accounting Officer has been advised of the implications of the result of their review of the system of internal control by the Finance Committee and a plan to ensure continuous improvement of the system is in place.

Statement on regularity, propriety and compliance

Although there is a straightforward model format included within the Accounts Direction which provides the contents, this statement is extremely important. It includes confirmation that public money has been spent for the purposes intended by Parliament (regularity) in line with the relevant authorities and legislation. The accounting officer must specifically make a formal declaration that they have met their personal responsibilities to Parliament for the resources under their control during the year.

Connected to this is the concept of 'propriety'; the accounting officer must confirm that appropriate standards of conduct, behaviour and corporate governance have been maintained when applying the funds under their control. There are no guidelines over what propriety could cover, but it could include matters such as fairness, integrity, the avoidance of private profit from public business, even handedness in the appointment of staff, open competition in the letting of contracts and avoidance of waste and extravagance.

Oversight of internal control processes should be performed throughout the year to ensure that the academy is working within the boundaries of regularity and propriety. This could include:

- review of management reporting documents;
- review of trustees'/governors' minutes;
- confirming compliance with the academy's scheme of delegation;
- ensuring outcomes and recommendations from the FMGS report have been implemented; and
- adherence to tendering policies.

The audit committee, responsible officer and internal auditor (or equivalent) also provide independent checking of financial controls, systems, transactions and risks which can be used to inform the accounting officer.

The accounting officer also has a responsibility to advise the board and the EFA of any instances of irregularity or impropriety, or non-compliance with the terms of the trust's funding agreement. The accounting officer must, therefore, confirm that there have been no instances of material irregularity, impropriety or funding non-compliance, but if there are they must confirm that such instances have been reported to the board and the EFA.

Statement of trustees' responsibilities

After the trustees' report, governance statement and the statement on regularity, propriety and compliance, a statement of trustees' responsibilities must be included. This acknowledges the requirements imposed by company law. Trustees are required to prepare the trustees' report and financial statements, maintain adequate accounting records, safeguard the assets and must not approve the financial statements unless they are satisfied that they give a true and fair view of the state of affairs of the academy. It should also set out the financial reporting framework that has been applied, which will comprise UK Generally Accepted Accounting Practice, and the Accounts Direction issued by the EFA.

Independent auditor's report on the financial statements

The auditors are independent accountants who are registered to carry out the auditing function. They certify that the accounts are drawn up in accordance with the requirements of the Companies Act and appropriate accounting standards including the Academies' Accounts Direction issued by the EFA.

The auditor also confirms that in their opinion the financial statements give a true and fair view of the state of the academy's affairs as at 31 August and of its incoming resources and application of resources, including its income and expenditure, for the year then ended.

Independent auditor's report on regularity

The auditor explains the basis on which the audit was conducted and confirms that nothing has come to their attention which suggests that in all material respects the expenditure disbursed and income received during the period has not been applied to purposes intended by Parliament and the financial transactions do not conform to the authorities which govern them.

COMMENT

Martin Wyatt, Partner at Whitley Stimpson LLP:

'Under the requirements of the Academy's Funding Agreement, the annual financial statements must be audited. The requirement for an audit of the annual financial statements is also set out in the *Academies Financial Handbook*, the Companies Act 2006 and Charities Act 2011.

The purpose of the audit is to provide an opinion to the members of the Academy as to whether the annual financial statements present a 'true and fair' view of the financial position and results of the Academy for the year/period.

There is also a requirement, under the *Academies Financial Handbook* and related guidance issued by the EFA, to report on the Regularity and Propriety of public funds. This is that public funding provided by the Government to the Academy has been used for the purposes intended.

What does this all mean?
It is about providing assurance to the EFA (and DfE), the Government and the public on the governance and accountability of the School and on the appropriate use and application of public funds

It is a process which is aimed at identifying whether there are any material oversights, accounting errors and over-optimistic predictions included within the annual financial statements. Sometimes, it can unearth serious issues such as fraud.

Gathering the evidence required to work out whether an organisation's claims about income and expenditure and its financial position are true and fair.

Auditors do not test and look at everything. It is about focusing on the "key" risks in each Academy and gathering sufficient evidence through various tests, observations and enquiries that can support a conclusion that the financial statements are "true and fair".

Auditors do not specifically test for fraud when undertaking an audit, but they do ensure there is review of areas where fraud could occur and ensure our tests and enquiries are directed at these areas. Auditors also have a responsibility to report to the Governors whether any instances of fraud have come to our attention during the course of the audit.

An important concept to remember is "going concern". The audit is carried out on the assumption that the Academy will be in a position to carry on its activities for the following 12 months.

If the auditor finds good reasons to doubt the Academy's ability to carry on, then this must be reflected in the Auditor's Report.'

Financial statements

Producing the statutory accounts is a complex matter and should be done by a qualified accountant or suitably experienced person. The process will vary depending on the accounting software used by the academy and what method is being used for converting the accounting records into the statutory accounting format.

Overspending is absolutely forbidden for academies, so meticulous budget monitoring is essential.

Statement of financial activities for the year (including income and expenditure account and statement of total recognised gains and losses)

The accounts are made up of a number of financial (or 'primary') statements:

- The Statement of Financial Activities (SOFA) is a record of income and expenditure, although it does not follow the format of a conventional income and expenditure account.
- The balance sheet provides a snapshot of assets, liabilities and capital as at 31 August. There is a model format included in the Accounts Direction.
- A cash-flow statement will record movements of cash into and out of the academy.
- Notes to the financial statements should provide further information including details of the academy's accounting policies. The notes provide a detailed analysis and are a major part of the accounts.

There has been some consternation about the requirement for staff governors' remuneration to be disclosed. EFA guidance has now relaxed the requirement so that disclosure is in £10,000 bandings for both staff trustees/governors and the accounting officer.

Approval

Once the annual reports and accounts are prepared they are formally approved by the board. The directors' report, the statement of trustees' responsibilities and the financial statements must be approved by the board of directors and all documents are signed on behalf of the directors, generally by the chair, with the date of approval and name of signatory stated.

The annual reports and accounts are also presented to the members. Historically this was done at the AGM however, private companies no longer have to hold an AGM unless their articles of association contain the requirement (some versions of the model articles include the requirement) (see Chapter 6). In these circumstances, the accounts must be sent to all members by the time they are due to be filed with Companies House.

It is feasible for the articles of association to be amended so that documentation including accounts can be provided to members by means of publication on a website. This is a provision more generally used by large companies with great numbers of members and is unlikely to be required by most academies. In any event, members will retain the right to request paper copies.

Filing

Academies must submit accounts to Companies House within nine months of the date to which the accounts are made up (i.e. by 31 May). Filing may be done through the Companies House e-filing service or through submission of a paper filing.

The deadlines for filing are initially set by the incorporation date of the company, which may not correlate with the date of conversion or the date when the academy commenced operations. For the first period, accounts may be prepared for a period of more than 12 months. These must be delivered to Companies House:

- within 21 months of the date of incorporation; or
- three months from the accounting reference date, whichever is longer.

EXAMPLE

Deadlines for filing

Presdales School Academy Trust:

- 14 March 2012 – Company incorporated
- 1 April 2012 – Converted to academy status
- 31 August 2013 – Accounts made up to ARD
- 14 December 2013 – Accounts due to be filed at Companies House

For filing, the copies of the accounts must state the following:

- the copy of the balance sheet must be signed by a director;
- the copy of the balance sheet must show the printed name of the director who signed it on behalf of the board even if the signature is legible;
- the copy of the directors' report must include the printed name of the director or company secretary who signed the report on behalf of the board; and
- the copy of the auditor's report must state the auditor's name. Where the auditor is a firm the auditor's report must state the name of the auditor and the name of the person who signed it as senior statutory auditor on behalf of the firm.

COMMENT

Martin Wyatt, Partner with Whitley Stimpson LLP sets out a timetable for submission and publication of accounts

'I would describe the current reporting deadline of 31 December as at the very least nonsensical and at the most as farcical.

With most schools concentrating on end-of-year plays and concerts in reality an academy has little more than three months to have its accounts completed, audited and agreed by the governing body and then signed by specific governing officers.

The example accounts in the Accounts Direction, Coketown Academy, consist of 39 pages. It is not unusual to have accounts with more pages than this, such are the disclosures currently necessary for the accounts.

Action required by 31 December – reporting to the EFA
The following documents must be submitted to the EFA by 31 December:

- A copy of the audited accounts, comprising:
- – a trustees' report – signed by the chair of trustees, or another trustee;
- – a governance statement – signed by both the chair and the accounting officer;
- – a statement on regularity propriety and compliance – signed by the accounting officer;
- – a statement of trustees' responsibilities – signed by the chair of trustees;
- – an independent auditor's report on the financial statements – signed by the auditor;
- – an independent auditor's report on regularity – signed by the auditor; and
- – a set of financial statements and supporting notes – including a balance sheet signed by the chair of trustees, or another trustee.
- A copy of the auditor's management letter. This will provide details of the auditor's findings from their audit, including any significant concerns if arising. The academy's response to the issues raised in the letter must also be submitted.
- A value-for-money statement.

The accounts and management letter must be submitted as scanned electronic documents only, in pdf form, to the following EFA e-mail address: AcademiesFinancialMonitoring.EFA@education.gsi.gov.uk.

The board of trustees should prepare, and agree with their auditor, an accounts preparation and audit timetable that enables the 31 December deadline to be achieved.

The timetable should incorporate the date of the trustees' meeting at which the accounts will be approved and signed.

The above is easily written in two very short paragraphs; in reality this can soon become a distant and moving target.

Accounts action required by 31 May – reporting to Companies House
In addition to submitting audited accounts to the EFA, academies must also file them with Companies House. Under section 442(2a) of the Companies Act 2006 accounts must be filed with Companies House within nine

months of the end of the accounting period. For academies this will be no later than 31 May.

However, where an academy is preparing accounts for its first period after incorporation and is preparing them for a period of greater than 12 months, then under s.442(3) CA 2006 the accounts must be filed within 21 months of incorporation, or within three months of the end of the accounting period, whichever is later.

Companies House will levy automatic penalties on a rising scale if accounts are filed late.

Accounts action required by 31 May – publication of accounts on academy's website
Academies are required to publish their accounts in full on their website. To maximise transparency and openness this should be done as soon as possible after the accounts are signed, but no later than 31 May 2014.

Accounts action no longer required – reporting to the Charity Commission
As exempt charities, academies are not required to submit their accounts to the Charity Commission.

Academies should notify HMRC that the entity is a charity or it will be asked to complete a tax return. This will require iXBRL tagged accounts at extra cost.

New academies

The Companies Act allows newly converted academies to have their first accounting period other than the usual 12-month period. As long as the period is more than six months, it can be up to 18 months from the date of incorporation of the company and ending with its accounting reference date (i.e. 31 August).

EXAMPLE

Martin Wyatt, Partner with Whitley Stimpson LLP provides a 2013 example:

- an academy incorporated on or before 28 February 2013 would have to prepare the first accounts from the date of incorporation up to 31 August 2013 because deferral to 31 August 2014 would take it beyond the permitted 18-month maximum period;
- an academy incorporated on or after 1 March 2013 may, if it wishes, defer preparation of the first accounts to 31 August 2014. The accounts would cover the period from the date of incorporation to 31 August 2014.

Note that it is the incorporation date (i.e. the date of company registration at Companies House), not the academy operational opening date which is relevant to these provisions.

Value for money statement

All academies must complete an annual 'value for money statement' (VFM) which is a free-standing return that is not part of the annual report and accounts. The statement does not need to be audited by external auditors. It is a self-assessment of what the academy has done to maximise the impact of their money.

The statement must be signed by the accounting officer and a copy of the signed statement emailed to the EFA by 31 December each year. It must also be published on the academy's website within one month of submission to the EFA.

COMMENT

Martin Wyatt, Partner with Whitley Stimpson LLP:

'Academy accounting officers are personally responsible and publicly accountable for achieving the best possible value for money in their academy. The governors will also come under scrutiny on the basis they should be challenging spending decisions to ensure that funding is used effectively. The purpose of the VFM is to provide accounting officers with an opportunity to demonstrate to parents and the public that the academy's use of public assets and funds has provided good value for money during the period and to identify opportunities for potential improvement.

Although the requirements of the VFM are not prescriptive, you must include examples of areas where value for money has been achieved and where improvements could be made. You will need to demonstrate the policies and procedures in place which ensure you are achieving the best possible educational and wider societal outcomes through the economic, efficient and effective use of all resources in the Academy's charge.

The EFA have produced some guidance for academies in completing the VFM. Overall, there is no definitive structure or content of the VFM and all the information in the EFA guidance is merely suggested.

However, whilst the VFM does not need to be lengthy it should include the information that is most relevant and appropriate to the Academy, and should emphasise those issues that had the greatest impact on the Academy's use of resources during the period.

The headings included in the EFA guidance as suggestions of areas to cover and include the following:

- **Improving educational results**: Utilising current resources effectively to improve results (e.g. conducting staff reviews to ensure teachers are in the most appropriate areas and sharing resources with other academies).
- **Financial governance and oversight**: Using up-to-date financial reporting to review financial performance in line with budgets and identifying if there are spare resources that could be better utilised.

- **Better purchasing**: This could include where contracts have been reviewed or renegotiated, or working with other academies to generate economies of scale.
- **Better income generation**: Identifying areas where additional income has been generated, such as lettings or other fundraising events. This could also provide evidence of how the academy has been providing benefits to the wider community.
- **Reviewing controls and managing risks:** Each academy will have prepared a risk register but it is important to demonstrate this is reviewed regularly and that new risks and opportunities are recognised on a timely basis and appropriate action taken.
- **Lessons learned**: What has the academy learned from its previous decisions and strategies in order to make the budget go further?'

Auditors

The funding agreement requires that accounts be audited annually by independent auditors. The auditor must be independent of the academy and hold a current audit-practising certificate issued by a recognised supervisory body. The audit will be carried out in accordance with International Standards on Auditing and will examine evidence relevant to the amounts and disclosures in the financial statements.

Members appoint the auditor who will produce a report stating whether the academy has prepared financial statements in accordance with company law and relevant accounting standards and the financial reporting framework. The auditor will also state whether the accounts give a true and fair view of the affairs at the end of the financial year.

An auditor can be removed from office at any time during their term of office. The members or directors give 28 days' notice of the intention to put to a members' general meeting a resolution to remove the auditor. A copy of the notice of the general meeting must be sent to the auditor who has the right to provide a written response which must be circulated to members. The auditor also has the right to attend and speak at the meeting when the resolution will be considered. Members will pass an 'ordinary resolution' to remove the auditor on a simple majority (i.e. at least 50% plus one of the votes cast). It is not possible to remove an auditor using the written resolution method.

Within 14 days of the resolution being passed, Form AA03 'Notice of resolution removing auditors from office' must be filed at Companies House (see Chapter 6).

Care should be taken when removing an auditor during their term of office as they may be entitled to damages for breach of contract or another form of compensation. A better approach would be to consider not reappointing the auditor for a further term.

When an auditor ceases to hold office, for whatever reason, he must deposit a statement at the registered office setting out any circumstances connected with his ceasing to hold office that he considers should be brought to the attention of the members and the EFA. The company must send a copy of this statement to all members or apply to the court to avoid having to do so within 21 days of the statement being deposited with the company. If the auditor does not receive notification of an application to the court within 21 days, they must send a copy of the statement to Companies House within a further seven days.

Where the auditor resigns or is removed, the auditor and company are obliged to notify the 'appropriate audit authority' (i.e. the EFA) under ss 522–525 CA 2006.

Whole of Government Accounts

Academies are classified as central government public sector bodies any must comply with central government accounting practices. This means that they are required to produce returns in respect of Whole of Government Accounts (WGA) each year.

COMMENT

Martin Wyatt, Partner with Whitley Stimpson LLP:

'We are given no time for smug satisfaction that year-end accounts and documents have been submitted by the deadline of 31 December. The old adage "It's not over 'til the Fat Lady sings" is very true. In this instance it's not over until the Academies Accounts Return (AAR) is submitted to the EFA.

Having completed, reviewed and indeed audited the AAR, I can confirm it is a voluminous spreadsheet to complete and you are inclined to break into celebratory singing on successful submission of the return.

In order for the EFA to complete and submit its own accounts for the Whole of Government accounts it must first obtain data from all academies.

For academies who have completed accounts for the year ended 31 August they must complete and submit the AAR by, currently, the following 31 January.

For new academies who have not completed accounts for the preceding 31 August they must complete an AAR for the period from opening to 31 March and submit by 30 June. An existing MAT that has opened new academies will need to complete and submit an accounts return for each new academy for the period to 31 March.

The EFA issue a very detailed spreadsheet to academies to capture and collate the accounts data needed for the Whole of Government accounts.

On accountants' forums there is now an annual race for the first person to find an error and the greatest number of errors in the spreadsheet. For those school business managers completing the return always find out from your auditor which cells contain errors; this will help you to avoid burning too many midnight candles to complete the return.

In EFA Bulletin 44 issued on 23 January 2014, the EFA issued the following helpful comment eight days before submission to the EFA. "On the accounts return itself, a number of single academy trusts and their auditors have noted that error messages appear in the 'Funds – for multi academy trusts only' box (lines 828–935). Single academy trusts should ignore these messages." Helpful indeed.

Academy trusts will need to commission from their external auditors an assurance report on the preparation of the AAR.'

Summary

Accounting and tax

- The funding agreement requires compliance with the *Academies Financial Handbook* which sets out financial requirements.
- The *Handbook* is supplemented by the Academies' Accounts Direction, which is issued annually and sets out the technical details to fulfil the requirements to:
  - prepare an annual report and financial statements to 31 August;
  - have these 'accounts' audited by an independent auditor;
  - deliver a statement of regularity, propriety and compliance and obtain a regularity assurance report on this statement from the auditor;
  - submit the audited accounts to the EFA by 31 December;
  - file the accounts with Companies House as required under the Companies Act 2006; and
  - arrange an independent audit of regularity and include the auditor's report on regularity as part of the trust's accounts.
- As charitable companies, accounts must be prepared under the Charities' Statement of Recommended Practice (SORP).

Annual report and accounts

- Accounts must be produced for the 12-month accounting period ending on 31 August.
- The annual report and accounts must be filed with Companies House by 31 May comprising:

- reports covering a trustees' report, governance statement, a statement on regularity, propriety and compliance, a statement of trustees' responsibilities and an independent auditor's reports on the financial statements and on regularity; and
- financial statements including a statement of financial activities, a balance sheet, a cash-flow statement and notes expanding on the statements.
- The annual report and accounts must be approved by the board of directors. They are also presented to members.
- Academies must submit accounts to Companies House by 31 May, nine months after the end of the accounting period. There are alternative arrangements for the first period when accounts are prepared for a period of more than 12 months.

New academies
- Newly converted academies may have a first accounting period of up to 18 months from the date of incorporation ending with their accounting reference date.

Value for Money statement
- Academies must complete an annual VFM which must be e-mailed to the EFA by 31 December.

Auditors
- Accounts must be audited by independent auditors who state whether the accounts give a true and fair view of the academy's affairs at the end of the financial year.

Whole of Government Accounts
- Academies are central government public sector bodies and must produce returns in respect of Whole of Government Accounts each year.

12 Corporate governance

▨ In this chapter

This chapter looks at the way in which an academy ensures a robust and effective self-regulating management system including:

- mechanisms to promote corporate governance such as remuneration of directors, independent directors and obligations imposed by Ofsted;
- managing conflict of interests;
- delegation of authority and the remit of committees and the chief executive officer/principal; and
- establishing a vision and strategy for the academy.

There is no recognised definition of the term 'corporate governance' but it is generally used to refer to the way in which a company is directed and controlled with a framework that monitors actions and decisions. The interests of the various stakeholders need to be balanced through a system of rules and procedures.

Major scandals such as Enron, Parmalat and BCCI have already arisen in the corporate world and have led to an increased focus on corporate governance. The Cadbury Committee published a report 'Financial Aspects of Corporate Governance' in 1992 which made recommendations on the arrangement of company boards and accounting systems to mitigate risks and failures. The resultant UK Corporate Governance Code expanded this to state that the purpose of corporate governance is 'to facilitate effective, entrepreneurial and prudent management that can deliver the long-term success of the company'. The principles contained in the Code are primarily aimed at listed companies, although non-listed public and private companies are also encouraged to comply with the requirements. The principles relating to the operation of the board should be considered by free schools and academies, not least because they are the recipients of public funding:

- Every company should be headed by an effective board which is collectively responsible for the long-term success of the company.
- The board and its committees should have the appropriate balance of skills,

experience, independence and knowledge of the company to enable them to discharge their respective duties and responsibilities effectively.

- The board should present a fair, balanced and understandable assessment of the company's position and prospects.

Failure to observe these principles leaves a board of directors open to criticism that it has not acted appropriately and has failed to fulfil the requirements of their funding agreement.

Academies are autonomous organisations free of local authority control. This also brings greater emphasis on effective, accountable and more independent governance.

Corporate governance mechanisms

Academies must establish and adopt mechanisms to promote good corporate governance and increase accountability.

Directors in academies are generally not entitled to be remunerated and this is reflected in the model funding agreement. Apart from the chief executive officer (CEO) and any member of staff, no director may be employed by, or receive any remuneration from, the academy. The remuneration paid should be 'reasonable in all the circumstances' and the individual director concerned should be absent from any discussion of his/her employment, remuneration, or performance in the employment. Furthermore, the total number of directors employed by the academy must be no more than one-third of the total number of directors – this figure is calculated including the principal, executive principal or chief executive.

There is a widespread recognition of the importance of the role of the chair and there have been calls to allow academies to offer remuneration.

COMMENT

Janet Aldridge, Chief Operating Officer of FASNA:

'FASNA's position is that remuneration for chairs should be neither mandatory nor banned. We are not lobbying for it to be paid, but feel that academies should have this increased flexibility so that the board can debate and discuss payment to their chair and make an informed decision. The time implications for a chair of governors are significant and being able to financially remunerate an individual might enable the right person to be able to do the job!

For a school in a category, the chair needs considerable time and experience. The decision should be made by the school as to what is appropriate for them and it may not be forever but change according to the circumstances.'

High levels of remuneration for board members, particularly in public companies, have been the subject of much media criticism. It is essential that academies ensure that any pay or other rewards to directors are granted through transparent mechanisms. The UK Corporate Governance Code states:

> There should be a formal and transparent procedure for developing policy on executive remuneration and for fixing remuneration packages of individual directors. No director should be involved in deciding his or her own remuneration.

The Code also recommends establishment of a remuneration committee comprising three independent, non-executive directors (NEDs) which sets the level of remuneration for executive directors. With the greater freedoms available to academies in setting staff pay and rewards, this is likely to become of greater importance as time goes on.

Directors' remuneration must be disclosed in the annual accounts within £10,000 bands. Confirmation is also given that they only receive remuneration in respect of their staff roles and not for their services as directors.

The National Governors' Association recognises eight key elements of effective governance:

- the right people around the table;
- understanding roles and responsibilities;
- good chairing;
- professional clerking;
- good relationships based on trust;
- knowing the school – the data, the staff, the parents, the children, the community;
- commitment to asking challenging questions; and
- the confidence to have courageous conversations in the interests of the children and young people.

The board is required to plan strategically and to produce a board development plan which is both informed by and feeds into the school development plan, training and development plan and budget.

Independent directors

The role of non-executive director (NED) (i.e. a director who is not an employee of the company) has gained increasing prominence over recent years. The Higgs Report, published in 2003, called NEDs the 'custodians of the governance process'; they bring a level of independence which is essential for robust governance. Their impartial viewpoint will assist in developing policy and constructing effective development plans and, as they are not involved in the management of the academy, they can objectively monitor the activities of the executive.

It is important to note that directors who do not work for the academy may not necessarily be independent. A classic situation is where a director is married to an academy employee and may well have a personal interest in some of the decisions made. Whilst there is no need to exclude such individuals, it is extremely important that their relationship or circumstances are clearly noted and the situation managed appropriately.

Of course, although this type of director may not work for the academy, they may work elsewhere or have other significant commitments. Their role is fundamental to the running of the academy, helping to set the strategic direction and provide oversight of the day-to-day, yet they are volunteers and receive no benefit. Concerns are regularly expressed over the amount of time that directors have to devote to become truly involved in the business of the academy. There may be a tendency for directors to rely on the executive to draw attention to areas that need consideration and this is a weakness in the system of oversight. They must be proactive in seeking information and understanding the workings of the organisation.

The appointment of NEDs is extremely important and care should be taken over the process of selection (see Chapter 7). However, the Articles of Association may provide that certain appointments to the board are made through an election process.

Ofsted

Ofsted makes clear the requirements undertaken by governors which relate to directors in academies. 'Ofsted Subsidiary Guidance: Supporting the Inspection of Maintained Schools and Academies' published in September 2013 states:

> Inspectors must evaluate the extent to which governors both challenge and support the school and hold senior staff, including the head teacher, to account for the achievement of the pupils. ... they hold important strategic responsibilities for the development and improvement of the school.

Directors other than staff directors are not expected to be routinely involved in the day-to-day activity of the school and would only visit lessons where there were clear protocols and the purpose was understood by school staff and governors alike.

Ofsted also requires that:

'Inspectors should consider whether governors:
- carry out their statutory duties;
- understand the strengths and weaknesses of the school, including the quality of teaching;
- ensure clarity of vision, ethos and strategic direction;
- understand and take sufficient account of pupil data, particularly their understanding and use of the school data dashboard;
- are aware of the impact of teaching on learning and progress in different subjects and year groups;
- are challenging and supporting leadership in equal measure;
- are providing support for an effective head teacher, or whether they are hindering school improvement by failing to tackle key concerns;
- are transparent and accountable, including in terms of governance structures, attendance at meetings, and contact with parents and carers;
- understand how the school makes decisions about teachers' salary progression;
- performance manage the head teacher rigorously; and
- are failing to perform well and contributing to weaknesses in leadership and management.'

Any failure by directors to fulfil these requirements will indicate a weakness in the 'quality of leadership in, and management of, the school' and may lead to a school being judged as 'requires improvement' or worse. This would have significant repercussions for the school and the board.

Code of Governance

COMMENT

Lindsay Driscoll, the Independent Chair of the Governance Code Steering Group, explained:

'The Code of Governance was drafted for all voluntary and community organisations including registered and exempt charities and non-charitable bodies. The high-level principles are applicable to all these organisations. The examples given for the application of the Principles are not intended to be prescriptive and not all the examples given will be relevant for all organisations. We have tried to indicate where a point is only applicable to registered charities or to companies. The Code would need to be read in conjunction with any special rules for Academies but the Principles and much of the examples should be relevant.'

'Good Governance – A Code for the Voluntary and Community Sector' sets out clear key principles that organisations should abide by:

An effective board will provide good governance and leadership by:

1. Understanding their role.
2. Ensuring delivery of organisational purpose.
3. Working effectively both as individuals and as a team.
4. Exercising effective control.
5. Behaving with integrity.
6. Being open and accountable.

The aim of the Code is to help organisations improve their governance by applying the six principles. However, as its website points out: 'It is about flexibility and proportionality, not uniform standards' taking account of 'an understanding of people and their roles as well as policies and systems.'

Self-regulation

Although the principles of corporate governance should apply to academies, they are run by volunteers acting as directors who may lack the skills or experience to understand their obligations. They are not aware of the requirements, never mind ignoring them. Most corporate bodies have professional individuals involved with the administration of their corporate governance. If errors can occur in this situation, what hope is there for academies?

Just like the corporate governance scandals that occupied the media in previous years, the instances of failures in academies are few and far between. This is, of course, no reason to ignore the problems.

A robust process to ensure ongoing financial and regulatory oversight is required to ensure that all academies and their directors are appropriate guardians of funding and use it for the benefit of their pupils. One way of ensuring that the obligations are being met at school level is to engage the services of a company secretarial advisor who can highlight the areas of risk and ensure that a robust system in put into place.

Effective governance is something that the academy must put in place itself; it will not be imposed by any external body or via government intervention. In fact, DfE strategy appears to have noted its inability to get involved in the governance of each academy and favours the role of overseeing regulator.

COMMENT

Graham Burns, Partner with Stone King:

Removal of the Secretary of State's Powers of Intervention

One of the key recent changes made to the DfE's Model Articles has been the removal of the Secretary of State's power to become involved in the governance of the Academy Trust. Prior to the publication of the DfE's updated Model Articles in January 2013, the Secretary of State was able to exercise his powers to appoint Members and also to appoint Governors onto the board of the Academy trust. Since this power has been removed the Secretary of State is no longer able to 'flood' the board of Directors.

As a compromise the Secretary of State now has the power to terminate the funding agreement if an Academy is designated as requiring significant improvement.

This change in approach seems to indicate a realisation by the DfE that as the number of academies continues to grow the power to flood the board of an Academy trust is an increasingly impractical tool for a centralised regulator without the local resources to implement it. In addition, it does not seem appropriate for a seemingly independent charitable company to be subject to such intervention in its governance. In practical terms, it is envisaged the DfE would no doubt prefer to have greater powers to terminate the funding agreement.

▨ Conflict of interest

It is essential that a fair and just process is applied at all times in the governance process. One obvious way in which this may be skewed is where a person involved in that process has a conflict of interest (e.g. where the individual has other interests which could possibly influence or corrupt their motivation or decision making).

There is often a focus on financial or 'pecuniary' interests which are easier to quantify objectively. However, conflict can arise in connection with any interests such as recommending a specific group of people or personal promotion.

Section 175 of the Companies Act 2006 states:

A director of a company must avoid a situation in which he has, or can have, a direct or indirect interest that conflicts, or possibly may conflict, with the interests of the company.

A conflict of interest may arise both from a 'direct' personal interest and an 'indirect' interest (e.g. arising through a relative or another business that the director is involved with). Directors have a duty to avoid conflicts of interest and must declare any interest in any transaction or arrangement or any proposed transaction or arrangement prior to it taking effect.

There are also strict rules regarding the benefits which may be received by trustees under charity law. In general, trustees cannot be employed by, or receive any remuneration from, the academy in their role as a trustee except in the case of an Executive Principal. Trustees may receive a benefit from the academy in the capacity of a beneficiary of the academy (i.e. with no preferential treatment arising due to their role as trustee). They can sell goods, services or any interest in land to the academy, or receive interest on money lent to the academy, only if the amounts concerned are 'reasonable in all the circumstances' and 'it is in the interests of the Academy Trust to employ or to contract with that Governor rather than with someone who is not a Governor'. Any benefit received must be disclosed in the annual report and accounts.

It is essential that any potential conflict of interest is identified and managed. To ensure transparency, this should extend to situations where the director's interests may appear to influence the director's decision making or be seen to have the potential to do so. The conflict will be seen to arise if circumstances reasonably indicate a risk that decisions may be unduly influenced, whether or not an individual actually is, or would be, so influenced.

It is good practice to have a policy on conflicts of interest which, in the interests of transparency, is available publicly. Appropriate procedures to be followed when a trustee is subject to a conflict of interest, could include:

- the removal of the director concerned from the decision-making process;
- managing the conflict of interest once a decision has been made; and
- recording details of the discussions and decisions made.

It should be noted that where a director is absent from part of a meeting due to a conflict of interest, they will not count towards the quorum.

There is no longer a statutory requirement to maintain a register of directors' interests. However, it remains good practice to do so, noting any interests that the directors hold (see Chapter 5). It is good practice to extend this to include any key staff that hold delegated authority or have the ability to contract on behalf of the academy. The register should be presented at each board meeting for confirmation that the details contained are accurate.

Upon first appointment, directors should be asked to complete and sign a declaration indicating any interests that could potentially conflict with those of the academy. The declaration should be repeated and the register subsequently updated annually. If circumstances change for any director, they should update their declaration in respect of any actual or potential conflicts as soon as they arise.

A version of a Declaration of Interests form following the ICSA version can be used. It reflects the principles highlighted in 'The Code of Governance for the Voluntary and Community Sector', but remains accessible and user-friendly.

School Academy Trust
Company Number: 1234567
Declaration of Interests

I .... as Member/Governor of ********* School Academy Trust have set out below my interests:

Category	Please give details of the interest and whether it applies to yourself or, where appropriate, a member of your immediate family, connected persons or some other close personal connection.
Current employment and any previous employment in which you continue to have a financial interest.	
Appointments (voluntary or otherwise), e.g. trusteeships, directorships, local authority membership, tribunals etc.	
Membership of any professional bodies, special interest groups or mutual support organisations.	
Investments in unlisted companies, partnerships and other forms of business, major shareholdings and beneficial interests.	
Gifts or hospitality offered to you by external bodies and whether these were declined or accepted in the last 12 months.	
Any contractual relationship with the Academy.	
Any other conflicts that are not covered by the above.	

I certify that I have declared all beneficial interests which I, or any person closely connected to me, have with businesses or other organisations, which may have dealings with this school. To the best of my knowledge, the above information is complete and correct. I undertake to update as necessary the information provided, and to review the accuracy of the information on an annual basis.

Signed: ....

Date: ....

Below is an alternative version, produced by the Cabot Federation:

CABOT LEARNING FEDERATION

ANNUAL DECLARATION OF PECUNIARY AND OTHER INTEREST 2013/14

As part of the Cabot Learning Federation's financial regulations the Federation Board is required to maintain an annual register that lists each member of the Board, the Principal, senior members of Staff and records their individual pecuniary and other potential conflicts of interest.

Staff Interest:	*Board and Council Member's Interest:*
It is important that every staff member completes this record, even if there is nothing to declare, that individuals are aware that they should notify the academy immediately of any changes which would affect their declaration and that individuals should make an annual declaration that the information is accurate.	Board and Council Members are required to register any interest that they or their partners or immediate family may have which could have association with the trading activity of the Federation. This may mean a company or individual that is a supplier to the Federation or a company that purchases services from the Federation or its subsidiary, John Cabot Ventures Ltd. The obligation to disclose also relates to any non–business organisation that may hire premises from the Federation.

Please complete the sections below. **[NIL returns are required]**

1. Board / Council / Staff Member Name: _____

[Please Print]

2. Do you have a business/pecuniary interest? **Yes/No** [delete as appropriate]. If Yes, provide details below (please attach additional sheets if there is insufficient space below):

3. Names of Company / Organisations details:
   [1] ———————————————————————————
   [2] ———————————————————————————
4. Indicate the type of work carried out in each case:
   [1] ———————————————————————————
   [2] ———————————————————————————
5. Relationship of the Company or Organisation to the person completing this form:
   [1] ———————————————————————————
   [2] ———————————————————————————

Signature ———————————————————————————

Date   ———————————————————————————

Delegation of authority

The board is responsible for the operation of the academy as a company. It has authority as a body rather than individually so that any decision making is a collective process of the board; once a resolution has been passed it is binding on all directors, not just those that voted in favour of it.

However, the Articles permit the board to delegate the responsibility for tasks and grant the necessary authority to carry them out to:

- board committees;
- individual directors such as the principal/executive head teacher; and
- members of the Executive (e.g. the business manager) who have responsibility for finance.

Responsibility and accountability will, nevertheless, remain with the board.

The directors can decide on the limit of such delegation and the conditions that should be imposed. No committee or individual should have unfettered powers. The extent and remit of their authority should be made clear. Levels of expenditure are commonly established so that each level in the hierarchy knows what size of contract or purchase agreement they can legally enter.

It is, nevertheless, good governance that major decisions are made by the board as a whole and the matters 'Reserved for the Board' (i.e. which can only be decided upon at board level) should be established and made explicit.

When any delegated authority has been exercised, the person or committee must report to the board 'in respect of any action taken or decision made with respect to the exercise of that power or function'. They must, therefore, formally report to the next board meeting.

A Delegation Planner used at Rush Common School, a single primary academy in Oxfordshire, can be found in Appendix 5.

Committees

The board can set up as many committees as is felt to be appropriate.

A MAT will generally have committees known as local governing bodies linked to each individual school. The LGB is often delegated responsibility for oversight of teaching and learning.

COMMENT

Emma Knights, Chief Executive of the National Governors' Association:

'There may be others involved in governance of academies who are not directors or members. This is particularly the case in multi-academy trusts (MATs), where the trustees govern all the academies in the MAT, but then each school has a local layer of governance. Increasing number of academies now belong to MATs. These are often local governing bodies, and sometimes advisory councils. The roles of a local governing body differ between different academy trusts. It may involve full financial delegation to each school, possibly with a percentage slice for centralised services, or may be a structure that is much more centralised, with local governing bodies looking only at attainment and progression of pupils. The roles should be set out clearly in a delegation document.'

The *Academies Financial Handbook* states that, as a minimum, there should be a finance committee and, in some circumstances, depending on the turnover of the academy, an audit committee.

Constitution and terms of reference for committees should be drafted and reviewed annually. Non-directors can be appointed to committees and be given voting rights as long as the majority of the committee are directors. The Articles do not set out a quorum for meeting so an appropriate quorum can be decided by the board and incorporated in the Terms of Reference. The majority present and voting at any valid committee meeting must be directors.

However, apart from a finance committee, there is no requirement for the board to appoint any committees. There may be other ways of working which are more appropriate for an academy.

EXPERIENCE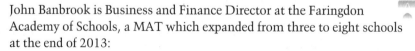

John Banbrook is Business and Finance Director at the Faringdon Academy of Schools, a MAT which expanded from three to eight schools at the end of 2013:

'Previously there was too much bottom-up in committees with consideration of the details. We now have a much more strategic approach and have introduced a business cycle which sets the business to be dealt with on the agenda at a particular point in the year.

The committees are not representative of all schools and this has helped to move to the strategic view.

We may, in time, give consideration to getting rid of the committees and migrate to a bolder model. We would have named leads for each area who would meet regularly with the executive responsible. Ad hoc meetings to deal with committee-type business would be called when required. The board will continue to set the strategy and check it is being done.'

Chief executive officer/Principal

The Articles recognise that day-to-day management of the academy will often be delegated to an individual. In a single academy this will be the Principal (Head teacher) and in a MAT the chief executive officer. This individual plays a central role in the academy but may be known by any one of a number of names: CEO, principal, head teacher, executive head teacher, Director of Learning, etc.

However, there is currently some conflict with regards to where that individual sits within the organisation. The CEO/principal is automatically a member of the board within the model articles. However, the Charity Commission are uncomfortable with this blurring of the board and senior executive.

EXPERIENCE

John Banbrook is Business and Finance Director of the Faringdon Academy of Schools, a MAT in Oxfordshire consisting of one secondary school (the Community College), five primary, one junior and one infant school. He explained:

'We were steered by the DfE to appoint our Executive Headteacher as a director as they should be accountable. However, we came up against opposition from the Charity Commission which did not feel that the Executive Headteacher should be a director but would prefer them as an advisor to the board.'

Different organisational structures may apply.

Vision and strategy

Fundamental to any successful organisation is a coherent vision that encapsulates core values and purpose whilst envisioning a future that the organisation hopes to become or achieve. That vision should set the core principles which underpin everything the organisation does and informs the creation of operational strategies and practices.

Strategy is the direction and scope of an organisation over the long term. That strategy puts into action the vision in a way that is both proactive and also responsive to change.

Academies should consider and set their own vision and strategy. That vision should be a constant that informs and underlies everything that the academy does in the long term. A strategic plan should flow from that.

CASE STUDY

Rush Common School in Oxfordshire:

Vision and Strategy

Our vision is to be an outstanding school where all learners have wide ranging opportunities to develop their talents and abilities.

In response to the ever-changing demands of the 21st century, the school provides a safe, continually improving and inspirational educational environment, making innovative and appropriate use of technologies, so that pupils, staff and the community develop as confident, independent learners with high aspirations. Effective teaching and learning ensures that all learners' capacity to be resourceful and adaptable individuals is developed, so that change and challenge is embraced and the qualities of resilience and self-confidence are fostered.

At the core of the vision is a concept of Rush Common School as the dynamic heart of a flourishing learning community, where high quality on-going professional training and development plus mutually beneficial relationships with wide-ranging agencies and organisations enhance the opportunities and experiences for all learners. Our partnerships encompass the local community and connect with wider learning communities nationally and internationally.

Underpinning the vision is the following set of core values. All pupils and staff are required to:

- Be self-respecting individuals who take personal responsibility for their own learning.
- Work hard and achieve their very best.
- Show respect for, and tolerance of, others and the world in which we live.
- Be sensitive to the needs of others with the capacity to empathise with the experiences of people from diverse communities and backgrounds.
- Display determination, self-discipline and perseverance and to be confident to take 'risks'.
- Be able to respond positively to the challenges they will encounter in the changing learning, work and social environments they will encounter in the 21st century.

Rush Common Academy Trust is a Multi-Academy Trust. The Board of Directors are discussing the school's long term strategy within the current educational landscape to develop the multi-academy status of RCAT.

The vision and strategy in an academy chain is more complicated. Strategy is, however, multi-layered and the over-arching strategic direction will feed down into the strategic plans of individual schools and departments. The board of an academy should be concerned only with the highest level of such strategic planning, but it will ensure that the strategy directs the executive and operational thinking throughout.

CASE STUDY

Vision and strategy is a bigger issue for MATs formed from a coming together of various schools with different histories and structures. A good example is the Faringdon Academy of Schools (FAoS) in Oxfordshire, a MAT consisting of a secondary school (Faringdon Community College), five primary schools, an infant and a junior school. Some of these schools had previously been Community schools whilst others were Church of England VC schools.

Bob Wintringham, Chair of the Board, explains:

'To understand our vision, we have to start long before schools were encouraged to become Academies.

'The governing body of the Community College (FCC) has been evolving over at least 20 years with a low turnover of governors and staff for the majority of that time. This has meant that the level of expertise has remained high and the strategic direction has evolved steadily, taking account of the perpetual change in education whilst always being aware of what is best for FCC. Governors see teaching as a vocation and schools only keep the best teachers if they can retain the motivation and challenge. This means that the whole school team (governing body and staff) need to be at the cutting edge of educational development, with every change part of the long-term push to continually raise standards and create a wider school partnership; a community school, a college, a specialist school, Charter mark etc., etc. – each has had a part to play in our development.

'A clear vision and strategy has meant that we have been able to assess the rainstorm of initiatives from successive governments; each carefully weighed against our own clear objectives to increase the quality of the education of our students.

'But an Academy must be built on trust particularly where schools agree to work together, and the Faringdon Partnership has a long history of mutual trust and support that provided the natural base for closer collaboration.

'So, the journey to Academy status took more than two years to complete. We shared and augmented the FCC vision for the future with our potential partners, and built on it to provide the overall FAoS vision. We were adamant that the pace of improvement would not relax; that smaller primary schools would not feel railroaded by the big secondary; that we needed to build on the successful parts of the local authority education provision and most importantly, that Academy status must bring added value.

'The single vision gives us stability and sustainability, future-proofing and credibility – more than a glib statement but a philosophy for the member schools to follow.

'All schools build their own plans around the strategic objectives which are derived from the central vision.

'The practical application of this vision has led to a proactive Academy School Improvement team, a programme of collaboration between schools towards an all-through curriculum and an altruistic sharing of resource to the greater good of the whole Academy.'

The Strategic Objectives & Key Indicators document used by Faringdon Academy of Schools is contained in Appendix 6.

Academy name

Choosing the name of an academy may not always be straightforward, especially where there is either a MAT or umbrella arrangement with a number of different parties involved. The name encapsulates the vision of that organisation for the future.

EXPERIENCE

One Twitter user, Brian Walton, Headteacher at Headley Park Primary School, summed it up:

@PrimaryHead1 'Thinking of names for our new multi trust academy... Inspire Learning Corporation ... It's like choosing a band name!'

Ensuring cohesion

Many MATs believe that it is important for the individual schools to unite in a single unit both legally and on a practical level. A strong and cohesive academy can share best practice and develop a single vision.

EXPERIENCE

Sujata McNab, Chief Operating Officer of the Cabot Learning Federation:

'The academy chairs meet as a group with the CEO and the chair of the board. They have a free agenda.

It is a really good way for them to air issues and talk through the details. They can share good practice, for example that a particular teacher has achieved a specific qualification which could be of benefit to other academies. They also have an opportunity to discuss things or to escalate anything they wish the board to consider formally. It is a key way that the board links itself to the academies.'

▦ Summary

Corporate governance

- 'Corporate governance' is the way in which a company is directed and controlled with a framework that monitors actions and decisions.
- Every company should be headed by an effective board which is collectively responsible for the long-term success of the company.
- The board and its committees should have the appropriate balance of skills, experience, independence and knowledge of the company to enable them to discharge their respective duties and responsibilities effectively.
- The board should present a fair, balanced and understandable assessment of the company's position and prospects.

Corporate governance mechanisms

- Academies must establish and adopt mechanisms to promote good corporate governance and increase accountability.
- Apart from the CEO and any member of staff, no director may be employed by, or receive any remuneration from, the academy. No more than one-third of the board can be employed by the academy.
- There have been calls to allow payment of chairs of governors.
- Any pay or other rewards to directors must be granted through transparent mechanisms.
- Directors' remuneration must be disclosed in the annual accounts.
- The board should have independent directors who can bring an impartial viewpoint.

- Ofsted makes clear how the requirements undertaken by governors relate to directors in academies. Failure to fulfil these requirements will indicate a weakness in the 'quality of leadership in, and management of, the school'.
- A robust process to ensure ongoing financial and regulatory oversight is required.

Conflict of interest

- Any actual or potential conflict of interest, whether direct or indirect, must be identified and managed. The director should be removed from the decision-making process.
- There are strict rules regarding the benefits which may be received by trustees under charity law.

Delegation of authority

- The board may delegate the responsibility for tasks and the necessary authority to carry them out to board committees, individual directors or members of staff.
- When any delegated authority has been exercised, the person or committee must formally report to the board.
- The board can set up as many committees as is felt to be appropriate. As a minimum there should be a finance committee and, depending on the turnover of the academy, an audit committee.
- Constitution and terms of reference for committees should be drafted and reviewed annually. Non-directors can be appointed to committees and be given voting rights so long as the majority of the committee are directors.
- Day-to-day management of the academy will be delegated to the principal/CEO.

Vision and strategy

- The academy should develop a coherent vision that encapsulates core values and purpose whilst envisioning a future that the organisation hopes to become or achieve.
- The strategy puts into action the vision in a way that is both proactive and also responsive to change.

13 Risk management

▨ In this chapter

This chapter looks at how the board should identify and manage risks that threaten the academy and explains:

- establishment of an appropriate risk management process;
- the particular risks attached to health and safety;
- other aspects for consideration including safeguarding, business continuity and disaster recovery plans and insurance;
- dealing with complaints and appeal panels; and
- review of effectiveness of the board and chair.

Every organisation faces risk in their everyday operation. However, management of risk by identifying and monitoring it is a key part of effective governance and is essential for the successful running of an academy.

The International Organization for Standardization (ISO) defines risk management as 'coordinated activities to direct and control an organisation with regard to risk'. The ISO has established International Standards which sets out principles and guidelines for managing risk in a 'systematic, transparent and credible manner'.

Every academy should develop and adopt a framework for effective risk management which is incorporated into the overall management and strategy as well as reflected in policies and procedures and underlying culture and values. The framework itself should also be subject to continuous review and improvement.

An effective risk management process involves:

- establishing a risk policy;
- identifying risk;
- analysis of specific risks;
- evaluation and, if appropriate, modification of risk; and
- ongoing monitoring.

The framework should be created to fit the specific risks faced by the particular academy reflecting the activities, structure and environment in which it operates. Possible risk categories could include:

- governance;
- operational risk, including health and safety;
- finance risk;
- environmental and external risk; and
- law and regulation compliance risk.

Risk management should consider the effect of uncertainty both in terms of positive and negative impact. Risk could arise as a result of an event that will occur to impact negatively on the academy as well as from the potential that something good will happen.

Risks are then prioritised according to the likelihood of occurrence and the potential loss or impact. Risks with the greatest potential loss and greatest probability of occurring should be managed first.

The resulting 'risk management plan' should identify mitigation strategies. One common mnemonic for a risk strategy is SARA:

- **S**hare risk. Outsource the activity or transfer the risk through insurance.
- **A**void risk. Change the activity or plan so that the problem will not arise.
- **R**educe risk. Take steps to control or mitigate the risk.
- **A**ccept risk. Take the chance that some or all of the potential risk will arise.

Academies are effectively 'service' businesses, so some consideration should be given to 'knowledge risk' where there is deficient knowledge either in academy staff or board or 'relationship risk' where there is ineffective collaboration from departmental level to across schools in an academy chain. These risks will reduce staff efficiency and/or effectiveness, potentially impacting on pupil performance and results and, consequently, increasing reputational risk.

Despite the importance of risk management, it is important that the cost in time and resources on risk management is proportionate and balanced against other pressing needs of the academy.

One key aspect of risk management is effective financial oversight. The *Academies Financial Handbook* contains detailed requirements that must be observed by academies. As the recipient of public money, the obligations on an academy are understandably onerous. Financial monitoring and appropriate internal controls are considered in detail in Chapter 10.

The risk management process should be continually or periodically re-assessed and enhanced and improved whenever possible. The process should become integral to the corporate governance processes, informing board decision-making.

Examples of a risk assessment and risk register are included in Appendices 7 and 8.

Figure 13.1: Faringdon Academy of Schools Risk Management Model

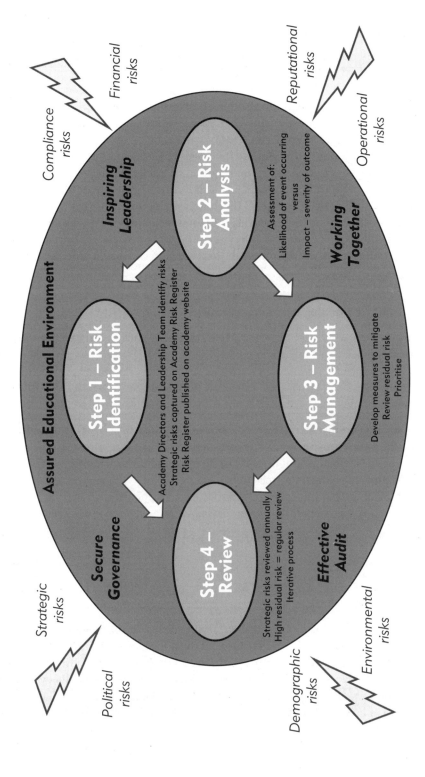

▓ Health and safety

Academies are an employer of staff and must ensure, as far as possible, the 'health, safety and welfare at work' of all employees as well as protecting other people such as pupils or visitors who might be affected by their activities. Further, as an academy will generally also have responsibility for maintenance and repair of its premises, it must ensure that they are 'safe and without risks to health' (Health and Safety at Work Act 1974).

The provisions of the Act are qualified by the words 'so far as is reasonably practicable' so an academy is not required to eliminate the risks entirely if that would be technically impossible or the cost of doing so would be disproportionate to the risk. Academies are, however, required to carry out appropriate risk assessments and take sensible measures to manage any risks identified. Risk management for health and safety is an ongoing process that needs to be kept under constant review. In simple terms, there is a three-step process:

1. Know the risks.
2. Control the risks that need it.
3. Make sure that risks stay controlled.

However, there is a lot of regulation in this area and specialist advice is recommended.

More specific requirements on the academy as employer are set out in the Management of Health and Safety of Work Regulations 1999 (SI 1999/3242) These include:

- making arrangements for implementing the health and safety measures identified as necessary by the risk assessment;
- appointing competent people to help implement the arrangements;
- setting up emergency procedures;
- providing clear information and training to employees; and
- working together with other employers sharing the same workplace.

COMMENT

Solicitor Stuart Armstrong of SV Armstrong has developed a Health & Safety Leadership Checklist as an introduction for those managing academies:

In the event of a serious incident occurring on or off premises, it is likely that there may be an investigation by the police and/or the Health & Safety Executive. Individual governors, trustees, board members as well as officers and employees may all be required to demonstrate that they did everything so far as was reasonably practicable to prevent the incident from happening.

Do board members know what they should be doing to avoid incidents occurring?

The HSE and the Institute of Directors in their Guidance to Directors (INDG 417) suggest three essential principles of effective leadership in health and safety for governors, trustees, officers, directors and their equivalents. These are:

1. Strong and active leadership with:
   - visible, active commitment from the board;
   - established downward communication systems; and
   - good health and safety management integrated with business decisions.
2. Worker involvement that includes:
   - engaging the workforce in the promotion of safe and healthy conditions;
   - effective upward communication; and
   - high quality training.
3. Assessment and review processes that:
   - identify and manage risks;
   - allow access to competent health and safety advice and require that advice to be followed; and
   - include monitoring, reporting and reviewing of health and safety performance.

How should boards put these principles into practice?

- Agree a policy statement that the chief executive signs – for and on behalf of the board.
- Agree on the arrangements for managing safety (who gives the board its competent advice? This should be someone with the relevant training (Diploma in Safety and above) as well as relevant knowledge of the industry, experience in working with the same systems etc. The board should also consider carrying out a training needs assessment to identify who else may need additional training to carry out their roles (first response, manual handling, risk assessment etc). To what extent is everyone aware of their responsibilities for safety in their role etc.).
- Agree on the policies and procedures operating in the organisation.
- Agree on how to implement changes in policy/procedure, monitor the effectiveness of change, review whether the changes are working in practice and continue to review on a regular basis.
- Recognise that a formal management system may take 12–18 months to implement.

Consider whether you could answer the following questions:

- Who is responsible for health and safety in the organisation?
- How does the board demonstrate its commitment to health and safety?

- What information does the board receive to enable it to monitor health and safety performance?
- How does the board communicate and implement its policies on safety?
- What information does the board review?
- Who decides what risks to assess?
- At what level is competent advice given within the organisation?
- Who monitors contractors working on the premises?
- Are the principal risks from premises or activities?
- How does the board ensure adequate supervision of its employees?
- How do employees inform the board if there are problems? Are there examples of these problems, and how were the issues resolved?
- Who is responsible for managing asbestos, and how is it managed? In several school refurbishment projects recently the schools have been criticised for not managing asbestos properly.

If board members are unsure what they should be doing, or whether their organisation is doing the right thing, then they should consider their own health and safety training needs. There are varying levels of health and safety training available.

Particular areas that should be considered for health and safety hazards are:

- Provision of a safe place of work including workstations (Health and Safety (Display Screen Equipment) Regulations 1992 (SI 1992/ 2792)).
- Slips and trips.
- General fire safety.
- Machinery safety (Provision and Use of Work Equipment Regulations 1998 (SI 1998/543)).
- Plant and equipment maintenance.
- Gas and oil fired equipment (Gas Safety (Installation and Use) Regulations 1998 (SI 1994/3140)).
- Workplace Transport (Workplace (Health, Safety and Welfare) Regulations 1992 (SI 1992/3004) and the Provision and Use of Work Equipment Regulations 1998 (SI 1998/2306)).
- Electrical equipment (Electricity at Work Regulations 1989 (SI 1989/635)).
- Harmful substances including asbestos (Control of Asbestos Regulations 2012 (SI 2012/632)) and COSHH (Control of Substances Hazardous to Health Regulations 2002 (SI 2002/2677)).
- Outdoor play equipment.
- Managing health including sickness absence and return to work and work-related stress.
- Adventure activities using licensed providers (Adventure Activities Licensing Regulations 2004 (SI 2004/1309)).

EXPERIENCE

Catherine Barnes, Business Development Manager of The Propeller Academy Trust, a MAT of two special schools, Kingfisher School and Fitzwaryn School, which has the additional expertise of a sponsor organisation, Abingdon and Witney College:

'The head of health and safety at the college is a qualified individual. I can ask him to come to do a health and safety audit for me which he does in a friendly way, offering help and support.

He has a health and safety qualification and is able to provide expertise when we need it. For example, he can provide support in connection with COSHH – we have a Jacuzzi at Fitzwaryn and a swimming pool at Kingfisher which require chemicals.'

The HSE website has a great deal of useful guidance relating to health and safety and includes a health and safety checklist which can be used to identify issues in classrooms.

All staff should be given appropriate health and safety training, although this may only require providing basic instructions. Academies are also legally required to display the HSE-approved law poster or to provide every worker with a leaflet giving the same information. Care should be taken to ensure that any information, instruction and training is available in the worker's native language to maximise understanding.

Particular focus should be given to the specific risks faced by any people with disabilities and new and expectant mothers.

Specific parental consent will be required for off-site activities involving a higher level of risk management or which take place outside school hours. The majority of off-site activities do not require written parental consent although parents should be informed where their child will be at all times.

Academies must provide adequate and appropriate equipment, facilities and qualified first-aid personnel (Health and Safety (First Aid) Regulations 1981 (SI 1981/917)). Emergency procedures should be in place in the event of an incident and workers should be aware of the process to be followed (Management of Health and Safety at Work Regulations 1999 (SI 1999/3242)).

There are obligations under RIDDOR (Reporting of Injuries, Diseases and Dangerous Occurrences Regulations 2013 (SI 2013/1471)) to report certain serious workplace accidents, occupational diseases and specified dangerous occurrences known as 'near misses'.

Safeguarding

As with maintained schools, academies have an obligation under the Education Act 2002 to safeguard pupils by ensuring that there are arrangements in place to ensure that they:

- carry out their functions with a view to safeguarding and promoting the welfare of children; and
- have regard to any guidance issued by the Secretary of State.

These requirements should be reflected in all policies and procedures in place in the academy.

Allegations against staff and volunteers

Any allegation must be reported immediately, generally to the head teacher, who will refer the matter for discussion with the LA Designated Officer (LADO).

Business continuity and disaster recovery plans

A business continuity or disaster recovery plan should be developed and maintained to provide a strategy in the event of a major disaster. This strategic recovery plan would ensure that disruption is minimised in the event of a disaster. Obviously, the likelihood of such an occurrence is small, but the impact would be significant, hence the need for a plan.

Having a plan that staff and directors are familiar with, will ensure that the response to any serious unforeseen event will be prompt and will help towards restoring normal operations.

COMMENT

Philip Cruickshank, Group Sales Assistant at Lucas Fettes & Partners:

'Disaster recovery plans can be a key element to any insurance portfolio and often one that is overlooked. What to do in case of a disaster and what is the best strategy to ensure as little disruption to education as possible are important considerations.

It is important to have a document in place to cope with major disasters such as fire, flood etc.'

Insurance

Under the Employers' Liability (Compulsory Insurance) Act 1969, academies must secure employers' liability insurance which will cover the cost of any compensation payments granted to employees for any injuries or illness sustained as a result of their employment. This is a statutory requirement and an academy can be fined if they do not hold a current employers' liability insurance policy.

Other insurances are not compulsory but should be considered:

- director/governors' and officers' liability;
- absence management, rehabilitation and supply cover;
- buildings, contents and property damage – including accidental or malicious damage;
- business interruption;
- equipment breakdown for engineering and computer equipment, including statutory inspections of pressure, lifting and other plant;
- public liability;
- motor/minibus and occasional business use for teachers' vehicles;
- out-of-school clubs and holiday clubs;
- pupils' personal accident; and
- pupils' personal effects including educational trips.

Academies receive some funding to cover insurance as part of the GAG.

COMMENT

Philip Cruickshank, Group Sales Assistant at Lucas Fettes & Partners explains the importance of a proper valuation:

'Many schools insuring directly with insurers or via purchasing consortiums take their sums insured based on figures supplied by the LA. Often these figures are not a true representation of the cost of a full rebuild. In these cases "average" would come into play meaning that any claim would be reduced proportionately to the true value of the sums insured.'

Risk protection arrangement

The EFA has established a voluntary risk pooling scheme for academies and free schools with effect from 1 September 2014.

The risk protection arrangement (RPA) is not an insurance scheme, but a mechanism through which the cost of risks that materialise will be covered by government funds. The RPA will reimburse academies in the event of a loss outlined in the 'Academies Risk Protection Arrangement Scope' document including:

- loss or damage to property (including minor works);
- increased cost of working following damage to property;
- legal liability to pay compensation to employees for death or injury due to employment with the academy (including as a result of exposure to asbestos);

- legal liability to pay compensation to third parties for death, injury or property damage (including as a result of abuse or exposure to asbestos);
- loss of money and personal baggage whilst travelling on academy business in the UK; and
- loss of academy property due to employee dishonesty.

The RPA will not cover risks related to motor, overseas travel, statutory engineering inspections and works of art.

All academies and multi-academies can choose to opt in to the RPA. Whilst there is no cost or premium to join the RPA, a per-pupil deduction will be made from the academy's general annual grant (GAG) for the first two years.

Dealing with complaints

Under the Education (Independent Schools Standards) Regulations 2010 (SI 2012/2962), Schedule 1, Part 7 academies are under an obligation to set out a formal, written complaints procedure. In practice, this means drafting and approving a complaints policy. The procedure must set out the way that complaints from parents or pupils will be handled and the timescales for the management of the complaint.

Complainants should, in the first instance, always be directed to the academy itself where the majority of complaints will be resolved. If this is unsuccessful, the complaint can initially be considered on an informal basis, but the procedure should involve a requirement for the complaint to be made in writing, initial consideration by the chair of the board and then a formal complaint hearing before a panel constituted by the board and made up of at least three people who were not directly involved in the matters forming the complaint and at least one of whom is independent of the day-to-day management and running of the school.

If a complainant does not feel that their complaint has been satisfactorily resolved, they can, having exhausted the complaints procedure, appeal direct to the Secretary of State for Education through the EFA.

For converter academies, the funding agreement contains obligations relating to complaints arising in whole or in part in the 12 months prior to conversion to ensure that there is continuity and complaints are properly considered.

Although there is no legal requirement on academies to have a complaints procedure in respect of any parties other than parents or pupils, academies may wish to consider complaints made by other parties for the purposes of community cohesion. However, it will be for the board to decide.

Appeal panels

The process for permanent exclusion of a pupil follows that of a maintained school. It will occur only where there has been a serious or persistent breach of the academy's behaviour policy and allowing the pupil to continue in attendance would seriously harm the education or welfare of that pupil or others in the academy. The board must convene a panel to consider the exclusion and decide whether to uphold the decision or overturn it, in which case the pupil will be allowed to return to the academy.

However, any subsequent request for a review of the decision must be presented to an Independent Review Panel within 15 days of such a request being made. In an academy, it will be for the board to convene the panel which must have either three or five members, all of whom must have received training on the process and have a clear understanding of the legal requirements. Independent Review Panels do not have the power to reinstate an excluded pupil.

Similarly, an academy is its own admission authority and any appeal against a decision to refuse admission should be heard by an independent appeal panel comprised of a chair and at least two other panel members. There must be:

- at least one person without any personal experience in the management of any school or provision of education in any school; and
- one person who has experience in education or who is a parent of a registered pupil.

The panel members and the clerk appointed to the panel must be appropriately trained.

In practice, many academies contract with another body (e.g. the local authority) to carry out the admissions functions on their behalf.

▓ Review of board effectiveness

Having an effective board is central to the governance of the academy (see Chapter 12). It is good practice, therefore, to carry out regular reviews of the board and the governance structures in place to ensure that they are effective.

There are now numerous bodies offering external reviews at a cost. Most local authorities provide a service which can be part of wider school improvement services.

However, the board can carry out its own self-review and it is good practice for this to become a regular feature in the annual schedule of work for the board. Various self-audit tools are available

In 2012, the All-Party Parliamentary Group on Education Governance & Leadership published 20 key questions for governing bodies to consider. These can be used as the basis of a self-review:

Right skills
Do we have the right skills on the governing body?
1. Have we completed a skills audit of our governing body?
2. Do we appoint governors on the basis of their skills, and do we know how to find people with the necessary skills?

Effectiveness
Are we as effective as we could be?
3. Do we understand our roles and responsibilities?
4. Do we have a professional clerk and run meetings efficiently?
5. What is our training and development budget and does every governor receive the support they need to carry out their role effectively?
6. Do we know about good practice from across the country?
7. Is the size, composition and committee structure of our governing body conducive to effective working?
8. Does every member of the governing body make a regular contribution and do we carry out an annual review of the governing body's performance?

Strategy
Does the school have a clear vision?
9. Have we developed long-term aims for the school with clear priorities in an ambitious school development plan which is regularly monitored and reviewed?
10. Does our strategic planning cycle drive the governing body's activities and agenda setting?

Accountability of the executive
Do we hold the school leaders to account?
11. Do we understand the school's performance data well enough to properly hold school leaders to account?
12. How effective is our performance management of the headteacher?
13. Are our financial management systems robust and do we ensure best value for money?

Engagement
Are we properly engaged with our school community, the wider school sector and the outside world?
14. How do we listen to and understand our pupils, parents and staff?
15. How do we report to our parents and local community regularly?
16. What benefit do we draw from collaboration with other schools and other sectors, locally and nationally?

Role of chair
Does our chair show strong and effective leadership?
17. Do we carry out a regular 360° review of the chair's performance?
18. Do we engage in good succession planning?
19. Are the chair and committee chairs re-elected each year?

Impact
Are we having an impact on outcomes for pupils?
20. How much has the school improved over the last three years, and what has the governing body's contribution been to this?

A Governor Mark is a national award which gives an external evaluation of the quality of governance. It states:

governing bodies must have in place quality processes if they are to make a significant impact upon the achievements of schools. Intrinsic to this approach is a belief that if governing bodies have adopted such quality processes, the extent of their contribution and influence can make a real difference to the leadership and management of the school.

The Governor Mark Standards Document which sets out the framework criteria together with guidance is freely available on its website.

Following any review, it is essential that the board note the identified strengths and weaknesses and make an action plan for addressing any issues or areas for development.

The principles relating to board review should also be applied to the various committees.

EXPERIENCE

Naureen Khalid, Vice Chair of Governors at Newstead Wood School, has developed a committee/governing body self-evaluation:

'I requested people who attend the committee I chair to complete an evaluation form. The reasoning behind this was that in order to see if the committee was functioning as effectively as it could, I needed to see what everyone thought of our practices. Such evaluations are important for governing bodies and committees in order to highlight areas for development which would then feed into how the identified concerns can be addressed. These evaluations will also show what is working well. It is just as important to acknowledge and appreciate what is working well as it is to highlight what is not.'

A copy of this self-evaluation form can be found in Appendix 9.

As well as a regular review, it is sensible for the board to formally adopt a code of practice. The National Governors' Association has a code of practice which 'sets out the purpose of the governing body and describes the appropriate relationship between individual governors, the whole governing body and the leadership team of the school'. The board should discuss the provisions of whichever code it chooses and formally adopt and sign it at the first meeting in the academic year.

Chair of the board

The role of chair is key to the governance function in any academy and appropriate training and relevant experience is fundamental. The National College for Teaching & Learning offers a Chairs of Governors' Leadership Development Programme. Part of this involves a 360° review incorporating feedback from various sources such as the head teacher, other governors and the clerk. The review considers a number of aspects: leading strategically, leading services, self-management, leading in the community and leading people.

Incorporating some form of regular review into the annual schedule of the board is not only good practice from a governance point of view but it is also a learning opportunity for the chair.

EXPERIENCE

Naureen Khalid, Vice Chair of Governors at Newstead Wood School, has developed a 360° review of the chair's performance based on various sources available online.

'360 degree feedback is a tool which can be used to provide valuable feedback about the performance of the chair. It is especially important for chairs to seek such feedback because it will give them an idea how their performance is viewed by fellow governors, the clerk, the head teacher and other members of the leadership team. If conducted properly, it helps the chair to understand his or her strengths and weaknesses and areas where professional development may be required. The feedback can help highlight a weakness which may not have been evident otherwise. I feel that in the present climate, where performance of school staff is under greater scrutiny than ever before, it is only fair that the performance of the chair be evaluated too.' A copy of the 360° review form used can be found in Appendix 10.

▦ Summary

Risk management

- Every academy should develop and adopt a framework for effective risk management which is incorporated into the overall management and strategy as well as reflected in policies and procedures and underlying culture and values.
- The framework should also be subject to continuous review and improvement.
- An effective risk management process involves:
  - establishing a risk policy
  - identifying risk
  - analysis of specific risks
  - evaluation and, if appropriate, modification of risk.
- Ongoing monitoring.

Health and safety

- Academies must ensure, so far as possible, the 'health, safety and welfare at work' of all employees and others who might be affected by their activities. Premises should be 'safe and without risks to health'.
- The HSE-approved law poster must be displayed or every worker provided with a leaflet giving the same information.
- There are obligations under RIDDOR to report certain serious work-place accidents, occupational diseases and 'near misses'.
- There is significant regulation in the area of health and safety and specialist advice should be sought.

Safeguarding

- Academies have an obligation to safeguard pupils.
- Any allegation against staff or volunteers must be reported immediately, generally to the head teacher, who will refer the matter to the LA's designated officer.

Business continuity and disaster recovery plans

- A business continuity or disaster recovery plan should be developed and maintained.

Insurance

- Academies are legally required to hold employers' liability insurance.
- Other insurances are not compulsory but should be considered.

- Academies can opt into the EFA's risk protection arrangement which will reimburse academies in the event of a loss.

Dealing with complaints

- There must be a formal, written complaints procedure statement setting out the way that complaints from parents or pupils will be handled.
- A complainant can appeal direct to the Secretary of State if they have exhausted the complaints process and are still unsatisfied.
- For converter academies, the funding agreement contains continuing obligations relating to complaints arising in whole or in part in the 12 months prior to conversion.

Appeal panels

- An Independent Review Panel to consider a review of a permanent exclusion must be convened by the board and all members must have received training on the process.
- Similarly the board is responsible for convening an independent appeal panel to hear an appeal against a decision to refuse admission.

Review of board effectiveness

- Regular reviews of the board and governance structures should be carried out.
- Identified strengths and weaknesses should be noted and an action plan developed for addressing any issues or areas for development.
- A regular review of the chair's effectiveness is good practice.

14 Policies

▥ In this chapter

This chapter considers the policies which set the framework for the academy and its operations with specific reference to:

- statutory policies and other documents that must be in place;
- the practical aspects of policy drafting and the needs of academy chains;
- provision of access to policies and establishment of a review schedule; and
- the importance of a policy on social media.

'Policies' are the overriding principles, rules and guidelines with 'procedures' setting out the detailed methods used. Together they provide the framework for the academy to function smoothly and in accordance with agreed values and towards the vision embodied in the strategic plan. The policy should be a relatively short, high-level document with the detail contained in any connected procedures.

▥ Statutory policies

All schools are required by law to have approved and adopted a number of policies and other documents. However, the list of 'statutory policies' and other documents that schools are obliged to have is fairly limited. The statutory policies and procedures required by an academy are:

- *Admissions arrangements*: Academies are their own admission authority (although the LA or another organisation can be contracted to carry out the tasks associated with the role). The admissions policy must comply with the requirements of the admission code and must be reviewed and adopted annually, irrespective of any changes. A formal consultation for a period of at least eight weeks between 1 November and 1 March must be carried out where any changes are required. Admissions-related information should be uploaded to the academy website.

- *Behaviour policy*: Every school should have a behaviour policy which includes the school rules and which covers:
  - screening and searching pupils (including identifying in the school rules items which are banned and which may be searched for);
  - the power to use reasonable force or make other physical contact;
  - the power to discipline beyond the school gate;
  - pastoral care for school staff accused of misconduct; and
  - when a multi-agency assessment should be considered for pupils who display continuous disruptive behaviour.
- *Charging and remissions*: The Education Act 1996 provides that parents and pupils cannot be charged for any activity unless there is a policy in place. Charges per pupil cannot exceed the actual costs incurred so that no element of extra cost can be charged to cover pupils who cannot afford the activity or for a profit element. Charges for activities taking place during the normal school day can only be on the basis of voluntary contributions and pupils will be treated no differently whether they pay the contribution or not.
- *Complaints procedure*: This sets out the process by which any complaint is dealt with. Complainants should, in the first instance, always be directed to the school itself where the majority of complaints will be resolved. If a complainant does not feel that their complaint has been satisfactorily resolved, they can, having exhausted the complaints procedure, appeal directly to the Secretary of State for Education through the EFA (see Chapter 13).
- *Data protection:* Academies are 'data controllers' under the Data Protection Act 1998 and must have a policy outlining how and why any personal data is processed in order to comply with the provisions of the Data Protection Act. This applies to the processing of any personal data whether in electronic form or manually held data.
- *Freedom of Information*: The Freedom of Information Act 2000 gives a right of access to information held by public bodies including academies. The Information Commissioner's Office has a model publication scheme which may be adopted without modification whereby an academy will commit to make information available to the public as part of its normal business activities.
- *Equality information and objectives (public sector equality duty) statement for publication:* Academies must draw up equality objectives every four years which show how it will meet the aims of the general equality duty to:
  - eliminate unlawful discrimination, harassment and victimisation and other conduct prohibited by the Act;
  - advance equality of opportunity between people who share a protected characteristic and those who do not; and
  - foster good relations between people who share a protected characteristic and those who do not.

  The protected characteristics are:

- disability;
- gender reassignment;
- pregnancy and maternity (which includes breastfeeding);
- race;
- religion and belief;
- sex; and
- sexual orientation.

Each academy must also publish information annually showing how the aims of the public sector equality duty are being met.

- *Health and safety*: The Health and Safety at Work Act 1974 places a duty on academies to take reasonable steps to ensure the health and safety of employees, pupils and visitors. Academies must produce a policy and carry out a risk assessment.

- *Home-school agreement document*: This should be drawn up in consultation with parents and should apply to all pupils. Reasonable steps must be taken to ensure that parents sign the agreement confirming their agreement to participate in a partnership with the school.

- *Sex and relationships education*: Academies must have a policy which:
  - defines sex and relationship education;
  - describes how sex and relationship education is provided and who is responsible for providing it;
  - says how sex and relationship education is monitored and evaluated; and
  - includes information about parents' right to non-participation.

- *Special Educational Needs*: The Academies Act 2010 provides that academies must have regard to the SEN Code of Practice published by the DfE which includes adoption of a policy on SEN setting out the approach to meeting pupils' special educational needs whether with or without a statement.

Other documentation must also be kept:

- *Accessibility plan*: A plan or strategy must be put into place setting out how disabled pupils can participate in the curriculum and associated services, maximising access to the physical environment and written information provided to pupils.

- *Central record of recruitment and vetting checks:* Generally the responsibility for maintaining the record will be delegated to the head teacher who will ensure that it is dealt with in the normal administration of the academy. The record must contain details of DRB checks undertaken on members of staff. It is also a requirement of the articles of association that directors undertake DBS checking. If they fail to do so, or if any information is disclosed which would 'confirm their unsuitability to work with children' then that person shall be disqualified as a director.

- *Minutes of, and papers considered at, meetings of the governing body and its committees.*

- *Premises management documents*: Academies have responsibility for ensuring safe management and maintenance of premises including health and safety, asbestos, compliance with the Disability Discrimination Act, fire safety, electrical testing and water hygiene (see Chapter 13). Documentation and certificates must be held and, where appropriate, displayed.
- *Register of pupils' admission to school*: Generally, the responsibility for keeping the register will be delegated to the head teacher who will direct appropriate academy staff to maintain it.
- *Register of pupils' attendance*: Similarly, the head teacher will generally have delegated responsibility for keeping the register which will be maintained by appropriate academy staff.

In addition, statutory guidance also recommends various other policies and procedures which should be in place (e.g. Child protection policy and procedures, Early Years Foundation Stage (EYFS) and a Statement of procedures). Although it is possible not to have all such policies, it will be necessary to show very good reasons for so doing. It is, of course, best practice to ensure that they are all in place.

The DfE website has a helpful list of 'policies and other documents that governing bodies and proprietors are required to have by law' which gives further details. However, it is worth noting that:

- drafting of school policies can be delegated to any member of school staff;
- not all policies need to be reviewed annually; and
- not all policies need to be approved by the board.

Reference must be made to the DfE's list providing information on the review frequency (which is often set by the relevant legislation/regulations) and the level of approval required for any policy or documentation. The DfE has stated its ongoing commitment to review the requirements relating to policy documentation and will endeavour to simplify the legal obligations on schools wherever possible.

Consideration must be given to any particular requirements contained in the funding agreement. Nevertheless, academies have greater freedoms than maintained schools in relation to school policies and other documents.

In addition to the policies required by law or guidance, there are numerous others which should be considered and, where appropriate, adopted, such as:

- allegations of abuse against staff;
- collective worship;
- critical incident;
- curriculum;
- drugs;
- first aid and administering medication;
- governor/director visits;

- homework;
- lettings;
- recruitment, selection and induction of staff;
- staff appraisal;
- staff discipline, conduct and grievance;
- staff pay;
- teaching and learning; and
- whistleblowing.

Policy drafting

There are many precedent policies available from LAs, corporate providers and member organisations. However, it is important that whatever model policies in use are tailored to the specific requirements of the academy.

The board of directors is responsible for the strategic vision of the academy. The day-to-day practice and procedure must reflect this vision if it is to be realised. It is crucial that the policy establishes the overall framework for the management and operations in the academy. As a minimum, an academy is required to adopt each of the 'statutory' policies. However, directors should give careful consideration to what other policies are required to ensure a coherent and effective approach.

In practical terms, the head teacher and staff will often do much of the detailed work on producing policies in relation to the educational aspects of running an academy. However, many other policies such as health and safety, equal opportunities or freedom of information may well sit better with a committee or an individual director with specific training or experience in that area.

Development of policies may, from time to time, involve consultation with those likely to be affected by them. An obvious example is the need to consult over pay and appraisal policies which will involve negotiation with staff and unions. This means that the policy has the greatest possible chance of being successfully implemented and adopted by all!

There is no required format for a policy although it is useful to ensure that all academy policies follow a 'house style' with a consistency in the formulation. All policies should be written in 'plain English' and without the use of acronyms or abbreviations unless they are defined in the policy (no matter how well known these might appear to be!). A policy should be a concise document which is likely to be a maximum of two sides of A4 paper – the detail should be included in the procedures.

Procedures deal with the day-to-day implementation of the policy and are more generally draw up by the head teacher and executive in the academy. This may not always be the case, particularly in a MAT where a particular consistency of approach is required across a number of individual schools each headed up by their own senior leadership team.

Policies in academy chains

The board will generally wish to adopt a consistency of approach across a MAT. As one legal entity it is important to have a single policy based on the overall vision; it is also far more practical! Policies relating to staff, for example, must be the same across all schools as all staff are employed by the MAT. Some level of flexibility may be required in the procedures put into place to realise the policies – the procedure applied in a secondary school may not be appropriate in an infant school within the same MAT.

The same is not true of umbrella trusts or collaborative arrangements where the individual schools can choose to adopt whichever policies they wish. A consolidated approach is often used, not least because of the efficiencies that can be achieved in drafting!

CASE STUDY

Liz Holmes is Vice Chair of the Faringdon Academy of Schools, a multi-academy of eight schools including one secondary, five primary, one junior and one infant school:

'A multi-academy trust will require a hierarchy of policies which reflects those which must be applied across all the academy's member schools and those which are school specific.

A comprehensive list of all the policies in existence at each member school at the point at which the multi-academy trust is formed should be collated and used to inform the scope of work to be done to develop a unified approach to policies across all member schools. As new schools, their joint information should be added to the collated information.

Most of the decisions around what must become a single academy-wide policy will be determined by looking at the policies required of any academy or maintained schools.

Single academy-wide policies will in most instances be required where:

- the academy may be held to account;
- a statutory requirement or employer/employee duty exists; or
- consistency across all member schools is a requirement when specific actions are taken or decisions need to be reached.

When drafting an academy policy for all the schools within a multi-academy trust, the need to separate out procedural steps from policy aims or objectives is very important.

A policy's aims and objectives should, whilst satisfying all statutory requirements and legal duties, be applicable to all member schools.

The procedures which support the application of a policy in a multi-academy trust must allow for variances in organisational and/or operational structures within member schools to be appropriately reflected.

Academy policies must be agreed by the trust's board for subsequent adoption and use within individual member schools.

Clear guidance should be provided around which academy committees are responsible for the promotion and review of academy policies.

Additional guidance may be required around application of parts of a policy (i.e. where a pay policy requires an annual Pay Committee to be convened and responsibility for this has been devolved to each member school, some of the questions it must ask should be specified as should how the local governing body will report back to the appropriate academy committee).'

Access to policies

Aside from any legal requirement to publish policies it is important, for practical reasons, that easy access is given for staff, directors and parents as appropriate. Consideration should be given to the particular policy or procedure and the needs of the school and options include:

- uploading all policies onto the website or VLE;
- including policies in a staff handbook issued to all staff;
- providing hard copies in community languages or for the visually impaired; and
- holding a master file in the school office.

Review

Policies should be reviewed on a regular basis, although it is not necessary that they are all reviewed on an annual basis. Care should be taken to identify any statutory or recommended review periods.

An efficient process for managing policies must be established. It is not a good use of board time to consider the detail of policies and it is only rarely that a policy will need to be approved at that level. A better structure is for responsibility for policy review and approval to be delegated to the relevant committees which will then report back to the board to confirm that the delegated authority has been exercised. Academies will have a significant number of policies in place and sharing policies amongst the committees avoids it being an onerous task.

A centrally held schedule is a good idea, setting out the relevant review dates and the party or committee responsible. A simple schedule could be:

Policy	Committee/Individual responsible	Date approved	Date for review

In addition, regular monitoring should be carried out to ensure that the policy is embedded in practice and to establish whether it is achieving what was intended. Much of that monitoring will be done by the board considering reports from the head teacher and staff. Schools are used to ongoing monitoring, not least because of the tracking and monitoring that is done on pupil progress. Therefore, the head teacher will be in the strongest position to ensure that evidence is gathered and evaluated for presentation to the board.

Directors should also undertake their own monitoring and it is useful to put in place a schedule of visits identifying the areas or subjects that will be the subject of the monitoring visit. However, it is important to remember that director visits are not to consider or comment on the quality of teaching and learning taking place and should never attempt to make Ofsted-style judgements. It is crucial that there are clear protocols regarding director visits in place which should cover:

- how visits will be arranged (e.g. according to a schedule agreed by the head teacher);
- scope of the visit (e.g. subject area);
- the nature of the visit (e.g. observation of class or collective worship, or meeting with subject leader);
- who directors will meet (e.g. staff, pupils); and
- reporting back to the board (e.g. initial discussion with head teacher prior to reporting back via committee structure).

There should also be a standard director visit form setting out the purpose of the visit, the director's comments and any key issues arising.

Director visits are useful not only because of the evidence that can be used to generate debate or inform decision-making by the board, but because a well-structured programme of visits will give directors a better understanding of the day-to-day operation of the academy as well as fostering good working relationships with staff.

Evaluation of the impact of policies can also be undertaken through the use of comparative data such as RAISEonline (a tool which provides an interactive analysis of school and pupil performance data).

Social media

All schools now routinely use technology. Many schools have suites of netbooks or iPads that can be used wirelessly in the classroom, whilst other schools have started to issue iPads to all new pupils. Some teachers use blogging or social media to encourage pupil engagement and independent learning.

Therefore it is important to consider the use of social media, noting any potential risks and setting appropriate policies for adherence by pupils and teachers.

COMMENT

Peter Wright, solicitor and managing director of DigitalLawUK

Social media

Why social media is important in a school

Social media is changing the way that people communicate and how business works and is arguably the biggest change to the economy since the Industrial Revolution. People's movements and comments on social media can be used as evidence in courtrooms, while for employers, a lack of proficiency on social media can be a disadvantage when recruiting staff. Conversely, employees around the world are fired every day for inappropriate comments or use of social media. In educating the workforce of tomorrow, social media is an issue that can't be ignored in schools today.

Social media can be used to create a positive online view of a school

A decade ago prospective pupils and their parents would attend an open day and perhaps review a brochure when making a choice on which school they should attend. However, with the advent of social media, first-hand experience from those attending a school is now available at the touch of a button on Facebook, Twitter and other platforms. A well organised and run corporate account on Twitter or Facebook for your school will speak volumes to those looking for more information about an establishment than that contained on a website or in a brochure. Achievements in terms of awards for the institution or staff could be publicised, as could notable charitable fundraising. However institutions should refrain from showing pictures of any pupils on social media, in particular those under 16. Consent should be sought from any individual featured in any photographic content, including adults, prior to it being uploaded.

Important to pupils in their future careers

Social media is of crucial importance for pupils. In their professional careers they will be expected to develop their professional networks of contacts using systems like LinkedIn, while they may also be expected to use systems like Twitter in a professional capacity. Their knowledge of new and developing social media networks will give them an advantage in the recruitment market, and it will not be in the interests of the school for its pupils to be in any way disadvantaged compared to those from other institutions.

Majority of pupils are engaged on social media platforms and have smartphones

The majority of pupils will most likely already have their own smartphones and be active on social media networks of some sort, despite networks like

Facebook making it clear that their systems are for use by adults only. Consequently, their use is a matter for a school to regulate.

School corporate social media use

It has been known for schools to operate corporate social media accounts in the name of the institution. Issues to be aware of are:

- No photos of anyone below the age of 16 to be uploaded to social media accounts.
- Permission to be obtained from anyone featured in a photograph before it is uploaded.
- Have guidelines in place for acceptable use in terms of comment and content. Comment on sensitive subjects such as politics or religion may be specifically prohibited.
- Ensure that any corporate accounts do not follow or are not in any way linked to any other content, accounts or pages that could be inappropriate.
- Consider having clear guidelines in place on how and when the social media account is to be updated (e.g. only to be updated from a laptop or desktop machine rather than a mobile device to ensure the security of the account and to remove the possibility of inappropriate corporate social media use outside normal work hours by a member of staff who has been entrusted to update the account).

Social media use by staff

Social media use by staff in any organisation is extremely important when it comes to managing reputation. It is of particular importance in a school, but for other reasons in addition to those that may appear obvious:

- Staff should not be connected on social networks to any of their pupils below the age of 16. Connecting with pupils who are leaving/have left following GCSEs or A levels should be permissible at the discretion of the member of staff.
- There should be a clear social media policy in place governing interaction between staff on social media. Organisations with no employee social media policy can be held liable in any instance of cyber bullying by one member of staff to another.
- The school may wish to have a policy governing the use of social media by staff during work hours, both on equipment provided by the school and on mobile devices owned by staff themselves. Persistent documented use of mobile devices such as tablets and smart phones by staff in some organisations to engage on social media has led to dismissal.
- Staff should consider having rigorous privacy settings on any social networks they are active on such as Facebook, so that pupils cannot

identify any of their teachers, or see them in a social setting in any photographs or exchanges of comments with social friends that may be inappropriate. Social media content is usually searchable by search engines like Google and staff must be aware of images leaking online if not properly monitored.

- Staff should refrain from uploading comments or photos to either their own social media accounts or accounts belonging to a class or school. In the United States, one teacher was dismissed for uploading a photograph of a pupil restrained to a chair using tape. The teacher alleged the restraint was a prank carried out by the pupils themselves and that it was uploaded online in a moment of jollity in the classroom, but to the local press and school governors took a more unfavourable view. Clear guidance and training on social media should be provided to all staff.

Social media use by pupils

- Consider prohibiting pupils from using mobile devices either during school hours or on school grounds. This could be a time-consuming resource-intensive step, but it should be considered against staff time engaged in investigating unsuitable social media use or interaction by pupils.
- Pupils should be made aware that bullying online – inside or outside of school hours – is as unacceptable as bullying on school premises and will not be tolerated.
- Repeated online bullying and harassment can be an offence under the Protection from Harassment Act 1997. Threats of violence or intimating criminal acts can breach the Communications Act 2003 and can lead to a criminal record and custodial sentences. Such behaviour is not tolerated in society and should not be acceptable in a school. This should be made clear to pupils from an early age.
- A Code of Conduct on social media may be considered as being appropriate.
- Pupils approaching school leaving age should be given guidance on the use of professional social media sites like LinkedIn in the same way that pupils will receive guidance on CV drafting before entering the workplace.

▨ Summary

- 'Policies' are the overriding principles, rules and guidelines for the academy and 'procedures' set out the detailed methods.
- Academies must approve and adopt a number of statutory policies and other documents.

- Various other policies and procedures should also be in place.
- Drafting of school policies can be delegated to any member of school staff. They do not all need to be reviewed annually nor do they all need board approval.
- Precedent policies are available but should be tailored to the specific requirements of the academy.
- Development of policies may involve consultation.
- The board of a MAT may wish to adopt a consistency of approach with a single policy. Individual schools in an umbrella trust or collaborative arrangement can choose to adopt whichever policies they wish.
- Easy access to relevant policies should be given for staff, directors and parents.
- Policies should be reviewed on a regular basis and in accordance with any statutory or recommended review periods.
- A centrally held schedule setting out the relevant review dates and the party or committee responsible should be established.
- Regular monitoring should be carried out to ensure that the policy is embedded in practice and to establish whether it is achieving what was intended.
- Consideration of the use of social media should be enshrined in policies and procedures.

15 Information management

▨ In this chapter

This chapter looks at the obligations for handling and publishing information covering:

- the requirements to publish certain information on the academy website;
- Freedom of Information Act requests and the need for a publication scheme;
- data protection, the academy as 'data controller' and dealing with subject access requests.

▨ Website

The latest versions of the funding agreement for academies and free schools contain provisions requiring the publication of certain information on the academy's website. Information must be updated as soon as possible after any change and at least annually. Responsibility for meeting the requirement and authority to approve the content may be delegated to a committee, an individual director or the head teacher.

Earlier versions of the funding agreement may not have this requirement but it remains good practice to do so.

The specific information that should be published on the website is:

- If applicable, the most recent Key Stage 2 results under the following column headings:
  (i) '% achieving Level 4 or above in English and maths';
  (ii) '% making expected progress';
  (iii) in relation to English, '% achieving Level 5 or above'; and
  (iv) in relation to maths, '% achieving Level 5 or above'.
- If applicable, the most recent Key Stage 4 results under the following column headings:

(i) '% achieving 5 + A*–C GCSEs (or equivalent) including English and maths GCSEs';

(ii) '% achieving the English Baccalaureate'; and

(iii) '% of pupils making expected progress'.

- How to access the most recent Ofsted report.
- How to access the school performance tables.

As a company, academies must include certain information on their website or be liable to a fine. The requirements are:

- company registration number;
- place of registration (i.e. registered in England);
- registered office address; and
- the information must be in legible characters.

This information must also be included on 'business letters' and electronic documents such as e-mails. It does not need to appear on every page and on websites can easily be included in the 'About us' or 'Contact' pages.

There are various other types of information, which must be included on the website. These include:

- the funding agreement, memorandum and articles of association;
- information on the directors;
- the annual report and accounts;
- admissions arrangements;
- the amount of pupil premium received, what it was spent on during the last financial year and what it will be spent on in the current financial year;
- content of and approach to Key Stage 4 qualification options;
- any phonics reading schemes for Key Stage 1;
- how to obtain further information on the curriculum;
- behaviour and exclusions policies; and
- the complaints procedure.

Freedom of Information Act 2000

As academies are recipients of public funding, they are required to provide public access to information by reason of the Freedom of Information Act 2000. This transparency is to ensure that academies are accountable for their actions and can demonstrate the best use of public funds.

Information could include printed documents, computer files, letters, e-mails, photographs and sound or video recordings. It is not limited to formal documents but can include drafts, notes and letters received or other information provided by a third party. The Act only covers information that is already held in recorded form so it is not necessary to create documentation in response to a request.

Information held on behalf of the academy will also be covered even if the documentation is physically held off-site (e.g. by solicitors or someone acting as company secretary). Any documentation which contains purely staff private or trade union information will not be covered.

It is important that academies adopt good records management practice so that information can be easily retrieved. The Code of Practice, issued under s. 46 of the Freedom of Information Act, sets out good practice. All academies should:

- have in place organisational arrangements that support records management;
- have in place a records management policy, either as a separate policy or as part of a wider information or knowledge management policy;
- ensure they keep the records they will need for business, regulatory, legal and accountability purposes;
- keep their records in systems that enable records to be stored and retrieved as necessary;
- know what records they hold and where they are and should ensure that they remain usable for as long as they are required;
- ensure that records are stored securely and that access to them is controlled;
- define how long they need to keep particular records, dispose of them when they are no longer needed and be able to explain why records are no longer held;
- ensure that records shared with other bodies or held on their behalf by other bodies are managed in accordance with the Code; and
- monitor compliance with the Code and assess the overall effectiveness of the programme.

There should be a publication scheme (i.e. a policy) which sets out:

- the information that is published;
- how and where that information is published; and
- whether the information is available free of charge.

The Information Commissioner's Office has a model publication scheme which may be adopted without modification whereby an academy will commit to make information available to the public as part of its normal business activities.

Publication of information

Academies must proactively publish certain information so that members of the public can access it at will. The board must agree the classes of information that are safe to disclose and which will be set out in the publication scheme. Examples of information that is likely to be covered include policies and procedures, minutes of meetings and supporting documentation, annual reports, financial information and examination results data. Some of this information may also be available via other websites such as Companies House or Ofsted.

Ideally, the information should be disclosed on the website so that it can be accessed immediately. However, it should also be available 'promptly and automatically' to anyone who asks for it. In addition, it is good practice to make the publication scheme itself available on the website so that the classes of information available are clear.

Requests for information

In addition, members of the public are entitled to request information that is not listed in the publication scheme. An applicant does not need to give a reason for wanting the information and all requests should be treated equally irrespective of whether it comes from the parent of a pupil or a journalist. Information should generally be disclosed unless there is good reason for it to be confidential as recognised by the Act.

A request must be in writing but does not need to make reference to the Freedom of Information Act or be directed to a designated member of staff. Any letter or e-mail sent to the academy requesting information is a request falling within the remit of the Act. Nevertheless, most correspondence will be handled in the normal administration of the academy without recourse to the formal mechanisms of the Act unless:

- the requested information cannot be provided immediately; or
- the request specifies that it falls under the Freedom of Information Act.

Normally an academy must respond to a request within 20 school days or 60 working days if this is shorter (e.g. if the request is received over the summer holiday period). Working days will be any day other than a Saturday, Sunday, or public holidays and bank holidays.

A charge to cover the costs of communication such as printing, photocopying and postage may be made subject to a limit set by the Act. Such fees are, however, rarely levied and information will often be provided in electronic form removing such costs.

A request can be refused if:

- it would cost too much or take too much staff time to handle the request;
- the request is vexatious (i.e. the request is likely to cause a disproportionate or unjustifiable level of distress, disruption or irritation);
- the request is a repeat of a previous request from the same person.

The Freedom of Information Act also contains a number of exemptions which mean that information does not necessarily need to be released. However, the majority of the exemptions are unlikely to apply to academies. The most likely exemptions will relate to disclosures which would be 'likely to endanger the physical or mental health or the safety of any individual', complying with the request would be a breach of confidence or where someone requests their own personal data which should be sought as a 'subject access request' under the Data Protection Act.

Most of the exemptions set out in the Act require a 'public interest' test to be applied when considering whether information should be disclosed: the public interest considerations in favour of withholding the information should outweigh the public interest considerations in disclosing it. Exempt information would include information:

- contravening the Data Protection Act;
- which could endanger the physical/mental health or safety of an individual;
- given in confidence;
- intended for publication in the future; and
- available by other means.

Some documents may include parts which are exempt from disclosure. Despite this, they should be produced in a 'redacted' form with the exempt elements edited or obliterated.

If in doubt about information which should be provided following a request, academies are advised to seek professional help.

COMMENT

Peter Wright, solicitor and managing director of DigitalLawUK

Freedom of Information Act

Academy schools are subject to the Freedom of Information Act 2000 (FOIA) and need to have appropriate systems in place to deal with requests. Requests can come from anywhere, but are particularly common from journalists and authors in search of statistics and raw data.

Institutions subject to a FOIA request have 20 working days to respond and can be fined by the Information Commissioner's Office (ICO) for handling requests in a dilatory manner or not responding with sufficient disclosure to the request.

There are certain issues that a school should consider in order to make it easier to process and respond to FOIA requests:

- The majority of school data and material will be stored securely either on a server or online securely in the Cloud. By storing data electronically, it can be searched, securely retrieved, reviewed and disclosed quickly and cheaply.
- Be aware of the main exemptions under which material can be withheld. Personal data referring to a third party, such as the names of a pupil or teacher or anything that allows them to be identified such as an address, photograph, audio or video recording, national insurance number or pupil number, should be redacted and on no account should be disclosed.
- Commercially sensitive details such as contracts with suppliers, payroll data, financial records etc can also be withheld under the Act.

- Disclosure following a FOIA request can be made electronically via encrypted CD, USB or securely online. If made in hard copy, it should be sent securely via recorded delivery or courier.
- Consider the use of an online document management service for records to be securely reviewed, redacted and disclosed.
- Consider obtaining legal advice from a law firm. Some firms offer a fixed fee service to review each FOIA request and may turn out to be more cost effective than using staff time.
- Charges can be levied under the FOIA for making requests.

Data protection

The Data Protection Act 1998 provides for 'the regulation of the processing of information relating to individuals, including the obtaining, holding, use or disclosure of such information' and is based on eight data protection principles which state that personal data is:

1. Processed fairly and lawfully.
2. Processed only for the specified and lawful purposes.
3. Adequate, relevant and not excessive.
4. Accurate and, where necessary, kept up-to-date.
5. Not kept for longer than is necessary.
6. Processed in accordance with the rights of data subjects.
7. Protected from unauthorised or unlawful processing and against accidental loss or destruction or damage.
8. Not transferred to a country or territory outside the European Economic Area without adequate protection.

Every academy must register with the Information Commissioner's Office as they are 'data controllers'. In fact, academies process vast amounts of 'personal data' in respect of pupils and staff and great care should be given to ensuring that processing, whether by electronic or computerised means or in a structured manual filing system, fulfils the requirements of the legislation.

In addition, it is necessary to show that one of the following conditions has been satisfied in order to permit processing:

- the data subject has consented to the processing;
- the processing is necessary for the performance of a contract or to enter into a contract with the data subject;
- processing is necessary because of a legal obligation;
- processing is necessary to protect the data subject's 'vital interests' (i.e. in the case of life or death);
- processing is necessary for the administration of justice, or for exercising statutory, governmental or other public functions; and
- processing is in accordance with the 'legitimate interests' condition.

Stricter conditions apply when the information is 'sensitive'. Examples of this kind of information include:

- ethnic background;
- political opinions;
- trade union membership;
- religious beliefs;
- health;
- sexual health; and
- criminal records.

Individuals are able to make a subject access request to see any personal information that is held on them. The request should be made in writing and the data controller may require payment of a fee subject to a maximum depending on the circumstances and verification of the identity of the data subject making the request.

A response to a subject access request should be provided within 40 calendar days of receiving it.

There are very limited circumstances when information can be withheld, for example in connection with:

- the prevention, detection or investigation of a crime;
- national security or the armed forces;
- the assessment or collection of tax; and
- judicial or ministerial appointments.

Great care should be exercised when dealing with requests in connection with pupil data which are likely to be made by those with parental responsibility for the child. Consideration should be given to whether the child is mature enough to understand their rights and, as they are the data subject, the response should be made to them rather than a parent or guardian. Particular consideration should be given to:

- the child's level of maturity and ability to make decisions;
- the nature of the personal data;
- any court orders relating to parental access or responsibility that may apply;
- any duty of confidence owed to the child or young person;
- any consequences of allowing those with parental responsibility access to the child's or young person's information, especially if there have been allegations of abuse or ill treatment;
- any detriment to the child or young person if individuals with parental responsibility cannot access this information; and
- any views the child or young person has on whether their parents should have access to information about them.

The Information Commissioner can serve a data controller with an 'information notice' requiring certain information to be provided within set time limits. Failure to do so is a criminal offence. If the Commissioner concludes that there has been a breach of the Act, then an 'enforcement notice' may be served preventing future processing. Failure to comply with an enforcement notice is also a criminal offence. Resultant fines may be unlimited, but the threat of being prevented from processing personal data is a far greater deterrent as an academy would be unable to operate.

Directors or members of the senior leadership team may also be found to be personally criminally liable if the offence has been committed with their consent, connivance or neglect.

Detailed consideration of the way that data is handled, processed and stored by the academy is absolutely essential and should encompass the following areas:

- cloud storage;
- back-up, disaster plan and disaster recovery;
- remote working/travel;
- devices/laptops/phones;
- Bring Your Own Device;
- destruction of IT hardware;
- e-mail encryption and security/data rooms
- administration system/finance and accounts systems/payroll/regulatory;
- website, privacy, cookies and website backup;
- social media, personal data and confidentiality;
- password security;
- CCTV/hearing loop/recording of calls;
- office procedures/file storage/desk storage;
- archived files/destruction/confidential waste; and
- post/confidential post/DX/fax.

Compliance with data protection legislation is a necessity. Detailed practical guidance on the issues that need consideration, setting out the principles and examples of mistakes made by other organisations (along with the fines that they received) is set out in Appendix 11. The cases serve to illustrate why the practical steps outlined are being recommended and that they are not just examples of over-zealous regulation being implemented with no purpose.

COMMENT

Peter Wright, solicitor and managing director of DigitalLawUK

Data protection
Academy schools need to be aware of the catastrophic risk that they carry from being susceptible to a data protection breach. By their very nature,

schools hold huge amounts of personal data, everything from pupil attendance data, staff salary and payroll information, pupil qualifications, addresses, dates of birth, health screening records – the list goes on. All it takes is for some of this data to be transmitted to an incorrect recipient, stolen from an office or the car or home of a member of staff and a school could be facing a fine of up to £500,000 from the UK Information Commissioner's Office (ICO). The regulatory regime also applies should a school's IT system be compromised and data taken.

Schools should consider:

- The security of the IT system, be it on a server or a cloud hosted network.
- Having a workable disaster recovery plan in place should the school be inaccessible or key staff be unable to attend work.
- Remote access issues created by staff working out of school, including at home or during travel.
- Security risks from staff working on mobile devices, smart phones and laptops.
- The need for a rigorous Bring Your Own Device (BYOD) policy or prohibition.
- Ensuring the secure destruction of IT equipment belonging to the school including hard drives.
- Putting systems in place to ensure the secure transmission of personal data including encrypting email and the use of secure online data rooms if applicable.
- Proving the security of any third party supplied systems such as finance, administration and payroll systems, in particular those that are hosted on the cloud.
- The security of any school website, including the use of an accurate cookie policy and website backup.
- The need for a comprehensive social media policy, ensuring the confidentiality of personal data will be preserved online.
- Having a system in place to ensure that any passwords used for systems at the school are sufficiently complex and that different passwords are used for different systems and that they are regularly changed.
- Ensuring the security of any records from CCTV systems, hearing loops and recorded calls.
- Putting policies in place to ensure that there are minimal security risks in the workplace through having a clear desk policy to make sure cleaning or security staff do not have access to confidential data, and limiting access to confidential records only to those who need to use them to fulfil their roles.
- Having a clear method for archiving files and their secure destruction.

- Making sure personal data is not sent via first class post or unsecure fax but is sent by approved methods such as recorded delivery or courier only.
- Ensuring that all members of staff receive adequate data protection training, including all new starters, and that this is repeated regularly to ensure compliance, along with spot checks to ensure rules and policies are being followed in practice.

Finally schools need to be aware that the law relating to data protection is always evolving, and that a data protection professional should be consulted regularly to make sure the school is up-to-date with the latest risks and security measures.

■ Summary

Website

- Specific information must be published on the website:
  - Information relating to the most recent Key Stage 2 results.
  - Information relating to the most recent Key Stage 4 results.
  - How to access the most recent Ofsted report.
  - How to access the school performance tables.
  - Company registration number.
  - Place of registration (i.e. registered in England).
  - Registered office address.
  - The funding agreement, memorandum and articles of association.
  - Directors.
  - The annual report and accounts.
  - Admissions arrangements.
  - Report on pupil premium.
  - Content and approach to Key Stage 4 qualification options.
  - Any phonics reading schemes for Key Stage 1.
  - How to obtain further information on the curriculum.
  - Behaviour and exclusions policies.
  - Complaints procedure.

Freedom of Information Act 2000

- Academies must provide public access to information that is held in recorded form.
- There should be a publication scheme setting out the information that is published, how and where it is published and whether it is available free of charge.

- Members of the public can request information not listed in the publication scheme by a request made in writing.
- A response is generally due within 20 school days or 60 working days if this is shorter.
- A request can be refused if:
  - it would cost too much or take too much staff time to handle the request;
  - the request is vexatious; or
  - the request is a repeat of a previous request from the same person.
- There are a number of exemptions, most of which require a 'public interest' test to be applied. Documents with exempt elements should be produced in a 'redacted' form.

Data protection

- Academies must register with the Information Commissioner's Office as a 'data controller'.
- Stricter conditions apply when information is 'sensitive'.
- Individuals can make a subject access request in writing to see personal information held on them. A response is due within 40 calendar days of receiving it.
- Information can be withheld in very limited circumstances.
- Breaches of the Act constitute a criminal offence with unlimited fines. Directors or members of the senior leadership team may be personally criminally liable if the offence was committed with their consent, connivance or neglect.
- Detailed consideration of the way that data is handled, processed and stored by the academy is essential.

Appendix 1: Example registers

Register of members

Surname:	
Forenames:	
Former names:	
Address:	
Date of entry as a member:	
Expiry of term:	
Consent to act:	

Register of secretaries

Surname:	
Forenames:	
Former names:	
Service address:	
Date of appointment:	
Date of resignation:	

Register of directors/governors

Surname:	
Forenames:	
Former names:	
Service address:	
Business occupation:	
Other directorships:	
Nationality:	
Date of birth:	
Date of appointment:	
Expiry of term:	
Date of resignation/removal:	

Register of directors'/governors' addresses

Surname:	
Forenames:	
Address:	

Register of interests

Name	Name of business	Nature of interest	Self/partner/ close relative	Date registered

Register of gifts, hospitality and entertainment

Name	Date of declaration	Description of gift, hospitality or entertainment	Value

Appendix 2: Skills audit

Skills audit and training needs

Name ....

Please add any other skills you feel you have to offer:

Your skills	High level of skills and qualifications	Medium level of skills	Some skills	Would like to develop skills in this area
Financial management				
HR				
Facilities management				
Teaching and learning				
SEN				
Data analysis				

Royal Wootton Bassett Academy Governing Body Skills Audit Form

NAME _____ DATE _____

How would you rate your knowledge/ understanding/competence in the broad skill/experience areas listed in the table?

Skills/experience	Very good	Good	Adequate	Poor
Commercial /Strategic Development				
Marketing				
Pastoral experience				
Working as part of a team				
Communication skills: 　Written 　Oral				
Administrative/Organisational				
Mediation				
Strategic planning				
Problem solving				
Project management				
Procurement				
Public speaking				
Chairing meetings				
Taking minutes				
Monitoring, reviewing, and evaluating school performance				
School finances				
School curriculum				
School policies				
Human resources/staffing				
Equality and diversity issues				
Health and safety, including safeguarding				
Building maintenance/ facilities management				
Information technology/computers				
School data analysis (e.g. RAISEonline)				
Special educational needs				
Marketing/publicity/public relations				
Performance management/appraisals				

Skills/experience	Very good	Good	Adequate	Poor
Education				
PR				
Charity fund raising				
Further and Higher Education experience				
Risk assessment				
Quality assurance				
Director experience				
Legal experience				
Governor experience				
Business links/Community relations				
Others (details of any skills/ experiences not listed):–				

Training needs analysis

Name _____

Responsibility	No previous knowledge	Some knowledge	A lot of knowledge
Roles and responsibilities of a board			
Teaching and learning			
SEN			
Financial management			
Understanding school data			
Health and Safety			
Safeguarding			
Performance management			
HR			
School improvement planning			
Monitoring performance			
Accountability			

Appendix 3: The minute-taker's reminder checklists

Before you begin scanning the lists, please remember the following with respect to each one:

▓ The 'before' list

This list covers a wide range of activities in connection with pre-meeting preparation. You should review this list *well in advance*; some of the activities require a longer lead time for completion, whereas others will relate to activities on the day of the meeting itself.

▓ The 'during' list

This list covers all the points which need to be considered in relation to the meeting itself. However, it is unlikely that you will be sitting in the meeting attempting to take the notes while at the same time pondering the contents of the reminder checklist! So, the best approach is to consider the points prior to the meeting as a form of preparation and then review them again following the meeting as a form of evaluation. In time, the points will become well embedded in your mind and you will naturally reflect on some of these points *during* the meetings you minute.

▓ The 'after' list

This list covers all the activities which follow the meeting. Some relate to activities which should be undertaken straight after the meeting, some to the writing of the actual minutes and others to self-development activities and self-reflection. The conclusions you draw from your review of this list will naturally feed into your preparation activities for the meeting that follows.

▓ The minute taker's reminder checklist: before the meeting

Tick the following as completed:

☐ Do I clearly understand the meeting cycle for this meeting?
☐ Have I created a timeline plan to show how this meeting cycle dovetails with those for the other meetings I attend?

☐ Am I expected to contribute at this meeting in addition to taking the minutes?

☐ If I am expected to contribute for one item only, have I made arrangements for someone else to take the minutes for that one item?

☐ If I am expected to be the minute taker and full meeting contributor, have I explained to everyone that the minutes will be more concise than usual with the emphasis on noting action points? Have I explained to the chairperson that a summary would be appreciated at the end of each item?

☐ Am I fully aware of the layout and style of the minutes required in respect of this meeting?

☐ Do I fully understand all the procedural matters in relation to this particular meeting?

☐ Have I confirmed all the necessary administration arrangements for the meeting?

☐ Have I checked that all equipment is in good working order?

☐ Has the meeting room been arranged in the way the participants have requested?

☐ Have I read thoroughly the minutes of the last meeting?

☐ Have I read and fully understood the agenda?

☐ Have I read and understood all the supporting papers?

☐ Is there any additional information that I need to read and understand in order to be fully prepared?

☐ If I need help, what should my approach be for this particular meeting?
  - Speak to the participant(s) before the day?
  - Speak to the participant(s) before the meeting?
  - Speak to the chair in advance of the meeting?
  - Seek clarifications afterwards?
  - Talk to the chair during the meeting?
  - Interrupt during the meeting?

☐ Have I copied up all the necessary papers for the meeting including the minutes of the last meeting?

☐ Do I have enough copies?

☐ Is the chair required to sign the minutes? Do I have a copy for this purpose?

☐ With respect to this meeting, do I know who the chair is?

☐ If I have not worked with the chair before, what can I do to establish a professional relationship?

☐ Have I arranged a pre-meeting briefing session with the chair?

☐ If a briefing is not possible prior to the day of the meeting, have I arranged for a short discussion with the chair just prior to the commencement of the meeting?

☐ Have I made arrangements to sit next to the chair at the meeting?

☐ If it is not possible to sit next to the chair what arrangements can I make to ensure that the quality of my note-taking is not compromised?

☐ Have I created an attendance list for circulation at the meeting?

☐ Is all my paperwork well arranged and in good order?

☐ Have I created a minute taking template that I am comfortable with?

☐ If I am using loose-leaf sheets of A4, have I numbered the pages in advance?

☐ Do I have enough spare writing paper?

☐ Have I noted all the abbreviations, technical terms and jargon that may be used by participants at this meeting?

☐ Do I have all the pens and pencils I need including a choice of colours?

☐ Do I have my highlighter pens?

☐ Have I allocated time to undertake an initial review of my notes immediately following the meeting?

☐ Have I arranged to arrive a little earlier at the venue to check the final arrangements and converse with participants?

☐ Is my personal appearance appropriate for this particular meeting occasion; is it professional?

☐ Is my clothing comfortable?

☐ Have I eaten foods that will help to maintain my energy and concentration levels throughout the meeting?

☐ Have I brought a bottle of water to help maintain hydration levels?

☐ If I need to interrupt for clarifications, have I practiced my voice projection and assertiveness techniques to enable me to do so with confidence?

☐ *HAVE I PREPARED A PERSONAL CHECKLIST FOR ALL THE ABOVE POINTS?*

▨ The minute taker's reminder checklist: during the meeting

Tick the following as completed:

☐ Have I entered the room confidently?

☐ Does my body language give evidence that I am a professional person with every right to be at the meeting, in order to fulfil an extremely important role, or does it suggest that I am a second-class citizen who is attending the meeting only to perform the onerous task of note-taking?

☐ Have I taken the opportunity to mix and converse with participants in order to build rapport?

☐ Have I placed my papers on the table and arranged my working space in a neat and orderly fashion?

☐ Have I spoken to the chair just prior to commencement to clarify any last minute points of concern?

☐ Has everyone seen and signed the attendance list?

☐ Do I have a complete and accurate record of all apologies?

☐ Am I sitting properly with good back support?

☐ Is my writing arm positioned so as to minimise the stress on the wrist?

☐ Have I put all distractions out of my mind and am I fully focused on the meeting?

☐ For each item, am I formulating in my mind an idea as to the main emphasis of the discussion and the possible decisions, from the chair's opening summary?

☐ Am I working with the chair to ensure that all participants who want to contribute are able to do so?

☐ Am I getting the sense of the *message* or am I focusing too much on the actual words?

☐ Am I isolating the key points from each speaker's contribution?

☐ Am I relating the key points to the central matter under discussion?

☐ Am I tending to record the arguments verbatim or am I employing my personalised form of shorthand?

☐ From the discussion, am I clearly extracting and recording all the decisions and action points?

☐ For the action points, have I made a note of who is responsible and the deadline date for completion?

☐ Where points are unclear am I asking for appropriate clarifications?

☐ Am I maintaining concentration or is my mind beginning to wander?

☐ Am I checking periodically that my handwriting is still legible?

☐ Am I tending to write sentences or am I mastering the use of bullet points and abbreviations?

☐ Am I setting out my bullet points clearly and legibly in a vertical format with plenty of space in between, or am I tending to bunch them together in clusters?

☐ If a problem arises regarding understanding and it is inappropriate at that point to seek clarification, have I clearly highlighted this (perhaps with a different colour pen) in my notes?

☐ Am I moving my writing hand too much (thus contributing to tiredness) or am I moving the *paper* to create the writing space I need?

☐ Am I maintaining eye contact with the speaker in order to improve the quality of my listening or do I seldom look up from my notes?

☐ Am I being influenced or distracted by the voice tone of the speaker, the manner of delivery or the emotional nature of the contributions, or am I still focusing on the key points, actions and decisions?

☐ Although my notes will be structured to a greater degree during the writing up stage, am I trying to keep the key points to the fore in my note-taking?

☐ Am I intervening confidently and assertively when required or am I a little 'backward in coming forward'?

☐ Am I helping the chair to keep the meeting on track and, where necessary, to observe procedural conventions?

☐ When I am contributing to an item on the agenda, do I ask the chair to summarise the discussion in the interest of an accurate set of minutes?

☐ Am I *listening* effectively, remembering to employ the different forms of listening in order to create a rounded out understanding?

☐ Am I allowing anything to influence my listening in a *negative* sense, such as bias, prejudice, cynicism, indignation or vested interests?

☐ Have I clearly noted the time, date and place of the next meeting?

☐ Before the participants disperse, am I taking the opportunity to speak to anyone I need to in order to seek necessary clarifications?

▍ The minute taker's reminder checklist: after the meeting

Tick the following as completed:

☐ Have I taken the trouble to shake hands with and say goodbye to, all the participants or have I remained in my seat with my head in my notes?!

☐ Have I taken the time, after everyone has left, to analyse my notes and check understanding and legibility?

☐ Have I made sure that all the key points are highlighted while my memory is still fresh?

☐ Have I thanked the chair?

☐ Have I discussed any pertinent points with the chair prior to leaving the meeting room?

☐ Have I asked the chair to sign the minutes of the previous meeting (if necessary) so that they can be filed and archived?

☐ Have I started writing up the draft minutes as soon as possible after the meeting?

☐ Am I using the correct format and style having regard to the nature of the meeting and the level of formality or informality required?

☐ Am I using an appropriate numbering system?

☐ Am I using the passive voice and correct verbs, particularly where the minutes are of a formal nature?

☐ Have I checked the *level of detail* required for this particular meeting? Is the recording of decisions and actions enough or do I need to incorporate the 'flavour' of the discussion?

☐ When summarising the discussions, am I being crisp and concise, perhaps consolidating certain discussion points into one sentence or is the minute tending to be too drawn out and 'wordy'?

☐ Have I carefully *proofread* the minutes before sending them to the chair for approval?

☐ I am aware that the draft minutes need to be returned on time to adhere to the meeting cycle, but have *I given* the chair a clear deadline for their approval?

☐ When sending the minutes have I clearly highlighted the action points for the individual participants?

☐ Which background papers do I need to file with the minutes?
☐ From my perspective as minute taker, what went well at the meeting and what areas need to be worked on?
☐ What exercises can I undertake to practice my listening and note-taking skills?
☐ At the next meeting, what can I *personally* do to make it even more effective?

This is an excerpt from ICSA Publishing's book, *Effective Minute Taking*, reproduced with the authors' permission.

Appendix 4: Finance processes for month-end reporting

	Sep-13		
Finance processes for month-end reporting	**Done by**	**Date**	**Comments**
Mid-month			
1	Run supplier invoice payment run for invoices falling due. Record transactions in the finance system. Process banking and ensure all completed correctly.		
2	Review dummy payroll. Reconcile to budget, overtime claim forms etc. Ensure all changes correctly reflected. Follow up any differences. Update budget if necessary; consider if material and take appropriate action.		
3	Review credit card transactions. Ensure copy invoices attached to statement. Book expense to finance system.		
Last week of the month if not before			
4	Review live payroll. Ensure in line with expectations; any changes from dummy are understood and queries resolved.		
5	Journal/upload payroll entries.		
6	Enter all invoices and credit notes.		
7	Complete all banking – enter all paying in slips, nominally receipt any remittances direct to the bank account, reflect direct debits and payroll cashbook entries and any other transactions.		

	Finance processes for month-end reporting	Done by	Date	Comments
	At month end			
8	Perform bank reconciliation – make any adjustments as necessary			Dependent upon the number of transactions the school may wish to do this weekly, fortnightly or at least monthly.
9	Review all purchase ledger accounts and reconcile to statement. Request copy invoices and action as appropriate – if invoices missing from finance system book to finance system. Process further invoice payment runs as necessary.			
10	Post any sales invoices and reconcile any debtor balances.			Significance of this item will depend upon the activities of the academy.
11	Review all transactions in the month – check nominal codes and cost centres are correct – if not raise a journal. File journal and supporting documentation.			
12	Review trial balance. Ensure that income/expense amounts look right and reconcile balance sheet accounts. Investigate any errors or omissions.			
13	Review outstanding purchase commitments and ensure all goods received have been correctly reflected in the accounts.			

	Finance processes for month-end reporting	Done by	Date	Comments
14	Check Capex booked to the correct ledger codes.			
15	Process month end journal to correct any items identified above			
16	Run VAT reports and reconcile. When satisfied correct process VAT reclaim.			
17	Prepare month end reports to include actuals in the month and year to date against budget; bank balances and cashflow forecasts. Significant variances from budget should be explained and corrective action taken/reforecasts made.			

Thanks to Sarah Chambers FCA.

Appendix 5: Board of Directors (BoD) Decision Planner

KEY	
	Level 1: Decision to be taken by full Board of Directors
	Level 2: Decision to be delegated to a committee of the Board of Directors
	Level 3: Decision to be delegated to an individual Director
	Level 4: Decision to be delegated to Headteacher
	Level 5: Headteacher day-to-day management

Column blank: Action could be undertaken at this level.
Column blocked off: Function cannot be legally carried out at this level.
Column with lighter shading – not recommended at this level.

For Secretary	Key Function	Tasks	Decision Level				
			1 Board of Directors	2 Committee	3 Individual Director	4 Delegate to Headteacher	5 Headteacher Day-to-day
	Curriculum	To ensure National Curriculum (NC) is taught to all pupils (monitoring curriculum)				X	
	Curriculum	To consider any disapplication from National Curriculum for pupil(s)				X	
	Curriculum	To draft curriculum policy				X	
	Curriculum	To agree or reject curriculum policy			X		
	Curriculum	To implement curriculum policy					X
	Curriculum	To monitor and review implementation of the curriculum policy		X			
	Curriculum	To ensure that the school meets for 380 sessions in a school year.				X	
	Curriculum	To set the times of school sessions and the dates of school terms and holidays	X				
	Curriculum	To ensure that the curriculum contributes to community cohesion		X			
	Curriculum	To decide which subject options should be taught having regard to resources, and implement provision for flexibility in the curriculum (including activities outside school day)		X			
	Curriculum	To ensure that only approved external qualifications and syllabuses are offered to pupils of compulsory school age				X	
	Curriculum	To monitor standards of teaching					X
	Curriculum	To take responsibility for individual child's education					X

For Secretary	Key Function	Tasks	Decision Level				
			1 Board of Directors	2 Committee	3 Individual Director	4 Delegate to Headteacher	5 Headteacher Day-to-day
	Curriculum	To make and keep up to date a written policy on Sex Education		X			
	Curriculum	To prohibit political indoctrination and ensuring the balanced treatment of political issues				X	
	Curriculum	To set and publish targets for pupil achievement		X			
	Curriculum	To review and amend curriculum policies				X	
	Curriculum	To ensure that the school appoints a Special Educational Needs Coordinator (SENCO)				X	
	Curriculum	To review (amend) and monitor the school's SEN policy.		X			
	Curriculum	To discharge other duties in respect of pupils with special educational needs.				X	
	Curriculum	To review (amend) and monitor the Board of Directors' other policies to ensure inclusion (in regard to gender, social disadvantage, race equality and disability discrimination).		X			
	Curriculum	To ensure that the Headteacher sends the Early Years Foundation Stage Profile assessments and Key Stage 1 teacher assessments results to the DfE.				X	
	Curriculum	To monitor pupil achievement against set targets.		X			
	Curriculum	To approve off-site visits and activities of up to 1 day				X	
	Curriculum	To approve off-site visits and activities of more than 24 hours or which involve a hazardous pursuit or journey by air or sea.		X			
	Religious Education	To provide RE in line with school's basic curriculum. (Implementation)				X	
	Religious Education	To ensure provision of RE in line with school's basic curriculum. (Monitoring)				X	
	Collective Worship	Ensure that all pupils take part in a daily act of collective worship (after consulting BoD).				X	
	Collective Worship	To make application to the Standing Advisory Council for Religious Education (SACRE) to disapply the Christian requirements for collective worship (after consulting BoD).				X	
	Collective Worship	To make arrangements for collective worship in schools without religious character (after consulting BoD).				X	
	Behaviour	To decide a discipline policy.		X			

For Secretary	Key Function	Tasks	Decision Level				
			1 Board of Directors	2 Committee	3 Individual Director	4 Delegate to Headteacher	5 Headteacher Day-to-day
	Behaviour	Headteacher has powers to search, with or without consent a pupil whom they reasonably suspect is carrying a knife or other weapon.					X
	Behaviour	To exclude a pupil for one or more fixed terms (not exceeding 45 days in total in a year) or permanently					X
	Behaviour	To review the use of exclusion and to decide whether or not to confirm all permanent exclusions (and fixed term exclusions where necessary)		X			
	Behaviour	To direct reinstatement of excluded pupils		X			
	Behaviour	To review the overall pattern and use of exclusions within the school.	X				
	Behaviour	To monitor and review pupil attendance				X	
	Behaviour	To set attendance targets		X			
	Behaviour	To decide whether parenting contracts should form part of the school's		X			
	Behaviour	To implement parent contracts				X	
	Pupil Welfare	To decide the content, presentation, and cost of school food, and where there is a cash cafeteria system, set the standard meals allowance for those entitled to free meals.		X			
	Pupil Welfare	To ensure that school policy and procedure for Looked After Children are consistent with measures set out in the statutory guidance.		X			
	Pupil Welfare	To decide whether to appoint a designated Director for Safeguarding Children or to retain as a full Board of Directors task	X				
	Pupil Welfare	To carry out annual review of Safeguarding Children and Child Protection policy and procedures and report to the BoD.		X			
	Parents	To publish the School Prospectus.	X				
	Parents	To approve and publish the School Profile annually.	X				
	Parents	To plan and coordinate strategies by which the Board of Directors can demonstrate its accountability and consult parents and community.	X				
	Parents	To adopt and review home-school agreements.		X			
	Parents	To ensure that school lunch nutritional standards are met.				X	

For Secretary	Key Function	Tasks	Decision Level				
			1 Board of Directors	2 Committee	3 Individual Director	4 Delegate to Headteacher	5 Headteacher Day-to-day
	Community	To consider matters relating to the role of the school in the community, including public relations.	X				
	Community	To ensure that the school contributes to community cohesion.		X			
	Extended Schools	To research and review the opportunities/challenges arising from extended school provision (from a pupil learning perspective).	X				
	Extended Schools	To research and review the opportunities/challenges arising from extended school provision (from a premises and resources perspective).		X			
	Extended Schools	To decide to offer additional activities under extended schools provision – or to cease provision.				X	
	Extended Schools	To put into place additional services provided.				X	
	Extended Schools	To ensure delivery of services provided.				X	
	Planning	To ensure that recommendations following OFSTED inspection are incorporated into the School Business and Development Plan/School Improvement Plan.	X				
		To prepare and review a strategy for school improvement on the following outcomes: • Stay safe • Be healthy • Enjoy and achieve • Achieve economic well-being • Make a positive contribution.	X				
	Planning	To agree priorities for the School Improvement Plan	X				
	Planning	To approve School Improvement Plan	X				
	Planning	To monitor School Improvement Plan overall	X				
	Staffing	To develop, review and oversee implementation of the Board of Directors' personnel policies (with reference to Employment Law and HR guidance).		X			
	Staffing	To appoint Headteacher (on recommendation of selection panel).	X				
	Staffing	To appoint Deputy Headteacher/Assistant Headteacher (on recommendation of selection panel).	X				
	Staffing	To appoint other teachers		X			
	Staffing	To appoint teachers to leadership group (as defined by agreed staffing structure).				X	
	Staffing	To appoint non teaching staff outside the leadership group.				X	
	Staffing	To draft/amend and review whole school pay policy.		X			
	Staffing	To decide on recommendations relating to the pay of all members of staff.		X			

For Secretary	Key Function	Tasks	1 Board of Directors	2 Committee	3 Individual Director	4 Delegate to Headteacher	5 Headteacher Day-to-day
	Staffing	To implement disciplinary procedures.					X
	Staffing	To agree disciplinary/capability procedures NB *Based on model policy as agreed with unions.*		X			
	Staffing	To dismiss Headteacher (BoD must act through Dismissal Committee		X			
	Staffing	To dismiss other staff (BoD must act through Dismissal Committee but normally delegated to Headteacher).				X	
	Staffing	To suspend Headteacher.			X		
	Staffing	To suspend staff (except Headteacher).				X	
	Staffing	To end suspension (Headteacher).		X			
	Staffing	To end suspension (except Headteacher).			X		
	Staffing	To determine staff complement.	X				
	Staffing	To approve applications for early retirement, secondment and leave of absence not covered by local agreements.		X			
	Staffing	To establish and maintain a performance management policy.		X			
	Staffing	To implement the performance management of staff				X	
	Staffing	To implement the performance management of Headteacher.		X			
	Staffing	To draft and review a policy on absence management.				X	
	Staffing	To agree and monitor a training strategy for teachers, support staff and Directors.				X	
	Premises	To obtain buildings insurance.		X			
	Premises	To develop a school buildings strategy (including budgeting for repairs etc.) and contributing to Asset Management Planning arrangements		X			
	Premises	To procure and agree a maintenance strategy for new buildings including developing a properly funded maintenance plan.		X			
	Premises	To review security of school premises and equipment.		X			
	Premises	To agree level of maintenance service the school will buy from service providers.			X		
	Premises	To research and be involved in drawing up an Accessibility Plan for the school.			X		
	Premises	To recommend a hiring policy to the Board of Directors and to oversee its implementation.				X	
	Premises	To approve hiring policy and charges		X			
	H & S	To implement health and safety arrangements					X

For Secretary	Key Function	Tasks	Decision Level				
			1 Board of Directors	2 Committee	3 Individual Director	4 Delegate to Headteacher	5 Headteacher Day-to-day
	H & S	To monitor health & safety arrangement			X		
	H & S	To ensure that suitable risk assessments are prepared and action taken to minimise risk.				X	
	H & S	To monitor accident book and agree appropriate action.			X		
	Admissions Academy	To implement Admissions Policy.	X				
	Admissions All schools	To appeal against Local Authority directions to admit pupil(s).		X			
	Organisation	To draw up instrument of government and any amendments thereafter.	X				
	Organisation	To agree proposals to change category of school.	X				
	Organisation	To consider forming, joining or leaving a federation	X				
	Organisation	To appoint (and remove) the chair and vice-chair of a permanent or a temporary Board of Directors.	X				
	Organisation	To appoint and dismiss the clerk to the Directors.	X				
	Organisation	To appoint and remove Directors.	X				
	Organisation	To appoint and remove associate members.	X				
	Organisation	To set up a Register of Directors' Business Interests.	X				
	Organisation	To approve and set up an Expenses Scheme.		X			
	Organisation	To consider whether or not to exercise delegation of functions to individuals or committees.	X				
	Organisation	To regulate the BoD procedures (where not set out in law) e.g. Standing Orders	X				
	Organisation	To establish and Review Committees annually.	X				
	Organisation	Agree a policy and protocol for Director visits to the school.		X			
	Finance	See attached Financial Regulations Manual					
	Finance	To set a charging and remissions policy.		X			
	Finance	To ensure provision of free school meals to those pupils meeting the criteria.				X	

Thanks to Rush Common Primary School.

Appendix 6: Example strategic objectives and key indicators

1. Our aim is to be the best multi-school academy in southern England	
Performance Indicators	Target Date
All Academy Schools to have an Ofsted outstanding rating	April 2015
All Academy Schools to consistently achieve progress and attainment standards within the top 25% nationally (KS1 – KS5)	April 2015
Satisfaction survey with stakeholders and if possible benchmark against other schools	Half Yearly

Notes

How can we measure and directly contribute to improvements in attainment? This is not just about actual results but also perceptions, image and other subjective criteria.

2. We want to achieve seamless progression across all key stages	
Performance Indicators	Target Date
Implement a 'through-life' teaching and learning strategy	April 2013
Create a rich and motivating curriculum acknowledged through student and parental 'voice' feedback; and independent verification	Annually at year end

Notes

What will help us to achieve an enhanced educational experience for our students? How can we assess 'seamless progression' at each key stage transition?

3. Maximise engagement with students, their families and the local community to achieve a vibrant community dimension	
Performance Indicators	Target Date
Produce an Academy Community Strategy document, detailing development of all key partnerships and interactions	July 2013
Annually audit the Academy's delivery of a 'safe, creative and ethical environment' with staff, parents and the local community	Easter term annually

Notes

What are the key areas for community engagement and how can they be measured? This also includes wider development of our students to help develop 'responsible, capable and confident young people who are active citizens in the 21st Century'.

4. Build a viable and sustainable long term Faringdon Education Strategy	
Performance Indicators	Target Date
Produce and publish a Faringdon Education Development Plan (10 year vision) linked to the Faringdon Neighbourhood Plan	April 2013
Proactively support the conversion of Faringdon Partnership schools to Academy status with feedback via the Headteacher Steering Group	November 2013

Notes

How can we keep a strategic perspective on the wider development of education locally?

5. Ensure that our Academy proactively adds value to member schools	
Performance Indicators	Target Date
Academy Board to subjectively assess the quality of approved 'Added Value Projects' being successfully implemented each year; and / or assessment by Local Governing Bodies using questionnaires with ratings on added-value progress	September Annually
Additional investment made available per year by becoming a Multi-school Academy – whether derived via economies of scale or other savings (measured as absolute quantum or % of total budget)	June Annually

Notes

Given that we need to add value to each school (above what was being achieved previously), what approach should we take to ensure that the sum is greater than the parts?

Copy kindly provided by Faringdon Academy of Schools. Reproduced with permission.

Appendix 7: Risk Assessment Form

Category	Specific	Probability	Impact	Score	Controls	Residual Probability	Residual Impact	Residual Score
Data Security and Integrity	Loss of up-to-date student information re students' past / present education, behaviour, medical or domestic situation or contact details				Tight controls in place. Acceptable usage policy – all staff have to read and sign.			
	Protection of confidential data – failure to maintain confidentiality of data on various media (print, data sticks, laptops, emails)				Tight controls in place. Training given to all staff. IT security. Acceptable usage policy signed by all staff.			
IT Hardware	Catastrophic failure of IT equipment impacting on teaching/ learning, management and support systems				New back-up and servers in place with APSs. New ICT vanilla network in place. Cco in with G4S for more power into server room.			
	Impact of crisis financial constraints on support systems (IT, H&S, medical care, parent information systems, website maintenance/ development)				Crisis financial constraints no longer in place.			
	Failure to develop ICT infrastructure needed to keep RWBA ahead of the curve				Recognised as high priority by school. Plan in place. Allocate annual budget.			
Financial Risk	Loss of financial control				Quality Finance Manager (Accountant) Headteacher line manages. Overview F&P			
	Insufficient income (core and additional) to maintain planned Teaching and Learning				Increasing numbers. Advertising. Recruitment drive. Proactive in other schools. Curriculum choice wider.			
	Fraud by employees, Governors or third parties				System in place, signatures etc.. Over £50,000 requires 3 tenders etc. Insurance – theft/fraud. External Audit			
	Theft of property by employees, governors, pupils, or third parties				Buildings locked and secure from 4pm. Theft is negligible?			

Category	Specific	Probability	Impact	Score	Controls	Residual Probability	Residual Impact	Residual Score
	Unknown liabilities, not covered by PFI contract				Headteacher leading with PFI contract. Link governor and chair of F and P heavily involved.			
	Underestimate of cost of outsourcing to replace WCC				All costings checked before outsourcing is bought			
Governance and Strategy	Failure to develop a clear aim and strategy for WBS (and to engage all staff in its achievement).				There are clear aims and they are being revisited. (Job of LT and Headteacher and Governing Body)			
	Failure to manage financial, operational, compliance and H&S risks				Checks in place for finance and new Finance Manager. Other issues less likely but all are covered on Governor Committees and standing items on Full Governing Body agenda. External audit			
	Failure to establish, maintain and comply with a framework of governance (roles, authorities, terms of reference, delegated powers etc.)				Follow Academy Handbook. All procedures set up and followed External Audit Reviewer			
	Suboptimal outcomes of change projects due to incomplete evaluation of options and analysis of risk and/or ineffective decision making and project management				Extensive consultation with governors happening all the time. Checks and tendering process does exist for items over £80,000. Formal project management training being looked into for a member of team.			
Long-term loss of staff	Staff leave the school or profession due to pressures of resource constraints or changing Terms and Conditions				Replace them. No one irreplaceable. May require short-term replanning. We have already shown we can manage this risk with a huge variety of people leaving including Deputy Headteacher			

Category	Specific	Probability	Impact	Score	Controls	Residual Probability	Residual Impact	Residual Score
Short-term loss of staff	Loss of large number of staff at one time due to strike, illness, accident, transport problems...causing loss of teaching and learning time				Always short-term. Planned time, work given. Time made up			
Loss of Buildings	Risk of damage to buildings – fire accident, loss of power/heat/water, poor maintenance, environmental causes				G4 sort out any problems			
	Lime Kiln development reduces access for RWBA to sports and other facilities				New campus proposed if not Lime Kiln will be refurbished.			
Pastoral Care	Failure to engage parental support against absence/truancy				Truancy call. EWO input. Student Managers phone home. Tutors phone home after 2 days. Electronic registration. Appointed our own EWO.			
	Pupil behaviour standards erode through gradual slippage/contagion				Outstanding T&L. Quality Assurance. Behaviour policy – stages, B15 etc.. Outstanding C, G, S.			
	Risk that students/parents are not given appropriate guidance leading to students embarking on wrong course.				Outstanding IAG. Interviews. Aim Higher. Information evenings. Personalised curriculum. ECM days. Outside agencies			
	Failure to work with outside agencies (social care/policy/healthy minds/primary schools etc.) leading to insufficient "not joined up" support				School contracts outside agencies constantly. MAF. MA meetings. TWC meetings. Cluster CPD			
	Press Level' school incident (site damage, financial error, violence, drugs etc.) leading to loss of student numbers, inability to recruit high calibre staff				Press training for LT (Headteacher has had this). Many incidents dealt with in past			

Category	Specific	Probability	Impact	Score	Controls	Residual Probability	Residual Impact	Residual Score
	Accidents with school				Risk Assessment. Meet G4S. H&S Policy. Outstanding T&L. Outstanding Safeguarding. Annual staff training			
	Ineffective risk assessment on school trips				Forms completed before you go. Signed off and checked			
	Inadequate visitor control/ supervision				Outstanding safeguarding procedure. CCTV			
Student Numbers varying from plan	Higher = pressure on staff and buildings (6th Form Centre, in particular)				Constant review of numbers in and out of school. LT awareness of numbers and potential impact. AHT curriculum looking into this rooming and timetable impact.			
	Lower = pressure on finances				Constant recruitment in primary and secondary schools for Years 7-12 entry			
Teaching Quality and Standards	Fall in quality of teaching delivered				Quality Assurance. 1-2-1. Professionalism. Outstanding T&L			
	Failure to maintain performance in GCSE/A-level and resulting loss of outstanding status leading to inability to attract pupil numbers and high calibre staff				Quality Assurance. 1-2-1. Professionalism. Outstanding T&L. Recent Orqual interference in English gradings has made this even more crucial. Curriculum change ahead. Porgress checked in all years against targets. Intervention as necessary.			

Thanks to Royal Wootton Bassett Academy.

Appendix 8: Example risk register

Risk ID	Risk (description)	Date Raised	Academy affected	Risk owner	Probability	Impact	Severity	Aggravating factors	Mitigation measures	Status	Date Reviewed	Date closed
	Governance and Legal											
G1												
G2												
	Strategic											
S1												
S2												
	Financial											
F1												
F2												
	Human resources											
HR1												
HR2												
	Health and safety											
HS1												
HS2												
	Other legal and operational											

Continued overleaf

Risk ID	Risk (description)	Date Raised	Academy affected	Risk owner	Probability	Impact	Severity	Aggravating factors	Mitigation measures	Status	Date Reviewed	Date closed
LO1												
LO2	Educational											
E1												
E2												

Copy provided by Cabot Learning Federation. Reproduced with permission.

Appendix 9: Committee self-evaluation

Committee Self-Evaluation   Name:

	Agree. Evidence	Neither agree nor disagree. Steps we could take to improve	Disagree. Steps we could take to improve
I understand the purpose and goals of the Committee			
The committee has help and support of the key stakeholders			
Meetings are planned well in advance			
Meetings begin and end on time			
I know how to contribute to the agenda			
I prepare and send out papers supporting my agenda items			
Agenda is clear and self explanatory			
The time devoted to each agenda item is proportionate to its importance			
All paperwork is sent out well in advance			

	Agree. Evidence	Neither agree nor disagree. Steps we could take to improve	Disagree. Steps we could take to improve
I read the paperwork before the meeting			
We have an agreed policy for "Any other business"			
I note down the Action I am responsible for and report back in the agreed time frame			
When I speak I feel listened to and my comments are valued			

What do you like most about our meetings?

What would you like to see improve in our meetings?

What would you consider to be the main achievements of the committee this academic year?

Thanks to Naureen Khalid.

Appendix 10: 360° Review of chair's performance

Name:

The chair understands the role of the committee and communicates it effectively to other governors.			
Strongly Agree	Agree	Disagree	Strongly disagree
Comments			

The relationship between the chair and the deputy head and other members of SLT who attend the committee meetings is that of a supportive and critical friend and is not 'cosy'.			
Strongly Agree	Agree	Disagree	Strongly Disagree
Comments			

The chair understands the difference between the role of the committee and the role of the SLT and seeks to ensure that the committee has a strategic focus.			
Strongly Agree	Agree	Disagree	Strongly Disagree
Comments			

The chair encourages the committee to review its processes and practices.			
Strongly Agree	Agree	Disagree	Strongly Disagree
Comments			

The chair ensures that meeting agendas and the work of the committee focus on school priorities.			
Strongly Agree	Agree	Disagree	Strongly disagree
Comments			

All governors and members of SLT feel they can contribute to meetings and feel that their views are listened to.			
Strongly agree	Agree	Disagree	Strongly disagree
Comments			

Meetings are well organised and run to time. Decisions are clear and are minuted.			
Strongly Agree	Agree	Disagree	Strongly disagree
Comments			

The chair has a good understanding of the school and its ethos.			
Strongly Agree	Agree	Disagree	Strongly disagree
Comments			

Interpersonal Skills: The chair is friendly, approachable and accepts effective criticism			
Strongly Agree	Agree	Disagree	Strongly Disagree
Comments			

Communication skills: The chair is a good communicator and listener			
Strongly Agree	Agree	Disagree	Strongly Disagree
Comments			

Leadership: The chair encourages teamwork and delegates appropriately			
Strongly Agree	Agree	Disagree	Strongly Disagree
Comments			

The chair has your confidence			
Strongly Agree	Agree	Disagree	Strongly Disagree
Comments			

For the following, please give an answer rather than using the above scale.

1. What do you like best about the way I chair the committee?

2. Is there anything you would want to change in the way I chair the committee?

Thanks to Naureen Khalid.

Appendix 11: Data protection

The material in this Appendix has been compiled by Peter Wright, solicitor and managing director of DigitalLawUK.

Academies should comply with the Data Protection Act. What does that mean?

- If you have a breach – what do you do? It is now a matter of when, not if, you are breached.
  - Keep quiet?
  - Tell those involved not to do it again?
  - Inform the parents of pupils that are affected?
- Should you tell the Information Commissioner's Office (ICO)? There is no legal requirement to do so (*at present*), however:
  - Full and frank disclosure to those involved will be taken into account by the ICO should it issue a monetary penalty notice, which can be of the value of up to £500,000, following a Data Protection Breach
  - An academy is classed as the data controller for holding the data of its staff and pupils, and as the data controller and it is the data controller that is fined. An academy cannot delegate this responsibility. By the same token, academies can be fined for services they may have outsourced.

1. 'Cloud' storage
Principles
Andrew Jonathan Crossley (ACS Law) (10 May 2011)

- Firm specialised in pursuing copyright infringement on behalf of holders.
- Massive data requests sent to ISPs for 1,000s of IP addresses, ISPs would return requests with name and address data for each IP address. Would be saved to CMS by ACS.
- Some of those pursued would provide information about being elderly or infirm with chronic or serious illnesses or mental health issues, whereupon ACS would enter into compromise agreements. These could contain sensitive data including medical records or bank account and credit card info.
- AJC asked junior paralegal to find a new web hosting company as current one not fit for purpose. Neither AJC nor paralegal had IT qualifications. Carried out search and found web hosting company with 'home' package at £5.99 pcm. Not intended for business use. No guarantees given regarding personal data storage.

- High-profile litigation led to a targeted attack from activists to server. Server went offline and file containing ALL e-mails from ACS account made available online allowing spreadsheets and e-mails to be accessed. 6,000 sets of personal details leaked.
- ACS reported to ICO, stopped using cloud host, obtained report with 20 suggestions to improve security including a firewall and access control. Spent £20,000 as a result of incident, suffered loss of revenue and had to make 14 of 16 staff redundant.
- Breach of Principle 7 – Appropriate measures shall be taken against unauthorised or unlawful processing of personal data and against accidental loss, destruction or damage to personal data.
- No professional IT advice taken, had not followed guidance on BSO/IEC 27001.
- ICO felt that as a lawyer, the data controller should have been fully aware of his obligations under the Data Protection Act.
- Issued Monetary Penalty Notice of £200,000 as reasonable and proportionate.

Practical guidance

Cloud computing: Reasons not to do it:
- Still some unknowns.
- Lack of control.
- Security.

Reasons why you should do it:
- Exceptionally versatile.
- Less expensive and cumbersome than on-site servers.
- It is the future of data storage.

List of 10 questions to ask cloud service providers:

1 What is the reputation of the vendor? Are they well known or a new start up that could be 'here today gone tomorrow'? If possible, obtain references from other lawyers that use the same system.

2 Will I have unrestricted access to my data? The lawyer must have full unfettered access to data. Can be ensured through off-site back-up. Alternatively, have a secondary back-up in case provider restricts access for any reason.

3 What will happen when I stop using vendor's service – what will happen to data? Ensure all data can be recovered, ideally in a non-proprietary format such as .csv. If relationship ends in dispute (e.g. non-payment of bills) will you still have access to the data or have it returned? Some cloud providers are explicit on this point that users will still have access and have data returned even in event of non-payment of bills. You also do not want the vendor to retain any of your data, even as a back-up, after you have stopped using the service.

4   Are passwords required to protect access to data? Will two-stage verification be used and will this be using a RSA token or text message system? You may also be logged out after a period of inactivity to prevent unauthorised access.

5   What is the provider's policy for the handling of confidential data? You need to know how the vendor's employees will treat data to preserve confidentiality. You may want to ensure that the provider notifies you if they receive a request to provide your data (e.g. to the police as part of an investigation).

6   Does the vendor use encryption? Data movement should be covered by secure socket lawyers (SSL) encryption of at least 128 bit. Data is encrypted and authenticated with the recipient. Many vendors use 256 bit. Web addresses will display as 'HTTPS' if SSL is being used and a padlock icon should appear on the browser. Data should remain encrypted while at rest on vendor's server.

7   What measures will vendor take to back-up data? You need daily back-up to multiple locations including physical removal from vendor's primary location. Even if vendor has back-up, you should have your own back-up system. If vendor offers regular ability to export or download your data, ensure that this is done and logged to a secure location.

8   How does the provider protect the security of the network? There should be firewalls, virus detection systems and the provider should be able to easily provide you with documentation about this. There should be regular scans of the system and ports to detect any unauthorised access.

9   How does the provider protect physical security of the data centre?
    - Where is the centre located?
    - What is the security? Is there video monitoring and verification?
        - Are there uninterrupted power supplies and a generator?
        - Redundant climate systems to maintain systems?
        - Fire detection and suppression including offsite alarm and monitoring?
        - 24 × 7 system monitoring?

Few cloud providers have their own data centre, so try to insist on it and if they outsource, still find answers to these questions.

10 What are the vendor's terms of service? Review terms and any licence agreements. Look for terms about confidentiality, security and data ownership
    - Train staff.
    - Verify regularly.

Do not rely on the cloud 100%.

2. Back-up, disaster plan and disaster recovery
Principles
Buncefield (11 December 2005)
- Damaged 30 nearby buildings

Boston alcohol warehouse fire (14 July 2011)

- Massive fire led to huge response from emergency services, massive cordon around hazard due to risk of further explosion. Who knows if an illegal business is being operated from a nearby unit?

Sheffield flood (2007)

- Heavy persistent rainfall led to massive flood and attendant issues.

A disaster does not have to be a terror attack or emergency incident in your office or building. It could be something as mundane as a gas or water leak preventing access to your office, or a limited fire in a derelict building some distance away leading to the police restricting access to your office. Or even a power cut. What would you do if access to your office and systems were limited, even if just for an hour or two? This could be enough to prevent a major transaction or event.

Practical guidance

Rule of one's exemplified

- Have a back-up of all data. Daily back-up and weekly back-up. Have a back-up register completed by staff.
- Have a back-up of your back-up. Consider large monthly back-up after end of month procedures followed.
- Test and verify your back-up regularly.

Scenarios to consider:

#1 IT system goes down

- Have paper back-up of all crucial data such as payroll, HR and pupil records at the academy but in a secure fireproof and waterproof safe
- Had a digital file of all raw data in a .csv format that could then be used in any other system. Copy kept updated with all off-site digital back-ups.

#2 Rain in the academy – flood from roof leak above

- All papers in office scanned when they came in onto digital files and backed-up offsite.
- All original documents kept in fire and waterproof safe or an inexpensive hazard-resistant cabinet.

*Once you have a system, **USE IT** – then no need to worry in future.

3. Remote working/Travel

Principles

Jala Transport Ltd (26 September 2013)

- Small money-lending business. Owner driving to work when thief leaned through window and stole briefcase from seat of car. Briefcase contained external hard drive and documents.

- Hard drive protected by password but unencrypted. Contained all details of 250 clients including ID proof.
- £5,000 fine but far greater damage from loss of reputation and bad publicity.

Practical guidance
So it happens – be smart
Electronic
- Encrypted/secure access only.
- Monitored access so can identify who, when and where.
- Training staff on when and how to use (i.e. not using unsecure WiFi hotspots to access your secure academy server).
- Lock devices and keep as few data files on remote devices as possible.
- Encrypted USB drives using products like Trucrypt.
- Where – who can see your screen?
- What can people see?
- How you protect data:
  - first class travel;
  - never leave unattended;
  - work with redacted travel files.

Paper
- Use locked cases
- Who can see your papers? (How often have you seen others working on trains and been able to tell that they are working on confidential papers!)
- Never leave unattended. (Remember criticism of David Cameron leaving Red Box unattended on train.)

Use specific redacted files put together to be taken out of the office for this specific purpose that do not contain any sensitive personal data.

4. Devices/Laptops/Phones
Principles
Ealing & Hounslow Council (4 February 2011)
- Ealing operated 'Out of Hours' service with staff working from home in the evening and supplied staff with phones and laptops so that they could work remotely.
- Opportunistic theft at home of one of workers, two laptops stolen. Sensitive personal data on both machines, none of it encrypted. Breached Ealing's own professed data protection policy by not being encrypted. Staff received data protection training at induction, but staff member had been there for 12 years.
- Home working policy existed but management had not checked out of hours team was actually following it. No quarterly assessments carried out, despite being supposed practice.

- Hounslow subcontracted out-of-hours cover to Ealing as well. Contract had no details about security to be followed by Ealing as it would contain data on Hounslow users. No procedure for Hounslow to monitor if Ealing was in compliance with Data Protection Act. Hounslow itself had no security policy in place, just a series of 'Do's and Don'ts'.

Ealing kept its work from Hounslow, but would your clients stay with you after such a breach?

Practical guidance
- Anti-virus on phones and tablets.
- Careful of other apps on devices.
- Have Bluetooth off by default on all mobile devices. Only activate when necessary.
- Be aware of using open wifi networks in public locations like cafés.
- Ensure any site that is interacted with uses HTTPS not unencrypted HTTP connections. If you don't, anyone nearby can use Firesheep to see what you are doing.
- Easier to think about securing devices if they are perceived differently. Devices are mini vaults of vital information and portals to more vital information via remote access – treat them that way.
- Encryption
- Passwords
- Screen locks
- Anti-virus software – Can even download free anti-virus as a start, but better premium anti-virus apps are available.
- Limit the mixing of business and personal use on devices.
- Protect them like you would a million pound cheque. They are not to be left in a cab, bar, train or unattended car overnight.

Have a home working policy in place.

5. Bring Your Own Device

Bring Your Own Device (BYOD) is the use by staff of their own personal devices such as smart phones or tablet PCs to access academy related e-mails, contact lists, applications and data, including accessing remote working systems. However it is a practice that is fraught with risk:

- Evaluate – is it worth it?
- Reduced cost to academy in short term in having staff easily contactable and more productive.
- Therefore greater flexibility for staff **BUT** greatly increased risk of security breach.
- Increased chances of misuse of personal confidential data.

Don't do it or have very clear guidelines, policies and training with support on work-based applications on devices from IT support. Cannot be treated in a cursory or casual manner.

6. Destruction of IT hardware

Principles

Brighton & Sussex University Hospitals NHS Trust (1 June 2012)

- Destruction of hard drives. Contractor used sub-contractor to destroy drives for free. No contract directly between hospital and sub-contractor. Basic checks carried out against sub-contractor.
- Sub-contractor only occasionally accompanied on site.
- Generic certificate of destruction provided for all drives. Should have individual certificated containing serial numbers for each drive.
- Drives found for sale online on eBay – still contained medical records. Easily available info for anyone familiar with MS Access, no encryption.
- Hospital unable to confirm how large volume of drives were removed from their site without their knowledge.
- No audit trails or logs of destruction undertaken by sub-contractor.
- Fined hospital £325,000.

NHS Surrey (12 July 2013)

- Sub-contractor assured NHS IT that drives would be destroyed using industrial guillotine for free.
- Destruction certificates provided, but disposal process not observed. No written contract in place, but written assurances given.
- Public began buying refurbished PC equipment online containing hard drives that held medical records and other data.
- Certificates had been provided for these supposedly destroyed hard drives.
- Fined £200,000.

The largest fines to date by the Information Commissioner (ICO) have been for organisations that had large amounts of IT hardware, including hard drives, to be destroyed. This task was outsourced and led to hardware being found for sale online, despite the organisation being assured that the correct procedures had been followed and that the hardware had been destroyed. Generic destruction certificates had been supplied rather than specific ones and contractors had not been constantly supervised at all times. While the contractor had been at fault, it was the organisation that was fined and suffered negative publicity.

Practical guidance

Phones

- Probably the lowest security risk but still a risk – particularly smart phones which are themselves mini-computers.
- Destroy SIM cards.

- Ask providers to wipe phone memory and confirm with spot-checks.
- Safest? Destroy the phone yourself.

Tablets
- As risky as computers.
- If you have them recycled or destroyed, verify method and obtain a destruction certificate for each device.
- Safest – destroy them yourself.

Computers (Desktop and Laptop)
- Do not try to have them recycled or donated. Good intention but not a risk you can afford to take.
- If you have them destroyed by a third party, verify method and obtain destruction certificate for each device. Observe destruction.
- Safest – destroy hard drives yourself.

7. E-mail encryption and security/data rooms
Principles

Academies store large volumes of personal data. There can also be commercial and confidential data for commercial contractors. Spreadsheets of confidential data along with other documents can often be in use across a school. Any personal data includes:
- Full names
- Date of birth
- Address
- NI number
- Photograph or video footage
- Bank account details (e.g. sort code, account, IBAN)
- Biometric data – fingerprints, retina scans, height & weight measurements
- Personal e-mail addresses
- Passwords.

Personal data should not be sent via unencrypted e-mail. If a parent or other party refuses to comply with measures taken to encrypt communication, make it clear that data will not be sent and they will be charged to receive it special delivery or can collect from the academy if they show ID and sign for it. They should be pleased with the measures that you are taking to protect their data!

Practical guidance

All e-mail systems you use should be encrypted 64 bit.

Password access to the academy e-mail system should be via two-stage identification.

If you are encrypting individual files attached to e-mails, send a separate e-mail containing the encryption key after the encrypted data has been sent to the recipient and receipt of the encrypted data has been confirmed by the intended recipient.

Consider using a **secure** cloud site to share data with client (Virtual Data Rooms) – same safeguards as discussed under Cloud providers above

Confidentiality notices on e-mails:

- Best practice for an academy to use in all correspondence.
- Consider an additional notice when first sending an e-mail to a new recipient at the top of e-mail (e.g. as when hard-copy mail is sent private and confidential).

Doesn't work if all sensitive data and information is laid out BEFORE the warning is given in an e-mail footer. Consider having 'Protect: Personal Data' at the top of any e-mails.

There are numerous encryption systems from free applications like Winzip to encrypt individual attachments through to premium encryption that are less time consuming and more secure.

8. Administration system/Finance and accounts systems/Payroll/Regulatory

Principles

There are numerous time-saving systems on the market. However consider whether they are secure. Do they store data on your server or at their own facility? If so, ensure that the data is stored in the UK and enquire as to how it is transmitted to and from your school.

Practical guidance

- Who has access to any data? How can it be accessed?
- Contracts with any IT suppliers should allow for systems to be available for regular inspection and data protection audits.
- Ask the questions. Is the system secure? How secure?
- On-site, cloud or another system?
- Password access.
- Monitor and tracking of access by staff.
- Limit who is able to act as an administrator.
- Firewall options to lock out staff that are leaving.
- Consider giving department access only to specific parts of system that they require to fulfil their duties.
- Test back-ups regularly – at least monthly.
- Consider hard copy back-up printed once a month (e.g. after invoicing).
- Keep in fire/ hazard-proof safe.
- Where is system located?
- How is data transmitted?

■ Consider RSA token or similar access.

9. Website, privacy, cookies and website back-up
Principles
Cookies are items that a website installs on a user's machine when they visit the site. It can tell the website where the user is based and what pages they looked at. Products like Google Analytics install cookies on user's machines. More sophisticated cookies track a user's search patterns while they visit other sites, so that when a user returns, the site will display advert banners based on searches carried out by that specific user previously.

The ICO requires that all websites that use cookies need to have a privacy policy that makes it clear what cookies are used by the site, what data they collect and how a user can turn them off. This privacy policy is not generic – it must be specific to the site. It must be easily identifiable from the home page. The 'consent' button is not strictly required, but it is nonetheless good practice. It is likely that if your academy has a website, it will have cookies and the privacy policy must accurately reflect this.

Practical guidance
Limit access through website
■ Data collected from viewers
■ Limit information shared on website
   – Should all staff be on website – is it necessary?
   – Should internal policies and procedures be on the site?

Train staff on web surfing, cookies and downloading anything from web.

Search engines build search profiles of individual users from search history. Consider using 'DuckDuckGo' which does not store search data as Google and others do.

Have a 'consent to cookies' button installed on the homepage for a 'belt and braces' approach.

10. Social media, personal data and confidentiality
Principles
Many academies have engaged on social media, with their own pages on Facebook and/or LinkedIn along with a Twitter feed. This needs to be handled carefully. How should the 'corporate' social media accounts be updated? One business gave this task to a junior member of staff as they were felt to be the most comfortable with the technology. They proceeded to set up the corporate Twitter account so that it could be updated from their phone as they were more comfortable with this, only to forget that the phone was still enabled over the weekend. During an evening out, a friend picked up the phone and sent a 'joke' tweet, only for it to go

out on the corporate Twitter account. The member of staff lost their position due to this error, as they were still on their initial probationary period.

On personal accounts, academy staff must consider how much information they give out on social media. For example, 'Going to London for a meeting' is acceptable, as is 'Going to London for a conference' ... 'Meeting Mr & Mrs X to discuss Pupil Y' is not. This may seem obvious, but a quick look at news related to social media shows that users reveal confidential personal data all the time without considering the consequences.

Staff in organisations have also been known to talk about information relating to clients, customers, patients or other staff. If this continues with no policy or guidance from an employer, the employer can be held liable for any online bullying that takes place between staff members.

Make sure management are aware how to access any corporate social media accounts. Remember HMV, who made much of their head office staff redundant before realising one of those losing their job was in charge of the Twitter feed. Several tweets were sent under the #HMVxfactorfiring hashtag before the account was closed, leading to the story featuring in the national press.

Should staff be updating social media from their own devices during work hours? Staff at the DVLA have been disciplined for updating social media accounts from their own devices during work hours.

Practical guidance

- Make a proper appointment for an individual responsible for the corporate social media feed, or contract with a supplier. Don't just pick the first person in the office below the age of 30 and presume that they are comfortable with the technology.
- Have clear policies for how the firm is to use social media.
- Provide guidance for staff on how the corporate account should be updated – from what device, appropriate content etc.
- Guidance on who should be connected to, or followed, on social media – should staff be connecting with parents on LinkedIn or other networks?
- What should staff be saying about their employment and experience on a LinkedIn profile?
- Remind staff that their work is highly confidential and their pupils rely on their discretion
- Clear policy not to discuss work on social media
- Even technically savvy staff can make inadvertent mistakes. One US lawyer checked in on Foursquare at a location before confirming in the narrative that they were attending to take witness evidence. Given that their field was defending professional negligence it was clear who they were representing and what the meeting was in connection with. In such circumstances, a lawyer is very close to breaching their duty of client confidentiality

- Two-stage social media account authorisation (e.g. enter login, password and a unique token supplied via e-mail or SMS to the user).
- Avoid using services such as Foursquare that require location information.
- Advise staff to remove DOB from social media profiles and to be aware of what is posted online about them by their 'friends' such as being tagged in inappropriate photographs.
- Own your own social media accounts. Don't let a member of staff take your corporate Twitter feed and hard-won followers with them when they leave. It is up to you as an employer to make it clear what proprietorial right, if any, is exerted over social media contacts.

11. Password security
Principles
Social media accounts, e-mail accounts and other applications like remote access, virtual data rooms and document management systems often all require password authentication. This can lead to a plethora of passwords. However, if a password is easy to guess – and over 50% of passwords are apparently 'password1' – they can be hacked easily. Multi-nationals like McDonalds and Jeep have all had their corporate social media accounts hacked. This can lead to reputational damage, not to mention the loss of thousands of carefully acquired followers.

Practical guidance
- Two-stage social media account authorisation.
- Don't use same password across multiple accounts.
- Regularly change passwords (have a system for this).
- Mixture of upper and lower case, numbers and non-alphanumeric characters.

Change regularly, ideally monthly.

12. CCTV/Hearing loop/Recording of calls
Principles
Many CCTV systems record and store their footage to a server. A restaurant was fined by the ICO for having their CCTV footage stored on a server where it was unencrypted and could be accessed remotely. As more and more academies have rudimentary CCTV at their entrances or in reception areas for security purposes, consider the damage from a breach where the details of who had visited the school revealed the identities of pupils and parents. Security is advisable and can be provided at an increasingly lower cost as the technology becomes more widespread.

Many academies are also using hearing loops for pupils and parents who may be hearing impaired. While this should be encouraged, ensure that the system is secure – could it be accessed remotely? Is the audio recorded and stored? This could present a risk.

Some academies routinely record calls. Some parents have been known to request that calls are recorded. If calls are recorded, participants need to be aware of this and message should be played to all callers so that they are fully aware of this practice.

Practical guidance
- Check positioning of CCTV cameras. What is being recorded?
- Where is footage or audio stored? Is it over-written, logged or backed-up? Server or cloud?
- Ensure appropriate level of security applied to data.
- Ensure data kept for no longer than is necessary.

13. Office procedures/file storage/desk storage
Principles
Schools historically had large numbers of hard-copy administrative files, many of which stay on a desk while they are worked on over several days; they may pass from teaching staff to secretarial, admin staff or accounts. They often find their way onto the corner of a desk, in a large pile on the floor by the desk, under the desk, on top of cupboards and stacked on shelves as well as their intended home in filing cabinets or lockable cupboards. These are often kept unlocked or in cupboards that are never actually closed and locked. While this allows for easy access, it also leaves an academy dangerously at risk from a data protection breach. Cleaning or maintenance staff may have access to areas out of hours or when staff are absent, while security staff may also have the run of the entire building. Should their access to certain areas be limited?

Have clear procedures that MUST be followed

Practical guidance
Use the basic principle that if you can see it without unlocking, entering a password or other security hurdle, then others can see it too.
- Where are administrative files stored?
  - How are they accessed?
  - Who can access them (paper and digital)?
- How secure are your storage or archive rooms?
- Third parties present in office (parents, guests, health visitors, cleaners, security, maintenance)
  - Can they see administrative files +/or personal data on a desk, on shelves, or on the screen of a PC or device?
  - Can third parties access file storage, server rooms or other facilities from near reception areas (e.g. if visitor is directed to where the toilets are?)
  - Can third parties access data if they use your Intranet, or access your WiFi network?

'Clear desk' policy

- Before seeing third parties in an office.
- At the end of the day before leaving the school.
- All staff must comply – needs the academy leadership to lead for all to follow.
- Consider having certain rooms clearly marked 'Do not enter' and restricting access to all except those members of staff who truly need access to them to fulfill their roles.

Consider having key fob access to areas where administrative staff work and data is stored and even having specific fobs for specific areas.

14. Archived files/Destruction/Confidential waste

Principles

Scottish Borders Council (11 Sept 2012)

- Council digitised pension records. No contract in place with processor carrying out the digitising.
- Public noticed paper recycling bank overflowing with discarded files containing personal data – files handed to police.
- Council unaware after it received digitised images exactly what was happening to the old files.

Fined £250,000.

Practical guidance

The basic principle of filing and archiving. File archives are easily accessible. If material can be viewed by you without any security steps being taken, then someone else could see it too. It is not an excuse to blame a lack of security on needing to have regular access to the archive.

- Locked and secure archive storage. Don't assume out of sight out of mind.
- Review security regularly.
- Train staff and spot check to ensure that they are following procedures.
- Repeat training regularly.

Destruction

- On-site
  - Storage prior to destruction must be as secure as during archive.
  - Cross-cut, shred or incinerate (strip-shred is not enough).
  - Recycling is not an option unless documents are near pulp.
- Off-site
  - Storage before pick up to be as secure as during archive.
  - Have strong secure contract with destruction supplier that is up to date, valid and current and allows for regular audit. Any problems and YOU will be fined, not contractor.
- Verify that destruction is undertaken as they claim. Ideally can be shredded by contractor at your premises using their equipment and resources.

15. Post/Confidential post/DX/Fax

Principles

Bank of Scotland PLC (30 July 2013)

- Member of public received details of BoS customer's mortgage by fax in error.
- 1 digit difference between internal fax number and actual recipient's fax.
- Error repeated consistently over a period of time, despite remedial action having been taken with individuals involved.
- Recipient, tired with continuing to receive faxes from BoS, stopped contacting BoS about them and just referred matter to ICO. Supplied ICO with 60 faxes containing personal data, including ID.
- Faxes sent from multiple different locations in BoS but all intended for same internal department.
- Further breaches continued after notification to controller that ICO was investigating matter. Probable that it was not mis-dialling, but incorrect pre-programming of numbers into fax machine.
- Majority of faxes sent with no fax cover sheet which contained disclaimer.
- Fined £75,000.

Nursing & Midwifery Council (12 February 2013)

- DVDs and evidence sent to Fitness to Practice (FTP) hearing to be held at hotel. Instructions given for package to be sent securely via courier.
- Package delivered and opened at hearing but DVDs not inside. No encryption applied to DVDs. Contained interviews with witnesses. No policy in place requiring that such data be encrypted.
- DVDs never found. No evidence package was tampered with.
- Fined £150,000.

Plymouth City Council (22 November 2012)

- Council sent additional social work report pages from third-party matter to family. Contained sensitive details of child neglect.
- Human error and no system in place to check correct documents being sent to recipients. In this instance report picked up from printer containing correct report and three additional pages from another report. All pages then packaged and sent out.
- Revealed single printer was in use by five members of staff in a single 15-minute period. Created risk of reports and papers being picked up by other users.

Practical guidance

- Staff must be well trained.
- Best practice – consider that all post could be marked 'Private & Confidential'.
- Have a procedure for packaging sensitive/personal data; double skinning envelopes etc.

- Fax cover sheets to be used at all times. Follow-up call to ensure received by correct recipient; call to be logged.
- System for unintended recipients to be able to report receipt and for issue to be dealt with promptly, efficiently and sensitively.
- Have individual printers for each department and do not have large numbers of staff all using the same printer. If a specific department or staff member regularly prints sensitive, personal data, consider providing them with their own printer.
- Consider having an ID for individual users to key into printer that has to be entered before their document can be printed.

16. Data protection policy and training

All of these principles and procedural steps need to be codified for your organisation into a data protection and security policy which can form a large part of your school's employee handbook. This can provide real guidance and change the way that your academy operates.

This can only be done with good practical training for all staff and incorporation into the training given to all new members of staff joining the school.

For the policies to work, they need to be regularly audited and spot-checked. They need to be adopted from the top, with the academy leadership taking a lead and showing an example for others to follow.

It must not be a document that just sits on a shelf gathering dust. It will need regular review and updating, ideally on an annual basis. Refresher update training should also be provided to staff. A one-off training session is not an end in itself.

Training should not just be 'death by Powerpoint'. Allow staff to understand the risks and the possible damage to the business. Allow them to input and if they think of a way of implementing something that is sufficiently rigorous but allows them to get the work done more efficiently, consider their input and modify or implement accordingly. Have assessments or 'informal quizzes' where staff are questioned about different scenarios and asked what the appropriate action would be. Ask them for examples from their daily activity too and continually assess risks to your business as it evolves and changes.

17. Relations with the ICO

There is a vast amount of information on the ICO website including check lists. Use it. Use the ICO helpline, consult on any extraordinary issues. Make sure you are registered as a data controller. If you are unsure about a procedure your academy is following, call and query it with the ICO. See what established best practice should be.

Have a proactive relationship with the regulator, which can help if you subsequently do have a data breach.

18. Data protection changes in immediate future

New EU Data Protection regulation could come in imminently. They would not require implementation at UK level with an Act of Parliament, so the Data Protection Act 1998 will be replaced immediately.

In its current draft form, businesses would have to report breaches within 24 hours. Would need measures in place to detect and report such breaches quickly.

Regulators may be able to fine based on percentage of turnover rather than on fixed rate, as currently set at £500,000.

Regularly consult a specialist in data protection for clear guidance on new regulatory matters to be aware of and any changes in the law that could affect your school.

Glossary

Academy State-funded schools, independent of Local Authority control.

Academy chain Any collaboration between academies whether that is done through a legal structure (i.e. MAT or umbrella) or a more informal approach (e.g. collaborative agreement).

Accounts A statement of the academy's financial affairs which can refer to published accounts or internal management accounts.

ACMF Academies Capital Maintenance Fund.

Annual return A return of information that all companies must make to the registrar of companies within every 12-month period providing a snapshot of the company including its directors, principal business activities and registered office.

ARD Accounting reference date – the date that marks the end of a company's accounting year end for the purposes of preparation and filing of statutory accounts.

Articles of association The academy's main constitutional document which prescribes the internal management, decision making and running of the academy trust and its liability.

BME Black and Minority Ethnic.

Board of directors The collective term for the academy's directors acting together as the governing body of the company, having the powers and authorities that are bestowed upon it by the company's constitution.

Board meeting A formal meeting of the board of directors.

Board resolution A formal resolution or decision of the board of directors.

CA 2006 Companies Act 2006.

CEO Chief Executive Officer (in a MAT).

Charitable company A company set up and run solely for non-profit making purposes with the proceeds only to be used for the purpose of the charity.

Companies House An executive agency of the Department for Business Innovation and Skills, Companies House is the registry for companies incorporated in the UK.

Company limited by guarantee A company where the liability of the members is limited to a fixed amount that each member agrees to contribute to the assets of the company in the event of a winding up.

Company secretary An officer of a company with no legally defined role but who generally has responsibilities with regard to the administrative, governance and compliance aspects of a company's affairs.

Connected person Persons who are considered to be connected with a director such as a spouse or civil partner, any other person whom the director lives with in an enduring family relationship, the director's children and stepchildren, the director's parents and a body corporate in which the director has an interest in at least 20% of the share capital.

Corporate director A company which acts as a director of another company.

Corporate governance Principles and best practice concerning the way in which companies are run and directed. There is no one definition of what corporate governance is, in the broader view it also encompasses issues relating to corporate social responsibility and business ethics.

Date of Incorporation The date on which a company was formed.

DBS Disclosure and Barring Service – replaces Criminal Records Bureau (CRB).

De facto **director** A person acting as a director who has not been formally or validly appointed.

Derivative claim A claim brought by a member of a company against a director on the academy's behalf in accordance with the procedure set out in the Companies Act 2006.

DfE Department for Education.

Directors' general duties Seven general duties of directors which are set out in the Companies Act 2006.

Disqualification order A court order preventing a person from, among others, acting as a director of a company without the consent of the court for the period of time specified in the order. Breach of a disqualification order is a criminal offence.

DPA Data Protection Act 1998.

Duty of skill and care One of the seven codified general duties of directors set out in the Companies Act requiring directors to exercise reasonable care, skill and diligence.

EAG Earmarked Annual Grant – paid in respect of either recurrent expenditure or capital expenditure for specific purposes agreed between the Secretary of State and the academy.

EFA Education Funding Agency – an executive agency of the DfE.

Electronic communication A communication sent in electronic form such as by e-mail, text or on a disk.

Electronic filing A form or document filed with Companies House in electronic format using either approved software or the Companies House WebFiling service.

Executive director A director who is a full-time employee with management responsibility within the academy.

EYFS Early Years Foundation Stage.

FASNA Freedom and Autonomy for Schools – National Association – a national forum for self-governing primary, secondary and special schools and academies.

FE Form Entry (as in 2FE).

FE Further Education.

FFT Fischer Family Trust.

Filing The process of submitting or presenting documents or information to Companies House.

FMGS Financial Management and Governance Self-Assessment.

FMSiS Financial Management Standards in Schools (now replaced by FMGS).

FOI Freedom of Information.

Free school An academy set up by a 'proposer group' such as parents, teachers, charities or other groups.

FS Foundation stage.

FSM Free school meals.

GAG General annual grant – funding paid to cover the normal running costs of the academy such as salary and administration costs.

General meeting A formal meeting of an academy's members.

HSE Health and Safety Executive.

IAA Independent Academies Association – a membership organisation dedicated to supporting leaders of academies.

ICSA The Institute of Chartered Secretaries and Administrators.

Incorporation The process by which a company is created, also referred to as 'formation' and 'registration'.

INSET In-Service Education and Training.

KS1 Key Stage 1, age 5–7 'Infants'.

KS2 KS2 age 7–11 'Juniors'.

KS3 KS3 age 11–14.

KS4 KS4 age 14–16.

LA Local Authority.

LAAP Local Authority Associated Persons.

LADO Local Authority Designated Officer.

LGB Local Governing Body.

LGHA Local Government and Housing Act 1989.

LGPS Local Government Pension Scheme.

Maintained school A school funded by central government via the local authority.

Management accounts Accounts produced by an academy for internal decision making and monitoring purposes.

MAT Multi-academy trust – a single legal entity formed by a number of schools combining to form a single academy.

Member A person or corporate body whose name is entered in the academy's register of members.

Memorandum of Association Document confirming the three 'subscribers' who wish to form the academy and become its members. The memorandum has no ongoing significance once an academy has been incorporated.

Minutes A formal record of the proceedings of a meeting and the decisions made.

Model Articles The standard form articles for academies prescribed by the Secretary of State under powers granted by the Companies Act. There are various model articles available to suit the particular governance structure.

Natural director A director who is a real person.

NGA National Governors' Association.

Non-executive director A director who is not a full-time employee involved in the management of the academy.

NOR Number of pupils on roll.

Officer A director, manager or secretary of an academy (under s. 1173 of the Companies Act 2006). In the case of an 'officer in default' this is broadened to include any person who is to be treated as an officer of the company for the purposes of the provision of the Companies Act in question.

OFSTED Office for Standards in Education.

Ordinary resolution A decision/resolution requiring approval by a majority of an academy's members.

PAN Published admission number.

Poll vote A vote by way of a ballot, generally by completing a slip or paper in secret.

PPG Pupil premium grant – additional funding provided to support disadvantaged pupils and pupils with parents in the armed forces.

Principal regulator Responsible for overseeing the compliance of exempt charities with charity law. For academies, the principal regulator is the Secretary of State for Education.

PROOF 'Protected online filing' – an agreement between an academy and Companies House that the academy will always file certain information electronically.

Quorum In relation to a board meeting or a members' meeting, the minimum number of directors or members respectively who must be present in order for the meeting to be validly constituted.

RAISEonline Reporting and analysis for Improvement through School Self-evaluation (online).

RAP Raising achievement plan.

Ratification Formal approval of something that has been considered or agreed by somebody else, in order that it can become valid or operative. Can be used to validate an otherwise invalid act by retrospectively confirming or approving it.

Registered office An academy's official address at which legal and other documents can be validly served and at which certain company records must be kept if not kept at a SAIL. For a single academy this is likely to be the school itself.

Remuneration Payments and benefits that an employee is entitled to in respect of services provided by the employee to an academy.

Resolution A formal decision of directors or members.

Risk assessment The process of identifying risks, the persons affected by them, the severity of the likely injuries or loss that might result from them, whether the control measures in place are adequate and any further measures needed to control them.

SAIL Single alternative inspection location – a location at which certain company records can be kept as an alternative to keeping them at the registered office.

SCR Single Central Record of DBS.

SDP School Development Plan (see also SIP).

SEN Special educational needs.

SENCo Special educational needs coordinator.

SEND Special educational needs and disability.

Service address An address for correspondence that directors must provide to Companies House which can, and ideally should, be different from their residential address. Generally this is the academy's registered office address.

SGOSS School governors' one-stop shop.

Shadow director A person who has not been appointed as a director but who directs or gives instructions to an academy's true directors.

SIP School improvement plan.

SLT Senior leadership team.

SORP Statement of Recommended Practice.

Special resolution A members' resolution requiring a majority in favour of 75% or over.

Sponsor A body responsible for the performance and finances of an academy.

Stakeholder A person or group of persons with an interest in an academy or who are in some way affected by an academy's activities.

Statutory registers Books/registers containing information relating to an academy's directors, members, etc which academies must maintain in accordance with the Companies Act.

TPS Teachers' pension scheme.

TUPE Transfer of Undertakings (Protection of Employment) Regulations 2006.

Umbrella trust An academy chain whereby the over-arching academy, or umbrella, is a charitable trust in its own right and each of the individual schools is a single academy.

UTC University Technical College.

VA Voluntary aided – a maintained school with a majority of the board of governors appointed by a foundation or trust, usually a religious body, which may also own the land and contribute financially.

VC Voluntary controlled – a maintained school with a quarter of the board of directors appointed by a foundation or trust, usually a religious body. The foundation may own the land, but will have less direct influence than in a VA school.

VLE Virtual learning environment.

WGA Whole of Government Accounts.

Written resolution A document setting out one or more proposed resolutions that is circulated to an academy's members for approval as an alternative to holding a general meeting.

Y5 Year 5.

Directory

Charity Commission
www.charitycommission.gov.uk

Companies House
www.companieshouse.gov.uk

Department for Education
www.gov.uk/government/organisations/department-for-education

DigitalLawUK
@DigitalLawUK
www.DigitalLawUK.com

Disclosure and Barring Service
www.gov.uk/government/organisations/disclosure-and-barring-service

FASNA (Freedom and Autonomy for Schools – National Association)
www.fasna.org.uk

GLM Partnership – Governor Mark
glmpartnership.org/governor_mark.html

Good Governance Code
www.governancecode.org

Health and Safety Executive
www.hse.gov.uk

HM Revenue and Customs
www.hmrc.gov.uk

Independent Academies Association
www.iaa.uk.net

Local Government Pension Scheme
www.lgps.org.uk

National Association of School Business Management
www.nasbm.co.uk

National College for Teaching and Learning
www.nationalcollege.org.uk

National Governors' Association
www.nga.org.uk

New schools network
www.newschoolsnetwork.org

SGOSS (School Governors' One-Stop Shop)
www.sgoss.org.uk

Teachers' pensions
www.teacherspensions.co.uk

The Information Commissioner
www.ico.gov.uk

The Institute of Chartered Secretaries and Administrators
www.icsaglobal.com

The Registrar of Companies for England and Wales (Companies House)
www.companies-house.gov.uk

Whitley Stimpson
www.whitleystimpson.co.uk

Index